IMAGES
of America

JOHN GLENN'S NEW CONCORD

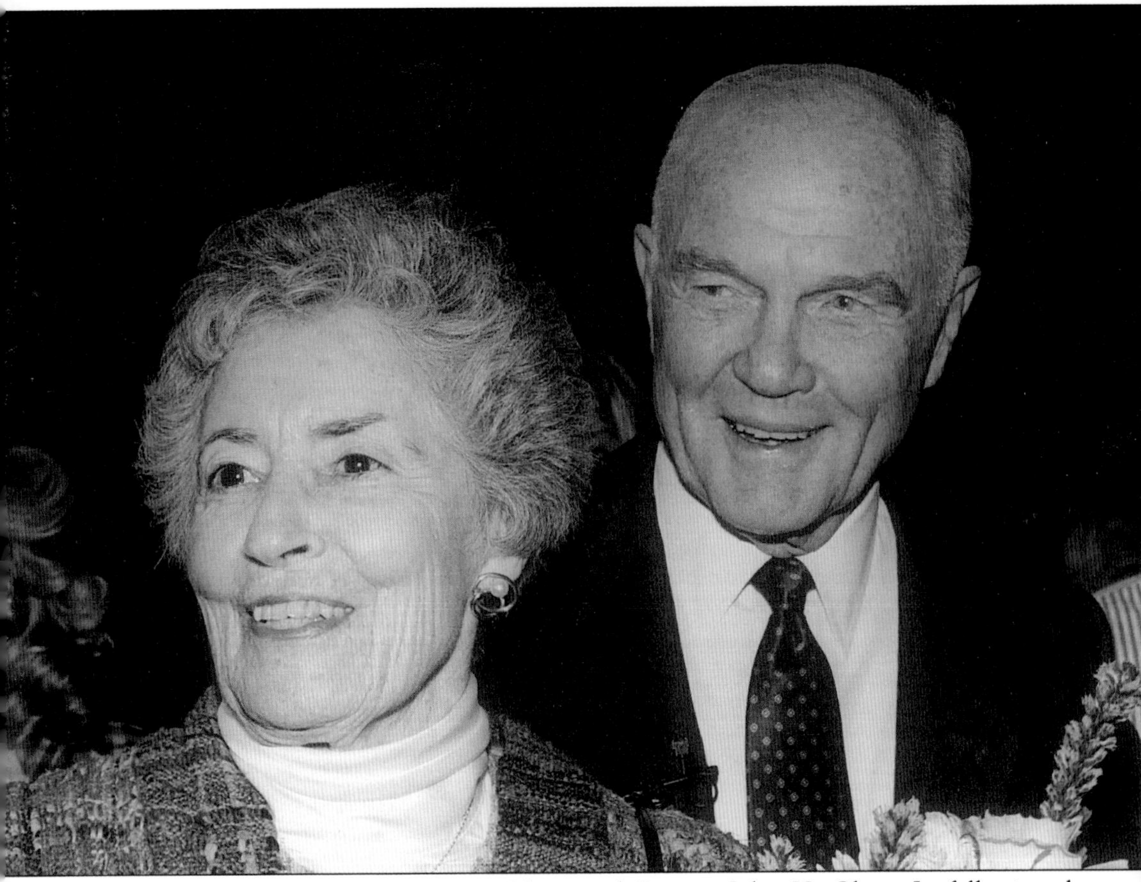

The camera captures Annie Castor Glenn and Senator John H. Glenn Jr. following the announcement of his retirement from the United States Senate, at Muskingum College, New Concord, Ohio, February 20, 1997.

IMAGES
of America

JOHN GLENN'S NEW CONCORD

Lorle Porter, Ph.D.

ARCADIA
PUBLISHING

ISBN 978-0-7385-0843-6

Published by Arcadia Publishing
Charleston, South Carolina

Printed in the United States of America

Library of Congress Catalog Card Number: 00-111090

For all general information contact Arcadia Publishing at:
Telephone 843-853-2070
Fax 843-853-0044
E-mail sales@arcadiapublishing.com
For customer service and orders:
Toll-Free 1-888-313-2665

Visit us on the Internet at www.arcadiapublishing.com

I've always believed that New Concord and Muskingum College are the center of the universe because if you get your start here, you can go anywhere.

John Herschel Glenn Jr.

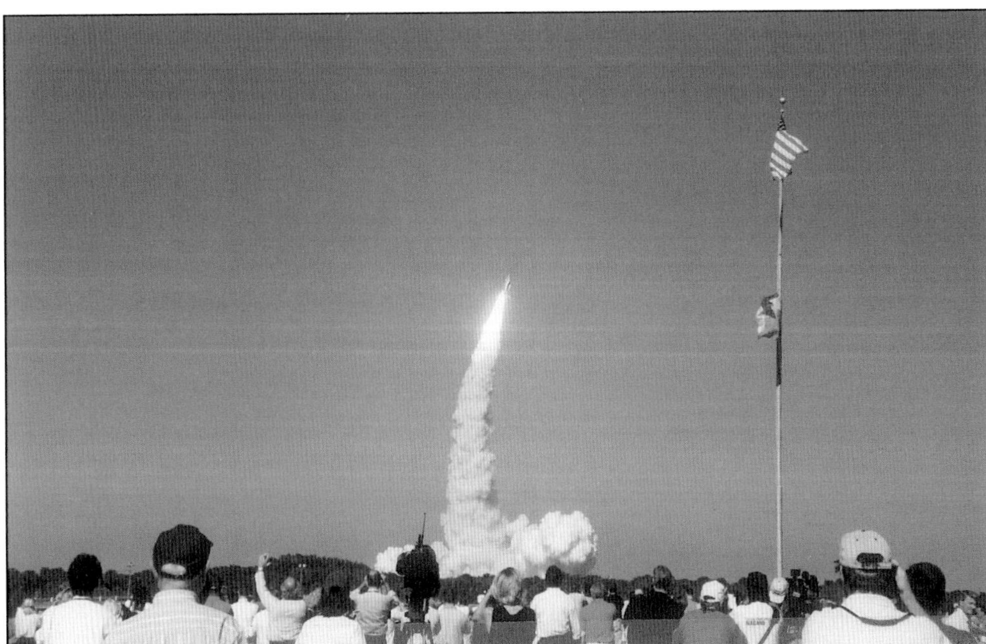

Above is the blast off of the *Discovery* Space Shuttle at Cape Kennedy, Florida, October 28, 1998. Students from the *Jon-Jee*—the newspaper of John Glenn High School, New Concord, Ohio—covered the event.

Contents

ACKNOWLEDGMENTS

Darlene Shryock
Janice Tucker McCloud
Dr. Donna Edsall
Beryl Besore
Bill Carlos
Cox Photography
Betty Grace Garrison Cupoli
Betty Flegal Cruickshank
Mary Ann DeVolld
Mary Doi
Vera Duff
East Muskingum School District
Eleanor Kettlewell Enevoldsen
Franklin Museum, New Athens, Ohio
Dick and Ruth Gault
Annie Glenn
John H. Glenn Jr.
John H. Glenn Jr. Collection, Ohio State University Archives
Margaret Park Himes
Jane Castor Hosey
Jon Jee Staff, John Glenn High School
Ken Kettlewell
Susan Leachman
Toni Leland
Barbara Mazeroski
Renée Morrow
Muskingum College Archives
Muskingum College Public Relations Office
Muscoljuan
Muskingum County Engineer's Office
Necohian 1939
Ohio Historical Society/Norris Schneider Collection
Leonard Reinhart
Shirley Riggle
Harrison Sawyer
Levi Shegog
Amy Shirakawa
Clair Stebbins
Mary Steele
Taylor Stults
Jack Taylor
Village of New Concord
Sharon Walker

OTHER PUBLISHED WORKS BY AUTHOR

A People Set Apart: Scotch-Irish in Eastern Ohio
by: Lorle Porter, Ph.D.
New Concord Press
P.O. Box 8016

Zanesville, OH 43702–8016

WELCOME

By: John Glenn

"I am a part of all I have met," wrote Tennyson, in *Ulysses*.

And for Annie and me, those "parts," those influences of family, friends, and community, of the values, ethics, and religious beliefs we grew up with in New Concord, have indeed formed the core of our lives.

In this book, Lorle Porter, with both prose and photos, shows us how that heritage developed.

From the Zane Trace to the interstate highway of today, New Concord was founded and developed along a vital travel route to the west that was key to opening up vast areas of the United States. The Ohio region did indeed become "The Heart of it All."

However, even more important than geographic expansion were the types of people who settled this area. They were an unusual people with a unique background and view of how life should be lived.

Lorle's extensive research gives us insight into their lives and into our own.

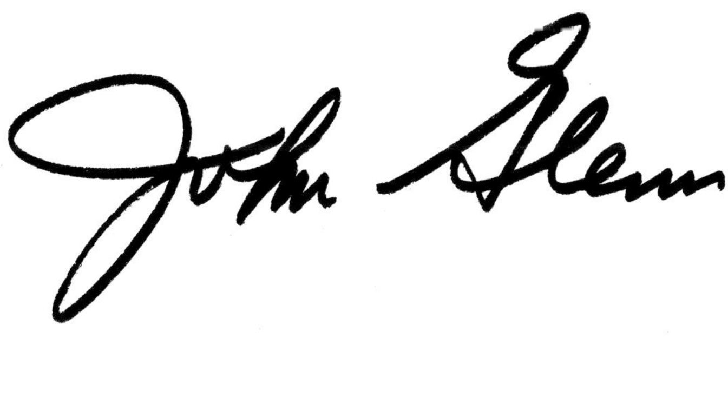

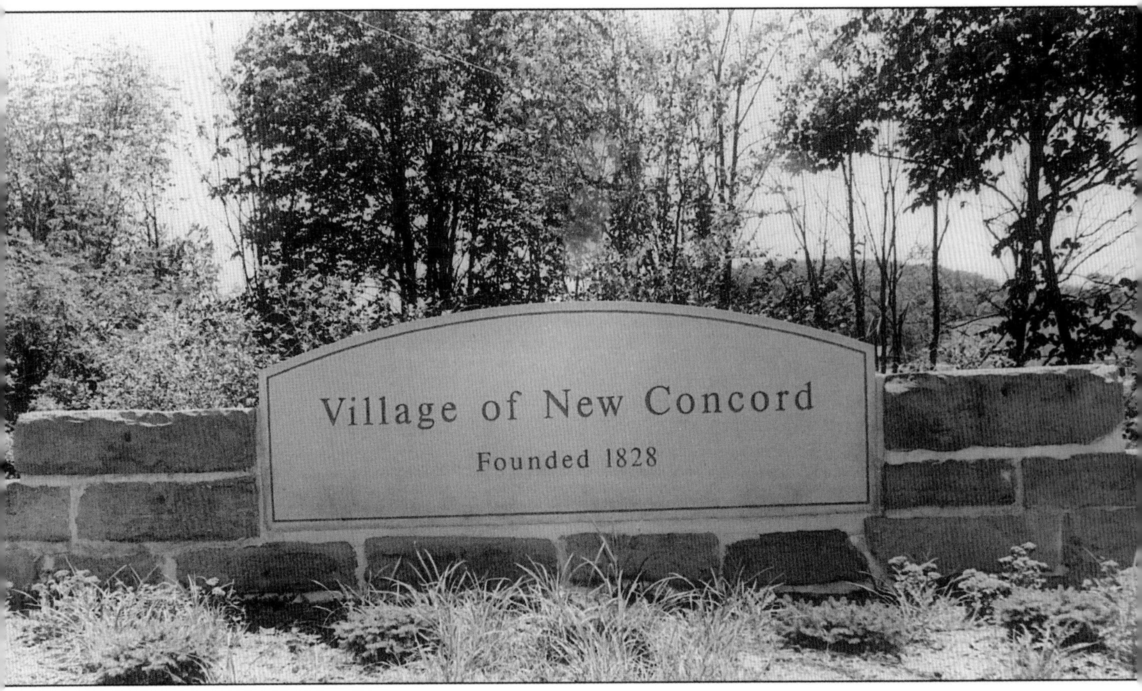

INTRODUCTION

The history of the Village of New Concord, founded in 1828, can be explained in a single sentence: New Concord was a Scotch-Irish/National Road town. These two elements make it unique.

The Scotch-Irish were Scots who were "planted" in Northern Ireland after 1600 to supplant the native Irish and Protestantize the rebellious Catholic country. Living as aliens amidst a hostile people, the Scots emphasized their characteristic clannishness and became "A People Set Apart." No longer Scots, certainly not Irish, they became Scotch-Irish. Migrating to America in the 18th century, the immigrants settled in enclaves in Pennsylvania and Ohio and down the Great Wagon Road into the Carolina Piedmont region. Wherever they went, their communities were marked by deep religious conviction and twin drives for education and public service.

In 1797, Congress commissioned the Zane Brothers of Wheeling to blaze a trail (trace) through the wooded wilderness of the Ohio territory. George Washington wanted the Zane's Trace to "open wide the gates of the West." Pennsylvania Scotch-Irish, already settled on that state's frontier, were unafraid of another frontier. They began to filter down the Zane's Trace, spilling off along the hills of its spine. John Glenn's ancestors settled in Guernsey County; Anna Margaret Castor's ancestors settled in the Crooked Creek Valley of Muskingum County. Settlements in eight Guernsey and Muskingum County townships developed. North to south, east to west, the Scotch-Irish community centered around what was to become New Concord.

From this tiny location in America, the community and its inhabitants would face many frontiers: The Zane's Trace, The National Road, the Railroad, U.S. 40, I-70 . . . and Space. Come with us on a visit to New Concord, Ohio, John and Annie Glenn's hometown.

One

AN OLD PEOPLE IN A NEW LAND

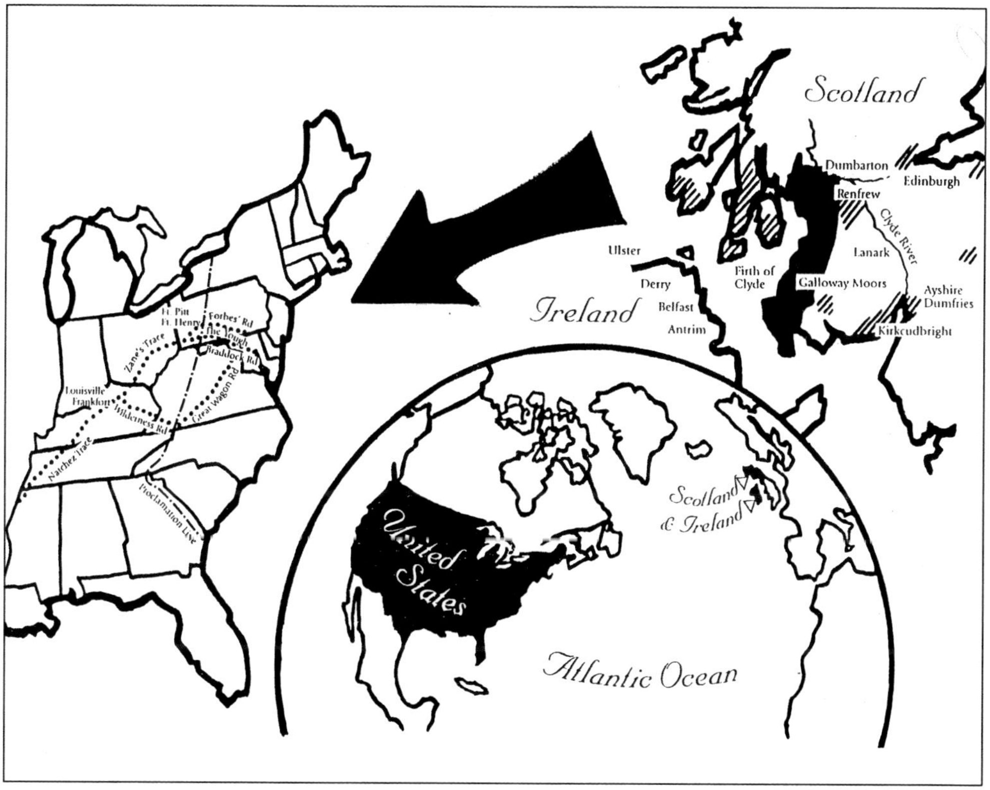

Beginning in 1600, tens of thousands of lowland Scots were transported to nine counties in the north of Ireland by their Scottish lords. The heaviest migration was from the darkened section on the map. This area bordered the Firth of Clyde in western Scotland.

The Scotch-Irish migrated from Ulster, Northern Ireland, to the American colonies beginning in 1700. Their settlements are located along the primitive roads carved out of the American wilderness in colonial times. By the American Civil War, some 300,000 persons had transplanted themselves to America.

Settlements sprang up in western Carolina and eastern Tennessee along the Great Wagon Road, in eastern Kentucky along the Wilderness Road, and down to Natchez along the Natchez Trace. The Ohio settlers entered the territory on the Zane's Trace.

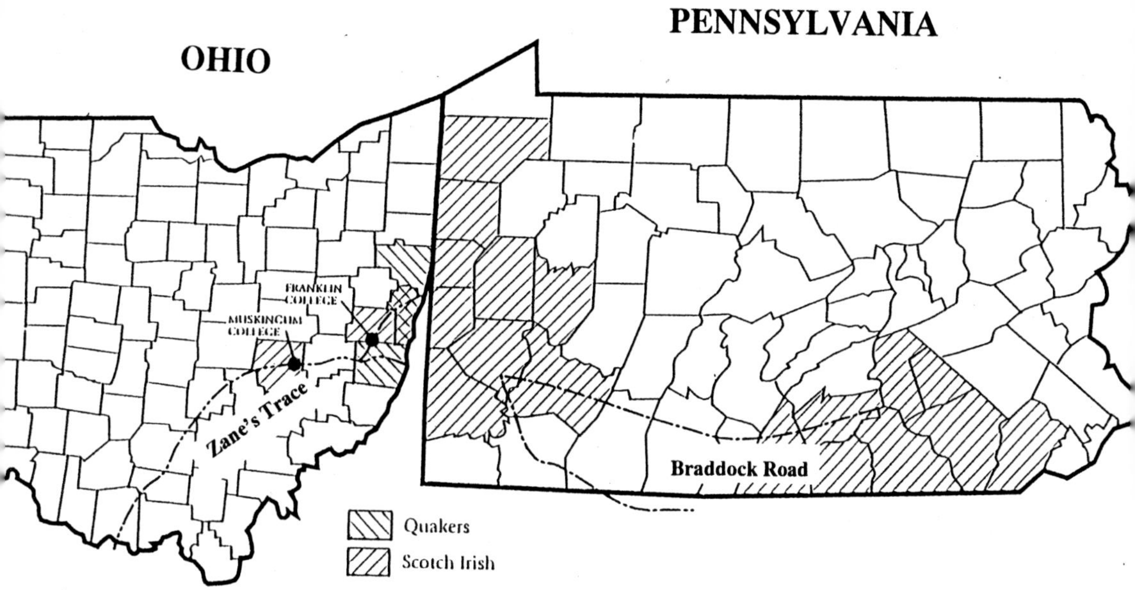

The Scotch-Irish dominated the settlement of southeastern Pennsylvania (Gettysburg) and western Pennsylvania (Pittsburgh). When the territory of Ohio opened, they began to spill over into eastern Ohio using Indian trails to penetrate the forests. The Zane Brothers carved out a "trace" from Wheeling to Maysville, Kentucky, in 1798. That accomplishment resulted in the settlement of Guernsey and Muskingum Counties in Ohio.

Wherever they settled, the Scotch-Irish insisted on promoting education. Thus in Harrison County they founded Franklin College, and in Muskingum County they founded Muskingum College; the latter remains a dominant presence in the region today.

The Findley Settlement

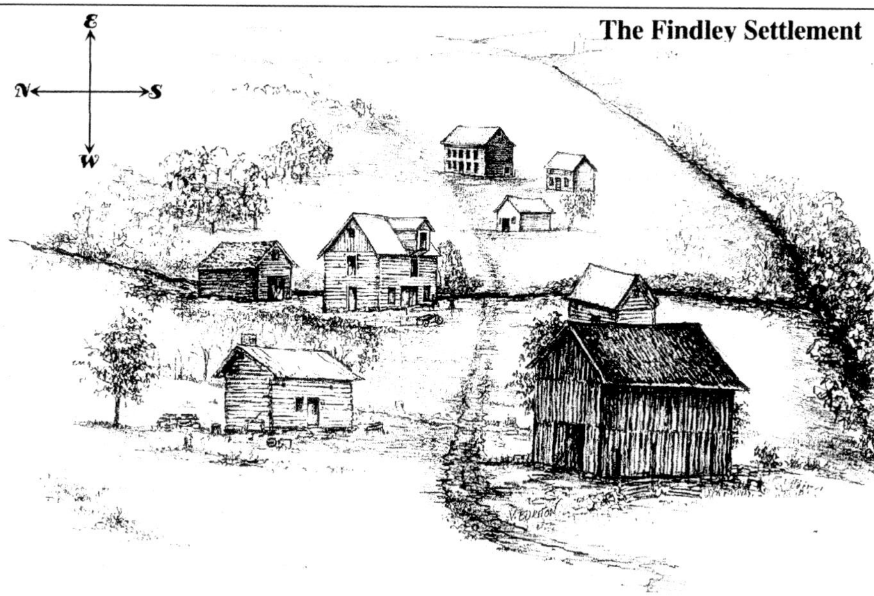

The Scotch-Irish settlement that became New Concord was laid out by Judge David Findley in 1806. The Judge and his sons carved out farms which ran from what is now Interstate 70 to the present day John Glenn High School. They raised log cabins, built a carding and fulling mill, a tobacco warehouse and a distillery. Tobacco was a common cash crop in the early 1800s. Corn was only marketable if it could be reduced to whiskey from its normal bulk. The greatest problem of these pioneers was getting crops to market. (Courtesy of Vicky Burton.)

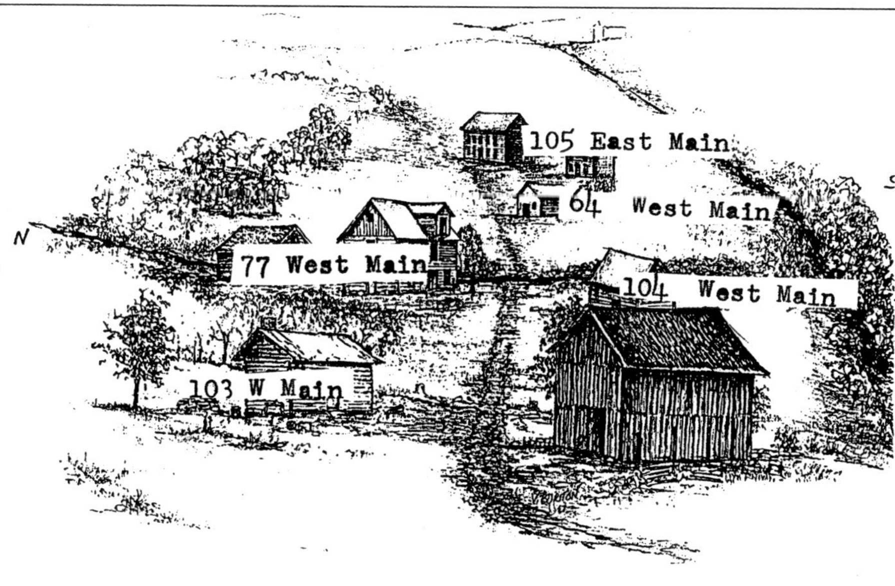

Artist rendering of Findley Settlement

The Zane's Trace was at best only a mule road. Ohio's rich land could not be tapped to its fullest potential as long as these "barebone counties" lay isolated and distant from eastern markets.

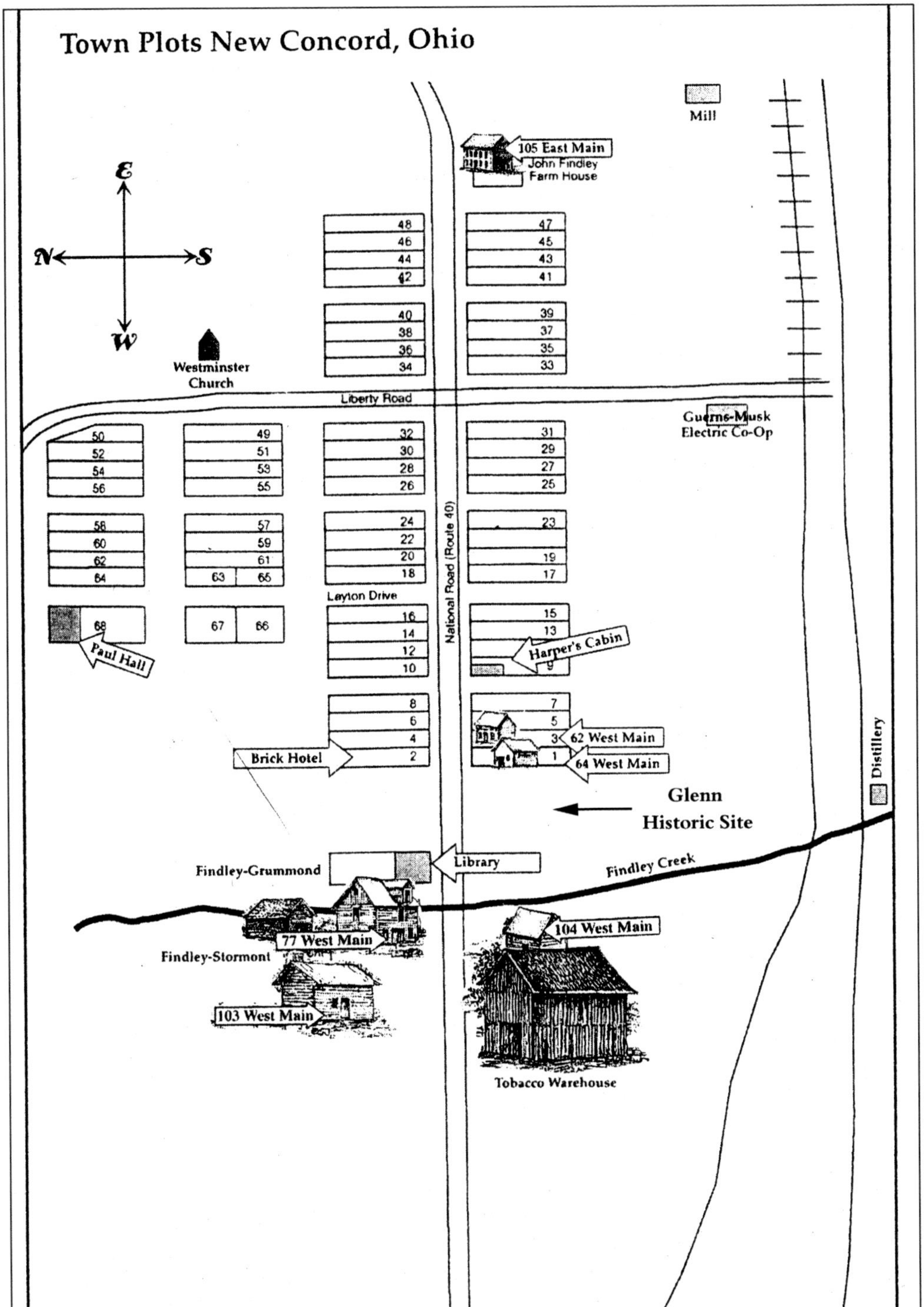

In the spring of 1828, Judge David Findley heard the sound of stakes being hammered into his pasture land. Surveyors were laying out the National Road. Findley laid out New Concord. The Pike town rapidly grew as the road builders inched across the county, tugging the nation behind them.

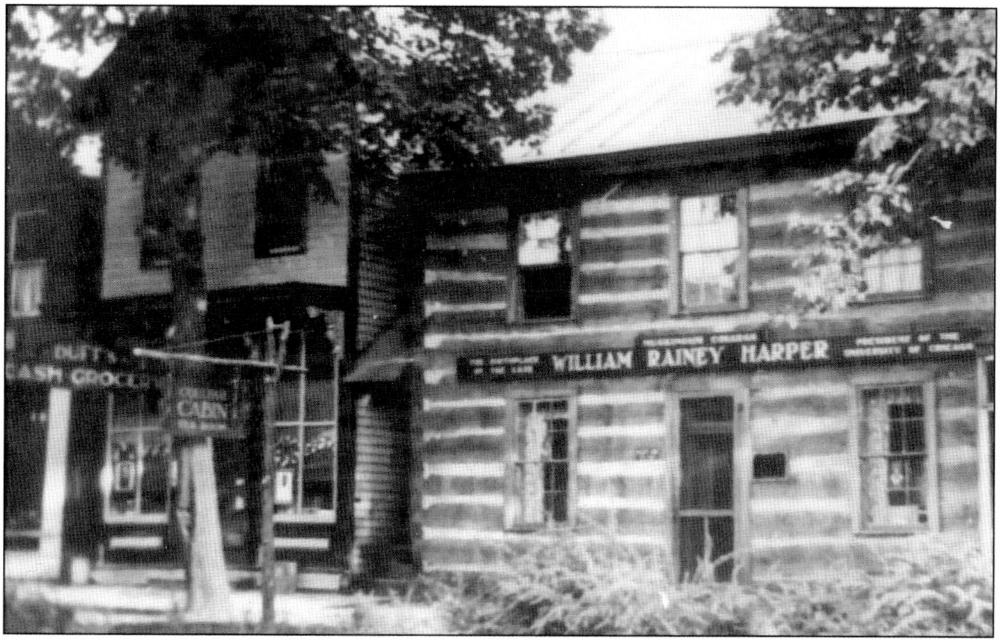

Log houses once lined the National Road in New Concord. "Harper Cabin" stands in the town center as a memorial to the village's National Road heritage.

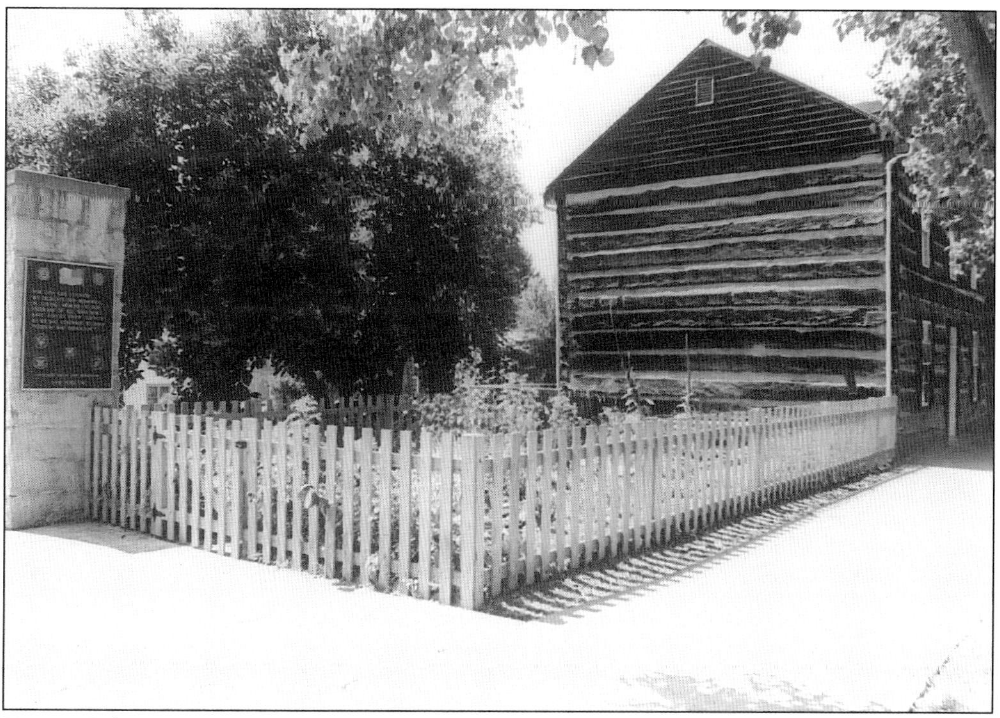

Harper Cabin sits on Main Street in its condition in 1920 and in 2000.

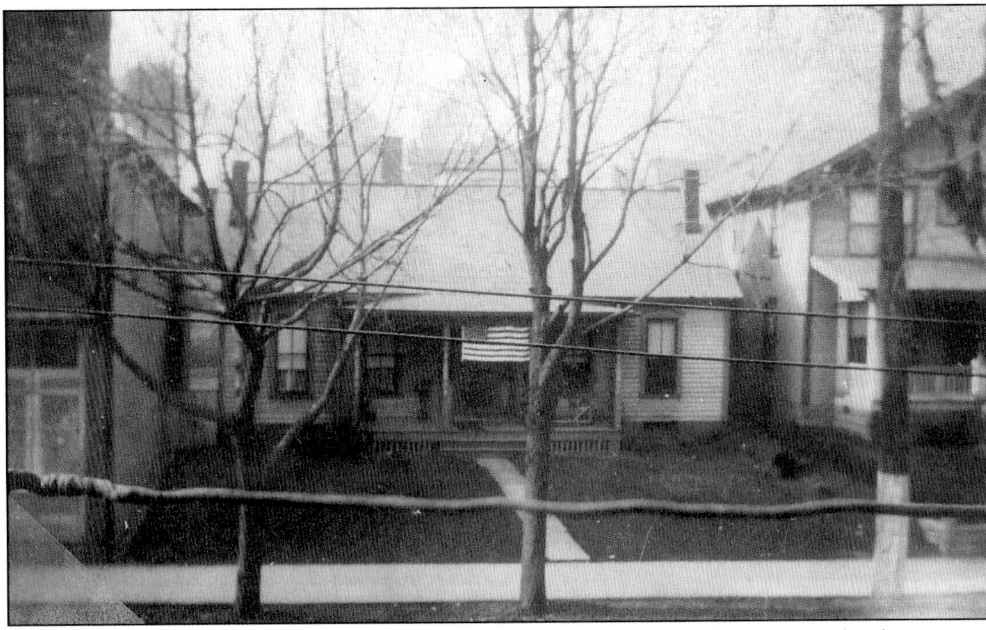

Reflecting the background of the settlers, log-houses and "Pennsylvania-Maryland cottages," such as this one, lined the muddy National Road. The cottage was the childhood home of William and Frank Harper, noted educators.

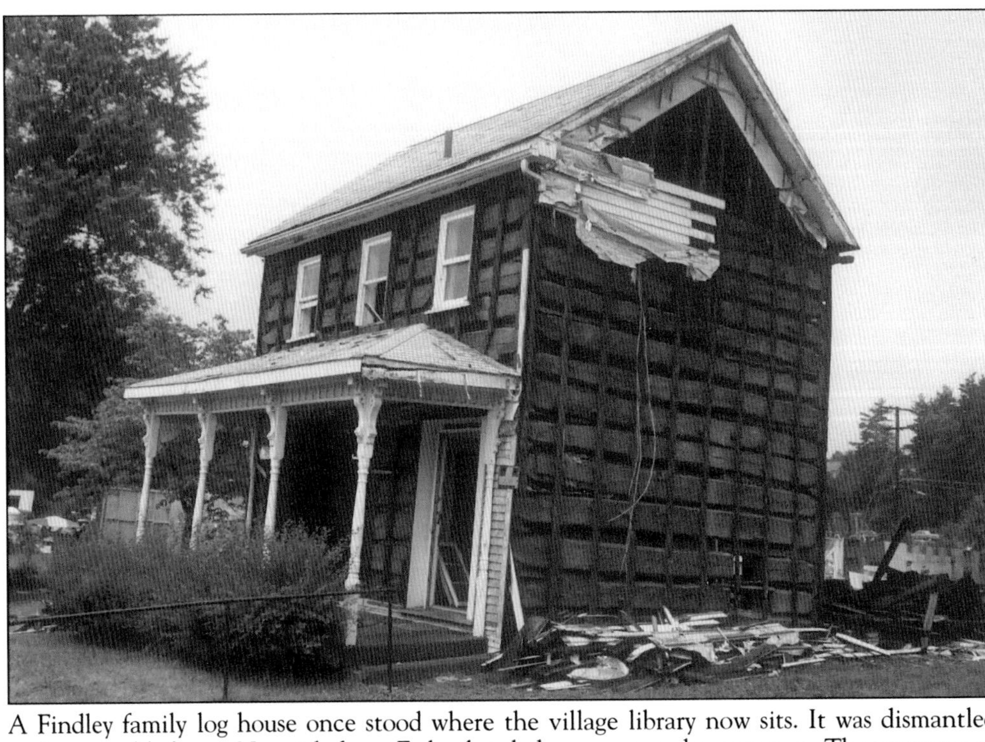

A Findley family log house once stood where the village library now sits. It was dismantled and reassembled on a Norwich farm. Federal-style houses were also common. The economy of the town blossomed as boarding houses, hotels, and blacksmith shops were opened to serve the heavy National Road traffic.

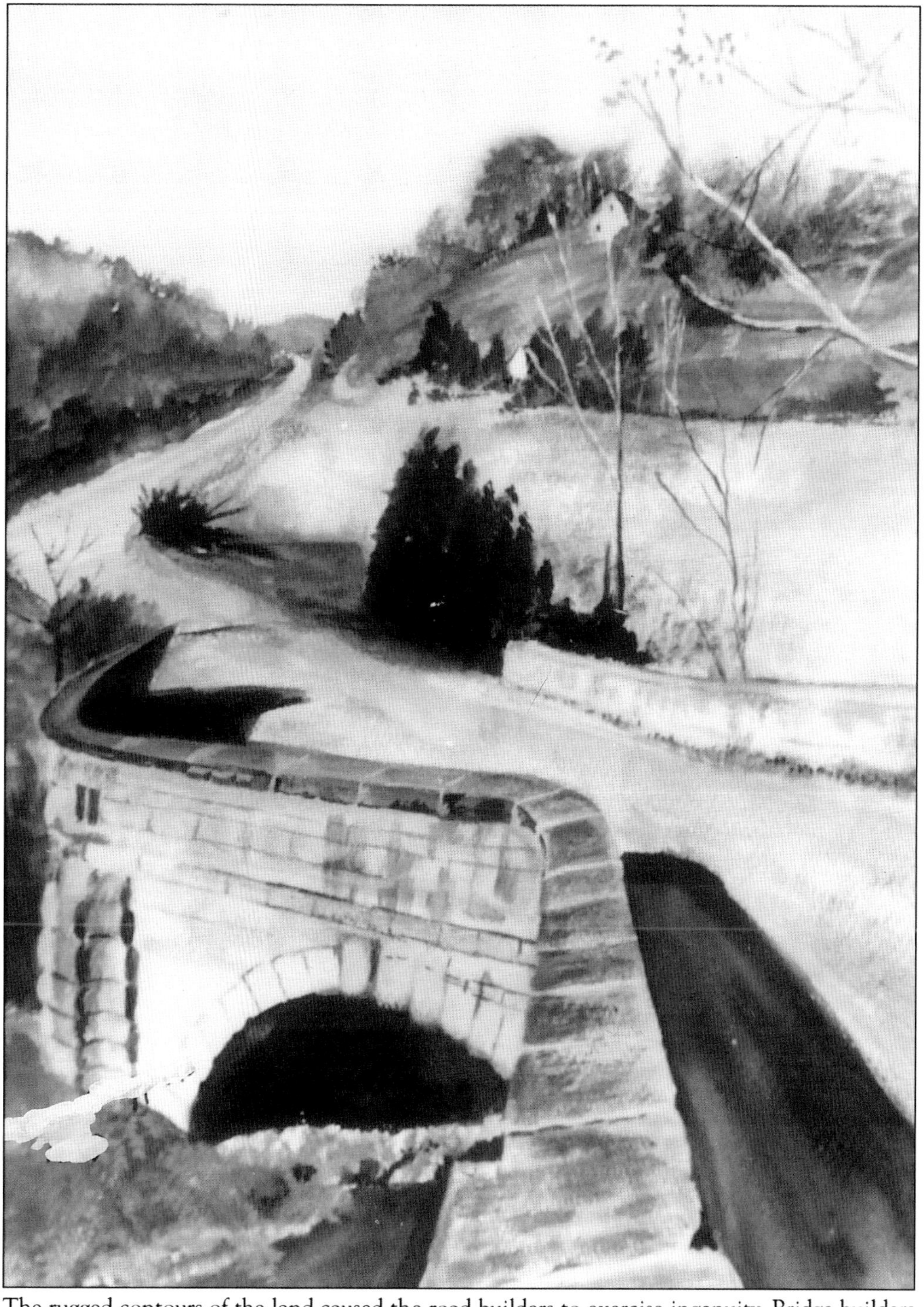

The rugged contours of the land caused the road builders to exercise ingenuity. Bridge builders had to cross a stream at right angles, thus they created the "S" bridges which once dotted the Road in Ohio. Crooked Creek "S" Bridge is an excellent example of this skill. Seen on the western horizon is Robert West Speer's home. He was a key player in the Underground Railroad stops which checkered the area prior to the Civil War.

The Scotch-Irish were distinguished by their adherence to various forms of Presbyterianism. New Concord once had five Presbyterian churches. The town's ethos was dominated by religious training. College Drive Presbyterian Church (the Castor family church) is the descendant of the United Presbyterian Church of Anna Castor Glenn's youth. In turn, this church was the descendant of the Associate Presbyterian Church (Seceders) and the Reformed Presbyterian Church (Covenantors). These denominations were famous for their strict adherence to rules and for their fervent anti-slavery stances. Because of their influence, New Concord, Norwich, Rix Mills, and Bloomfield were deeply involved in the secreting of runaway slaves on the Underground Railroad and in the area's fervent support of the Civil War as an anti-slavery crusade.

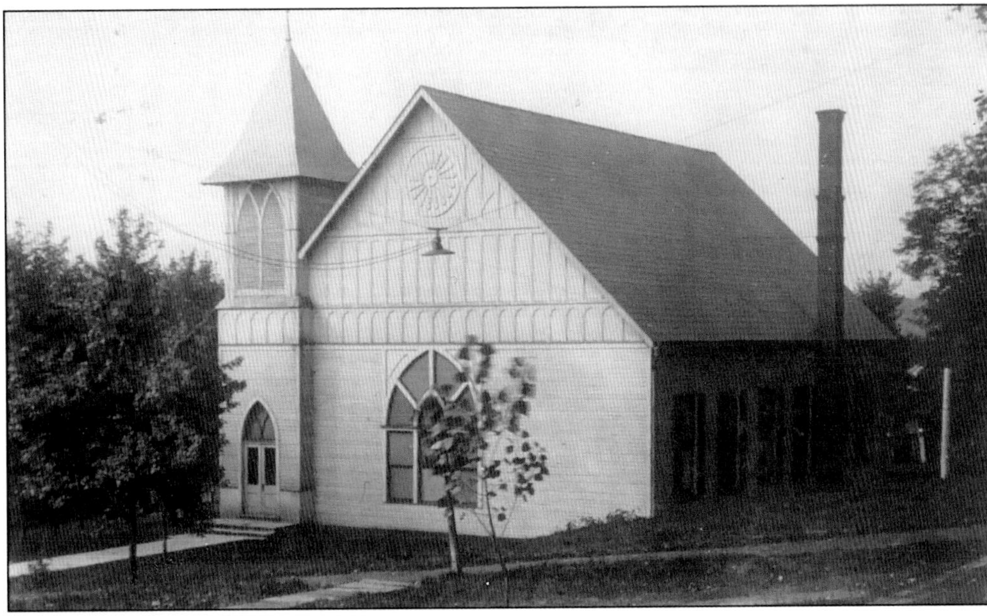

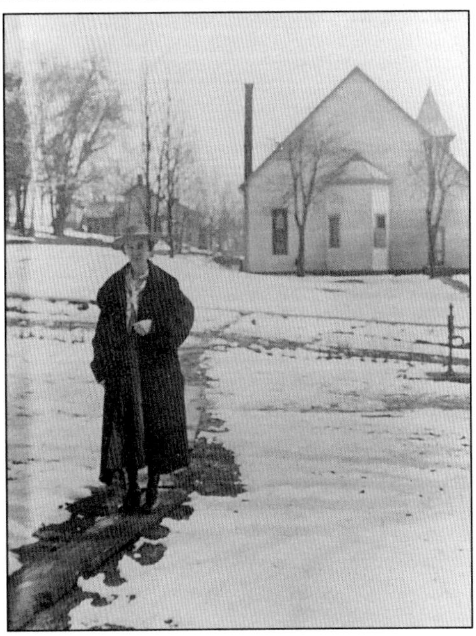

Here are two views of the United Presbyterian Church. The building faced Layton Drive. Helen McCreary walks away from the rear of United Presbyterian Church. The College Drive (road) was later built directly behind where she is seen in this picture.

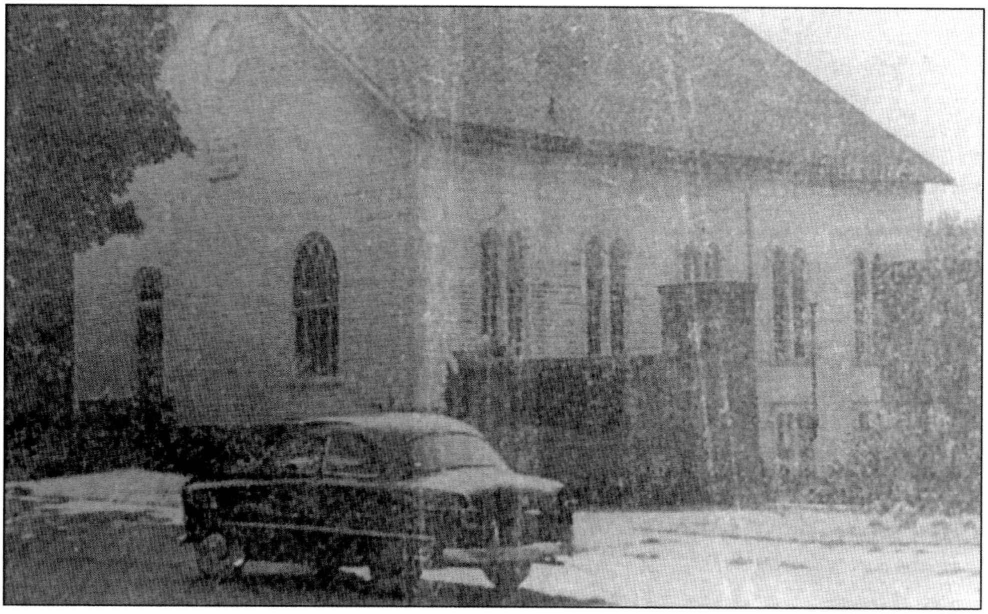

The Reformed Presbyterian (Covenantor) Church stood on Main Street to the west of the Village Hall. The Covenantors were among the most vocal opponents of slavery in America in the 1850s. Their influence turned much of the Scotch-Irish area into a bastion of Abolitionist sentiment. During the Civil War, a remarkable number of men and boys marched off to fight for a "holy cause." Two Muskingum College students were awarded the Medal of Honor for their actions, as was a third local resident.

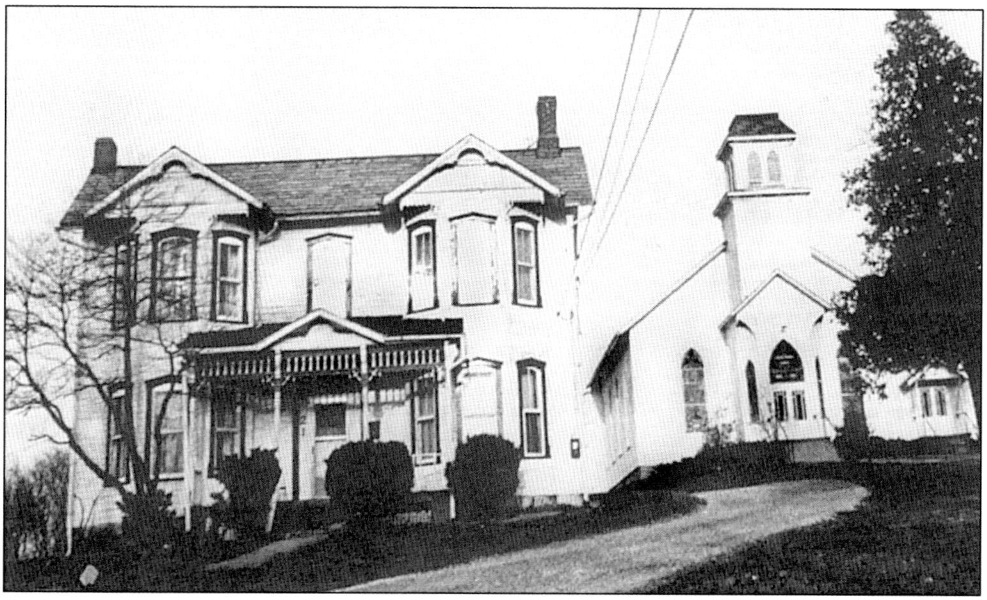

Westminister Presbyterian Church (the Glenn family church) was a part of the broader Presbyterian Church, which resisted taking a stand on the slavery issue. Even though the denominations merged in 1958 as the Presbyterian Church (U.S.A.), and though the reason for separate churches has long been forgotten, local sentiment still supports the two traditional church operations.

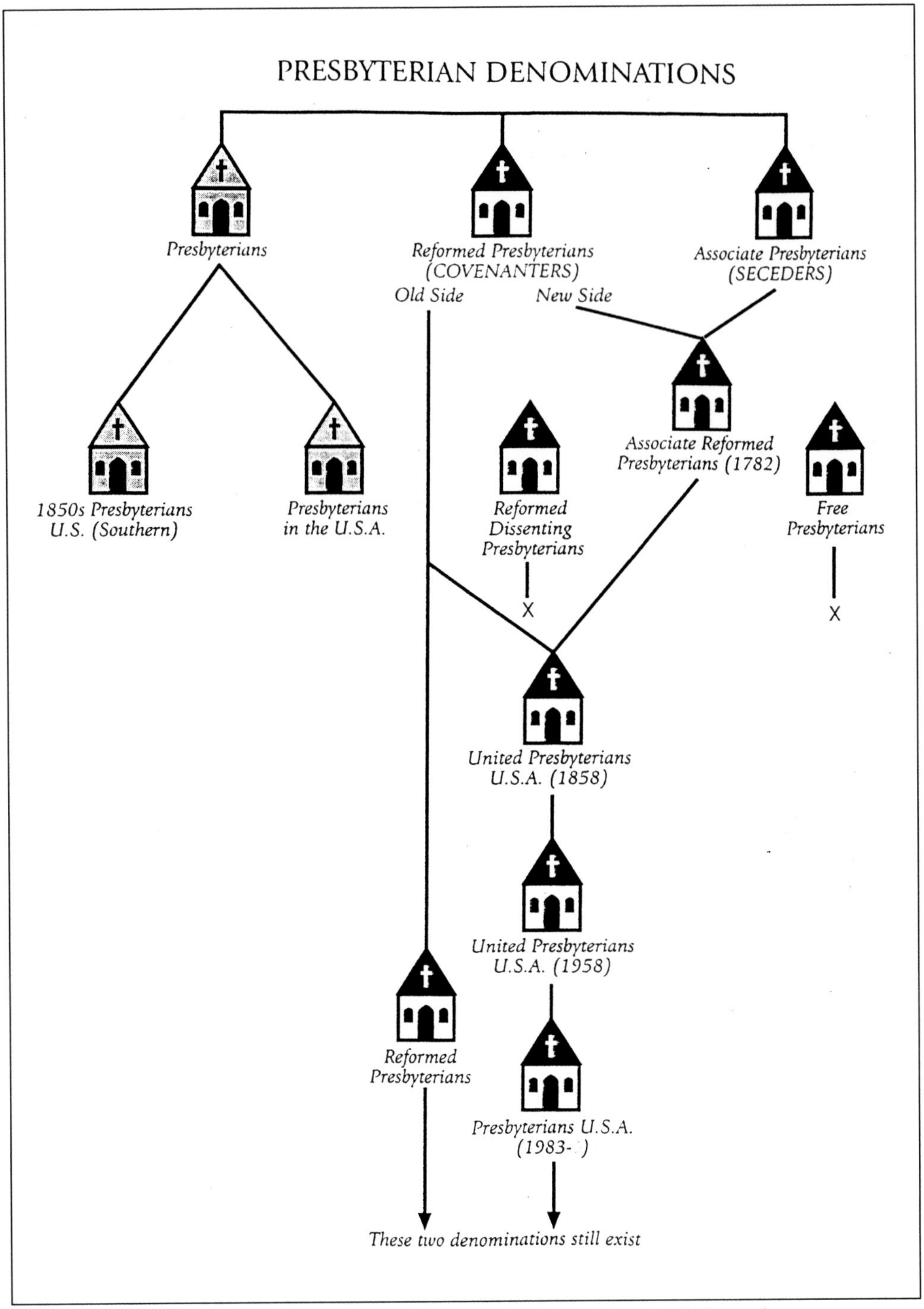

This chart shows the complexity of "Presbyterianism" in America. All these denominations—except the Free Presbyterians and the Reformed Dissenting Presbyterians—had a presence in the New Concord area.

The New Concord area was a staunch Scotch-Irish enclave favoring Presbyterianism. But some of its citizens followed other religious traditions, particularly in response to the religious revivals which swept the American landscape in the 1800s. The Methodists established a strong community in the village. The Baptists worshiped in the Muskingum College Hall in the early decades of the town's existence. The Baptists built their church on High Street and later sold it to the Methodist congregation.

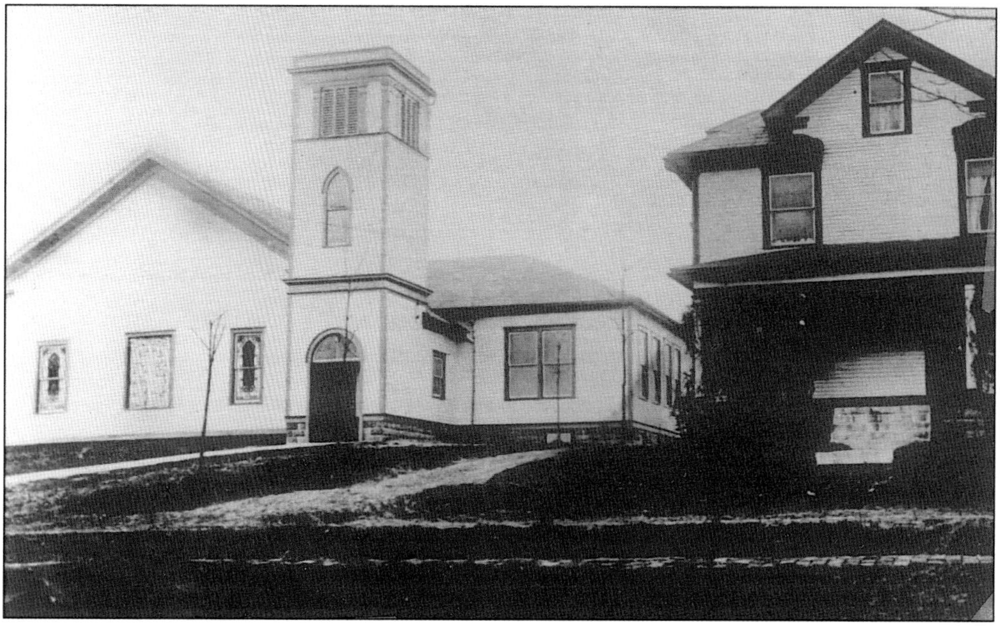

The New Concord Baptist Church is depicted in 1900 at 20 East High Street.

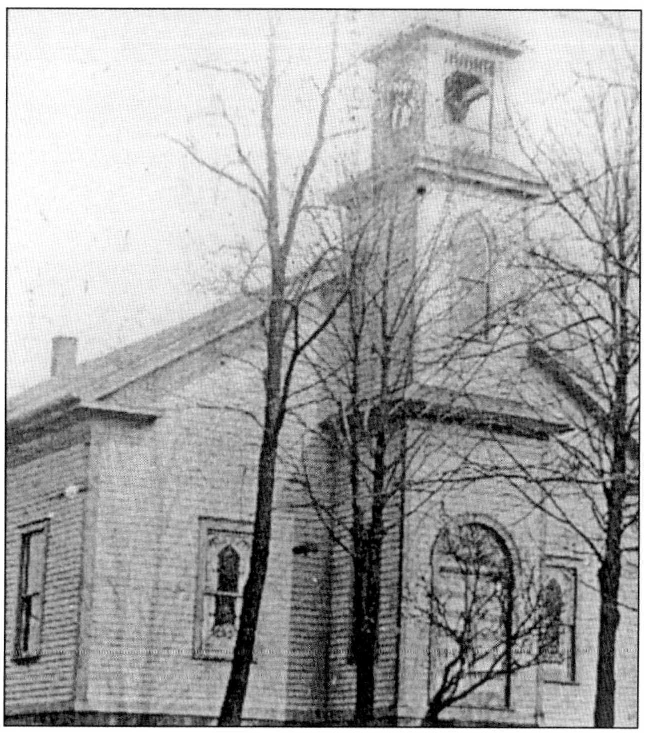

The Methodist Episcopal Church, 1904 (now the New Concord United Methodist Church), is located at 20 East High Street.

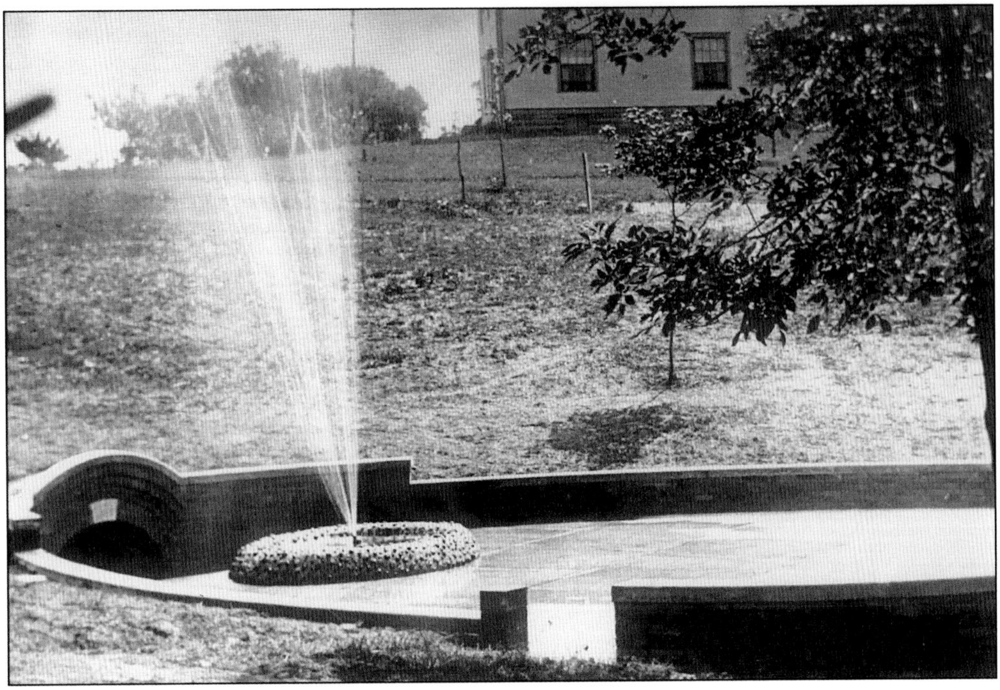

The religious atmosphere of John and Annie Glenns' youth was marked by church/village rules against dancing and drinking and by "keeping holy the Lord's day." Thus the major event on a Sabbath evening was a town gathering at the Muskingum College Spring for sacred music concerts. Sacred Music concerts were weekly events.

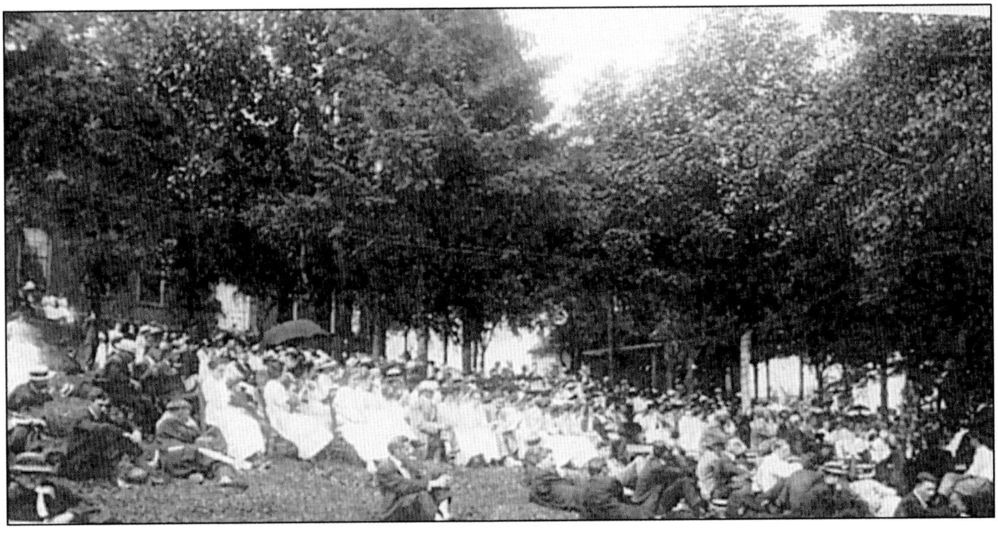

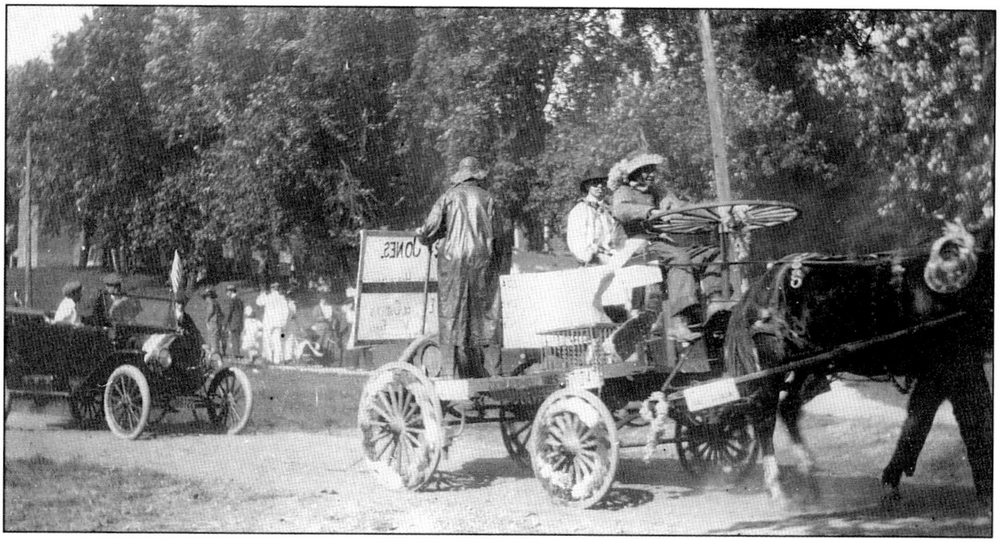

New Concord was a center of the Anti-Saloon League and of the Temperance Movement. John Knox Montgomery, the Muskingum College president, ran for Lieutenant Governor of Ohio on the Temperance Ticket in 1927. The Women's Christian Temperance Union (WCTU) was active in the village until the 1960s. These photos show a WCTU parade in the 1920s as it moved past the Muskingum College Manse.

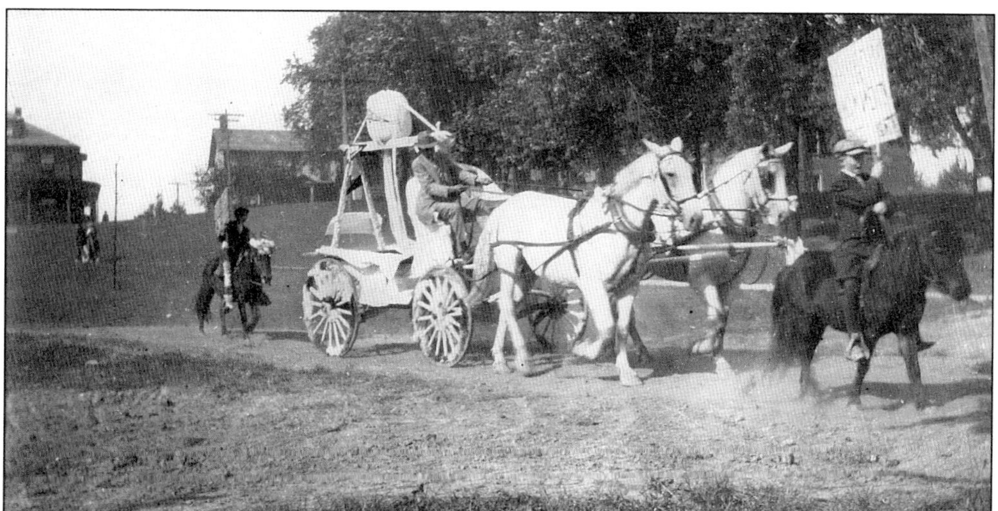

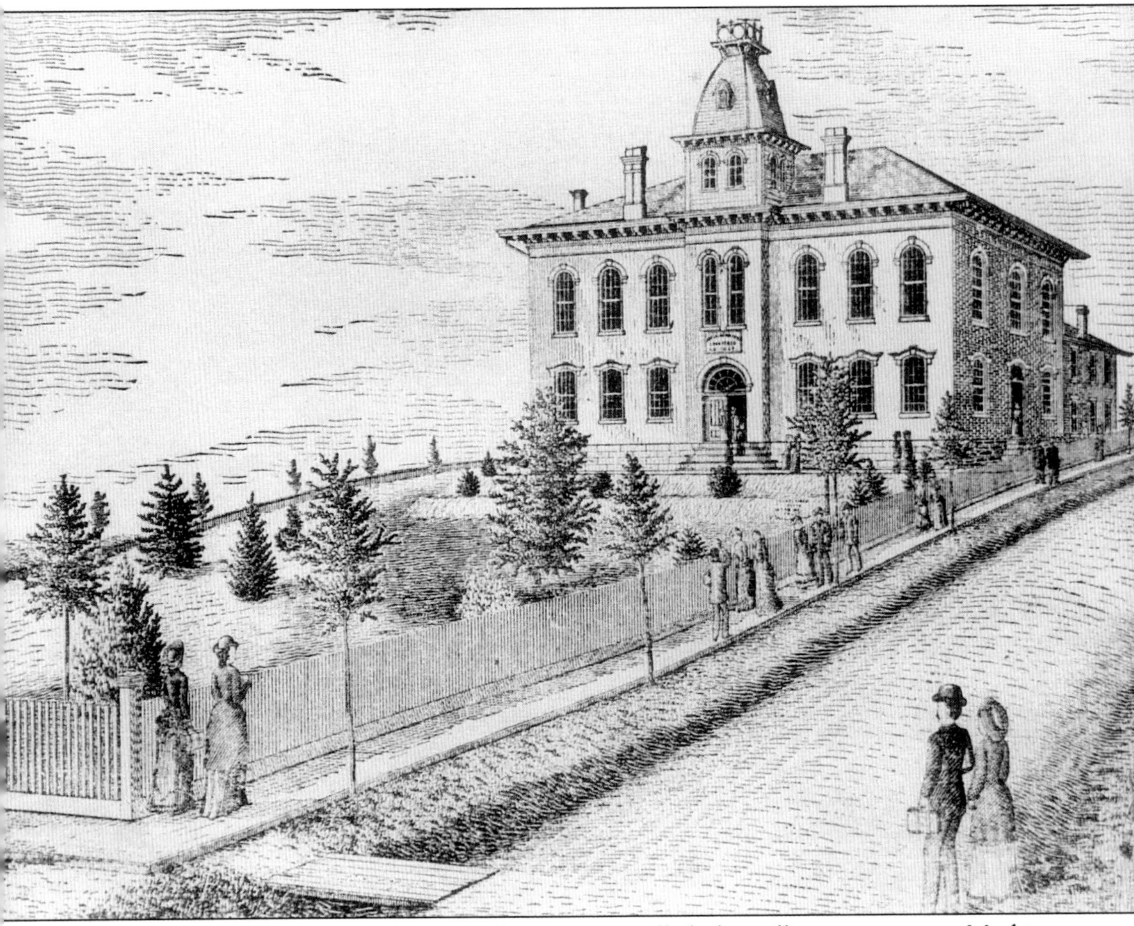

The Scotch-Irish commitment to education propelled the villagers to create Muskingum College in 1837. New Concord and Muskingum College have enjoyed a hand-in-glove relationship ever since. The original building burned in 1855. Paul Hall (the third building), built in 1875, is shown with the second college building to its rear. Layton Drive is the road on the right.

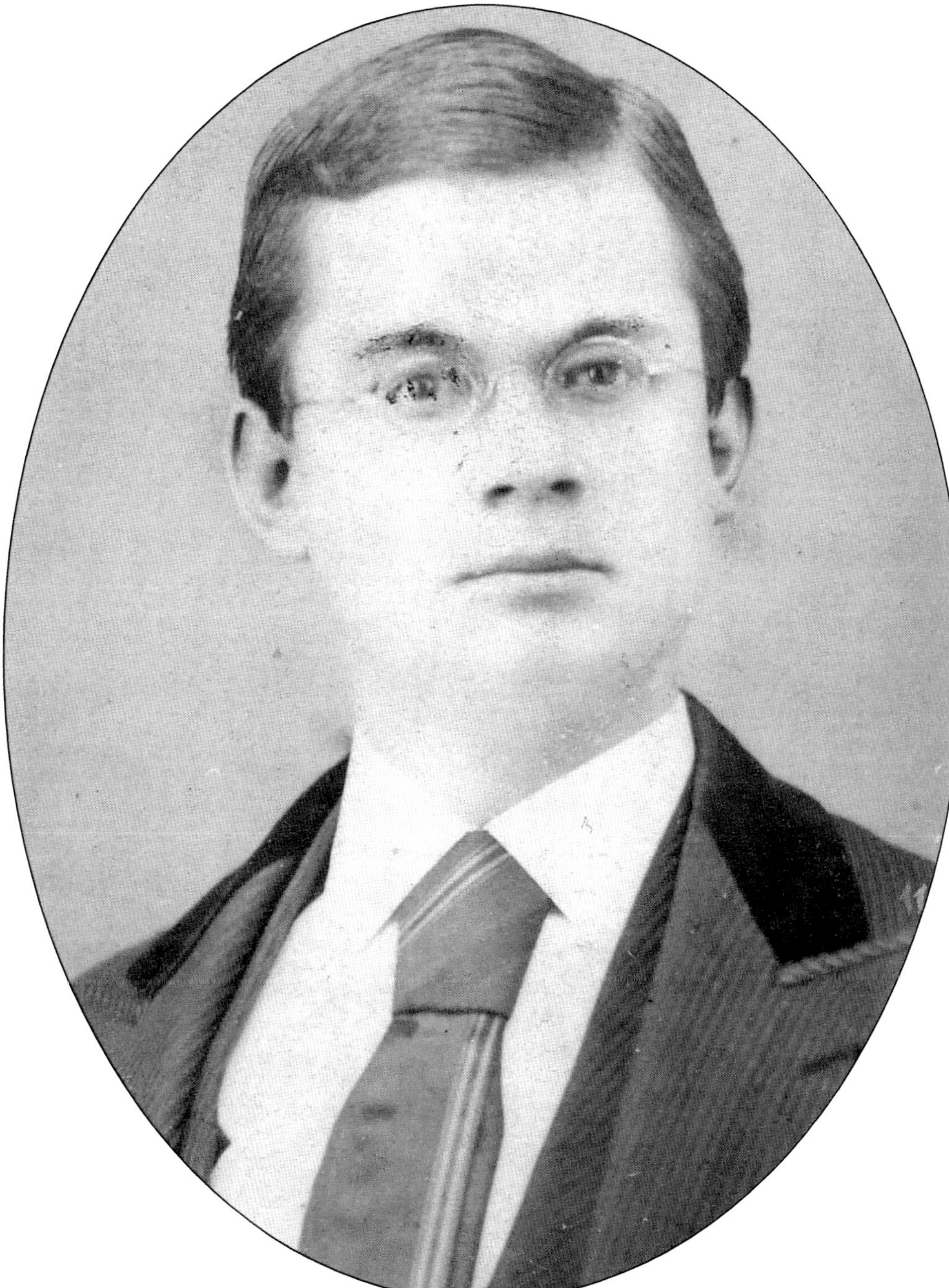

New Concord children were expected to go to school, then to college. The importance of education is exemplified by the lives of the Harper brothers. William Rainey Harper was born in a log house on the National Road (Harper Cabin). Harper graduated from Muskingum College while barely 14. After a renowned career in education, he accepted the challenge of John D. Rockefeller to build a European-style university in America. The University of Chicago is their legacy. This photo shows William Rainey Harper at 19, the year he received his Ph.D. in Semitic languages from Yale University.

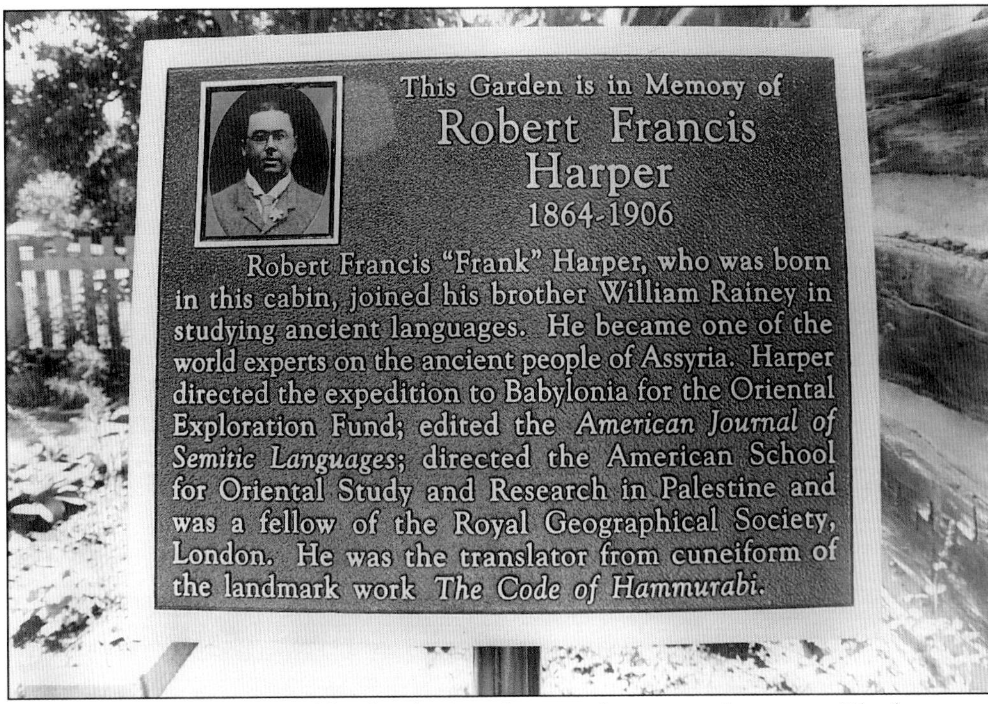

Robert Francis Harper shared his brother's enthusiasm for ancient languages. The boys grew up during the first exciting period of archeological discoveries in the Near East. Frank Harper became one of the world's authorities on ancient Assyria and translated from cuneiform *The Code of Hammurabi*.

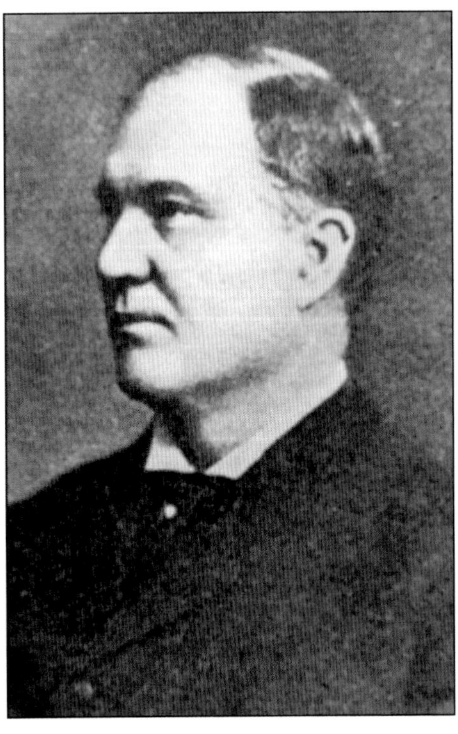

William Oxley Thompson, who boarded in Harper Cabin while a student at Muskingum College, transformed the Ohio State University from a land grant agricultural school to a world class university.

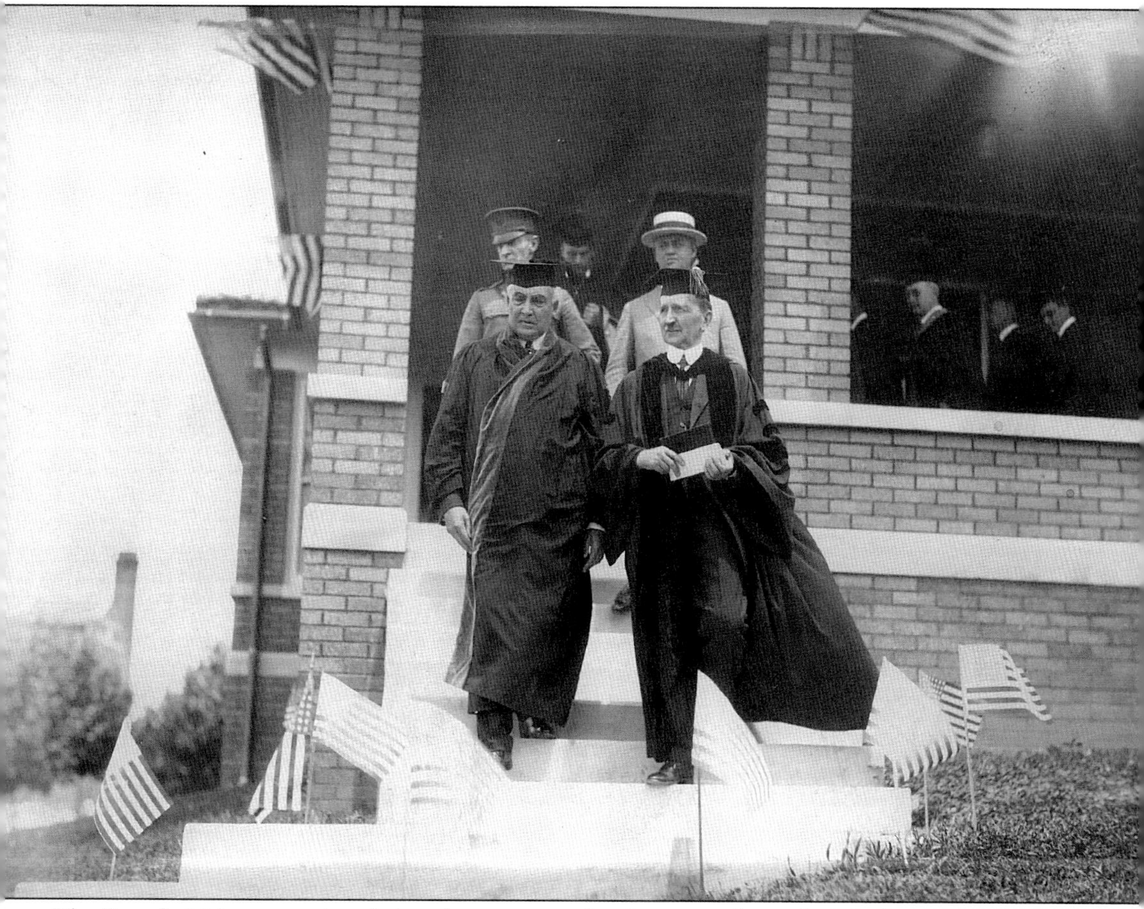

The Scotch-Irish connections led to the granting of an honorary degree by Muskingum College to sitting President Warren G. Harding. Harding was a graduate of the defunct Iberia College in Morrow County, Ohio. Iberia was the institution of the short-lived Free Presbyterian Church. Harding and Muskingum College President John Knox Montgomery are shown leaving the college manse for the ceremony in 1922.

Annie Glenn's parents, Homer Castor and Margaret Alley, were married by Dr. Montgomery in the Manse in 1918.

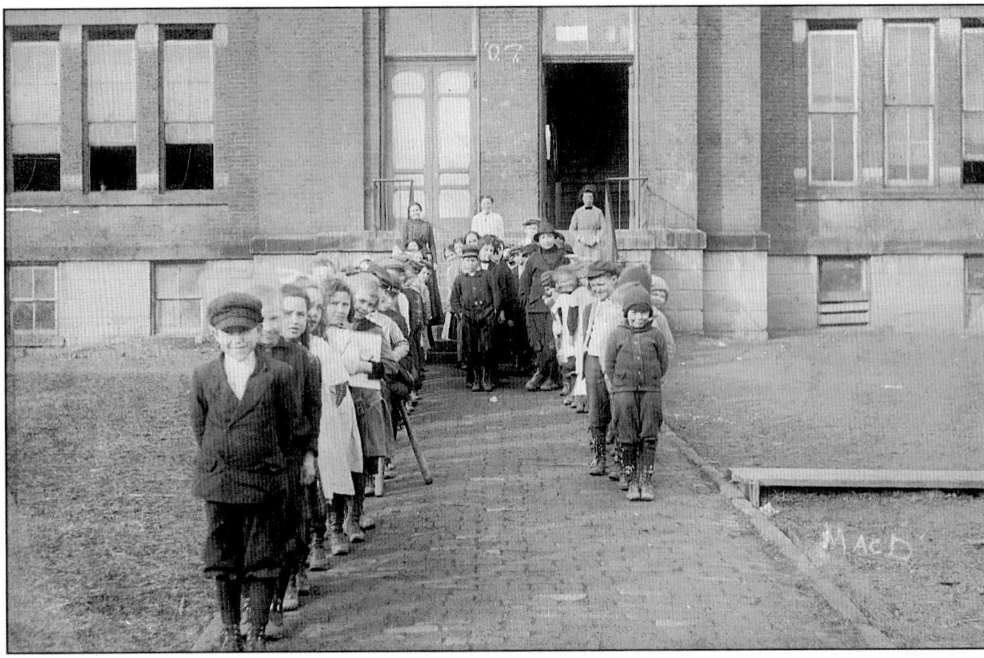

The educational traditions developed by the community called for hard work, order, and discipline. The ethic is reflected in these photos of children at the elementary school (*c.* 1910) and of the college's women's physical education class (*c.* 1900).

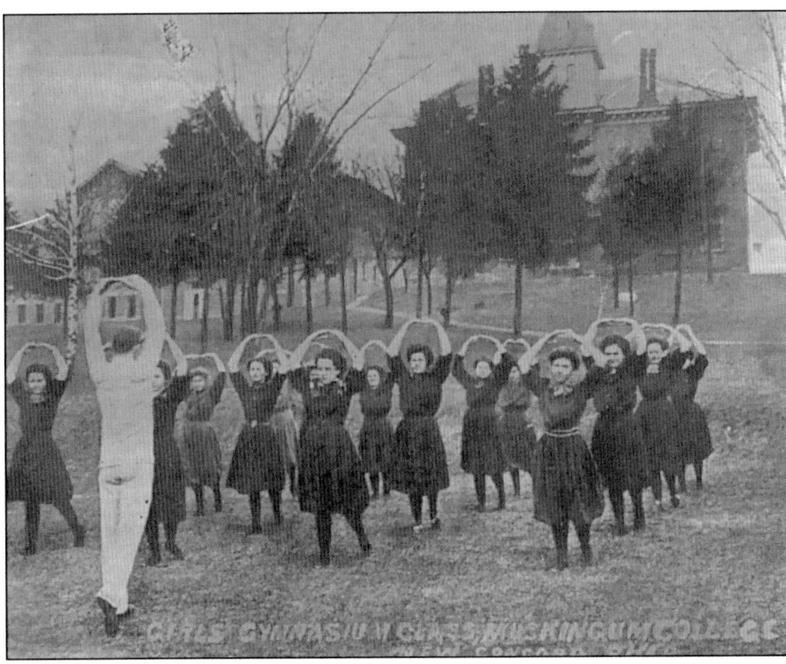

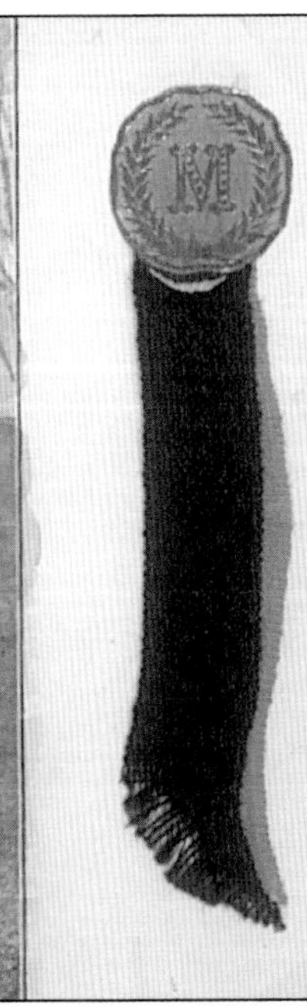

Two

THE AGE OF THE IRON HORSE

The Baltimore and Ohio (B&O) Railroad presented the next frontier. Nationally, the railroad's iron tentacles laced together the country in the 1850–60s. The railroad spurred a building boom when it skirted New Concord in 1852. The village expanded to embrace the rails. Maple Avenue and West Main Street are a legacy of that period.

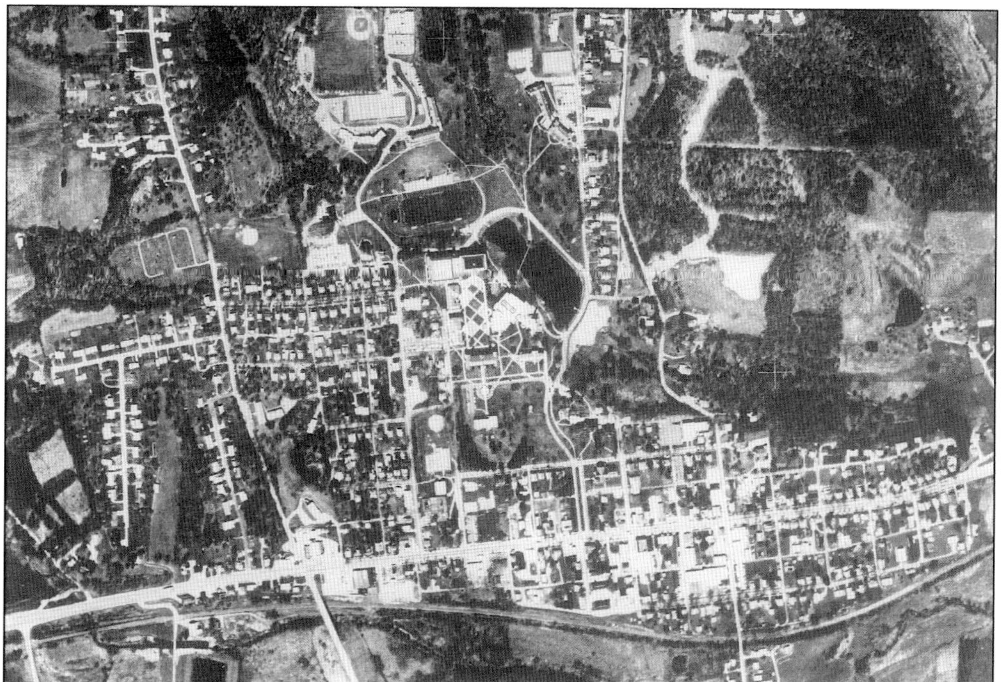

This aerial view of New Concord (1993) shows the orientation of the community along the National Road and the B&O Railroad. The railroad skirts the town on the extreme bottom. The National Road (U.S. 40) runs through the town east to west. Ohio Route 83 (Friendship Drive) runs north to south on the left hand side of the picture.

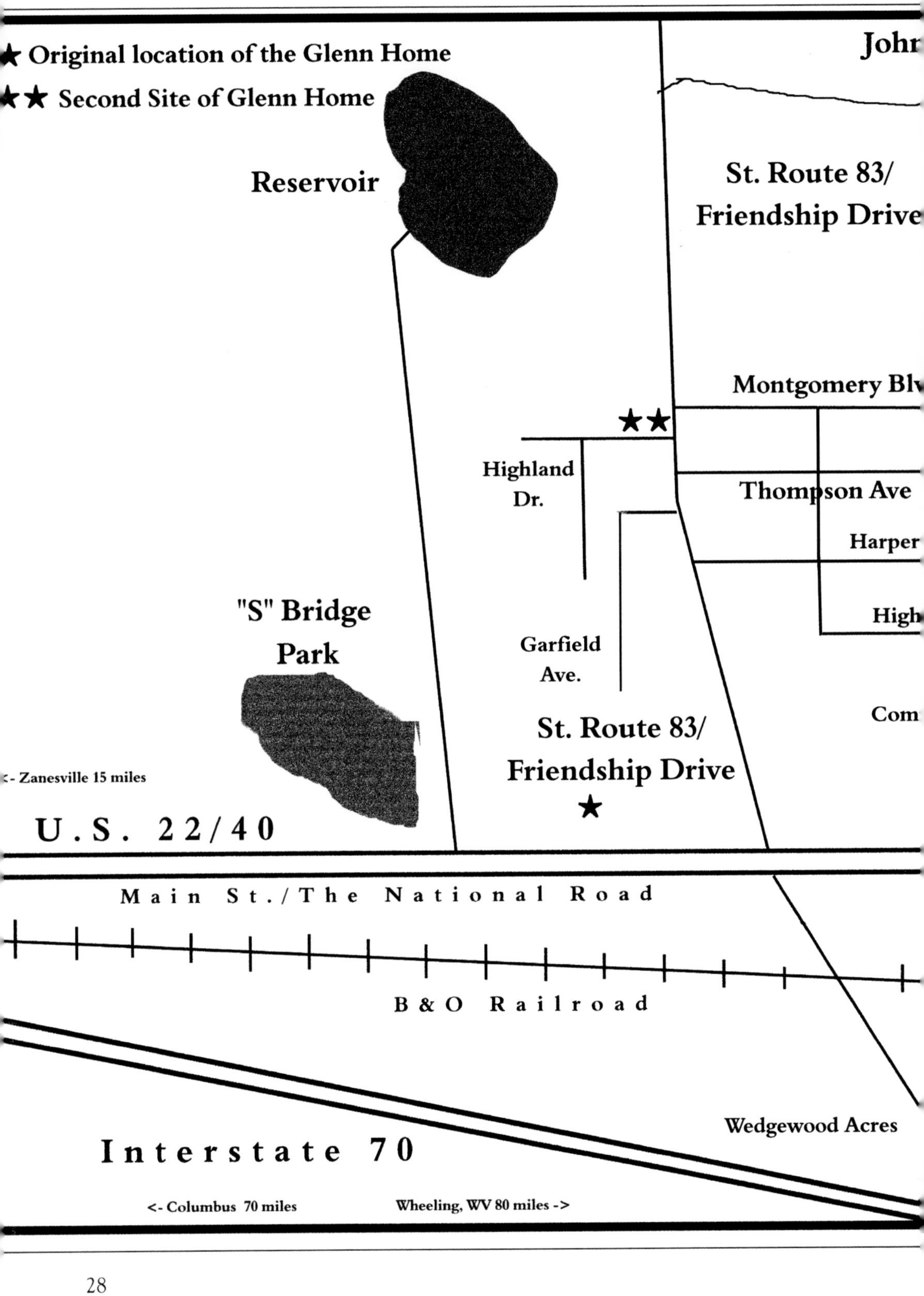
★ Original location of the Glenn Home
★★ Second Site of Glenn Home
Reservoir
Johr
St. Route 83/
Friendship Drive
Montgomery Bl
★★
Highland
Dr.
Thompson Ave
Harper
"S" Bridge
Park
High
Garfield
Ave.
Com
St. Route 83/
Friendship Drive
★
<- Zanesville 15 miles
U.S. 22/40
Main St./The National Road
B & O Railroad
Wedgewood Acres
Interstate 70
<- Columbus 70 miles
Wheeling, WV 80 miles ->

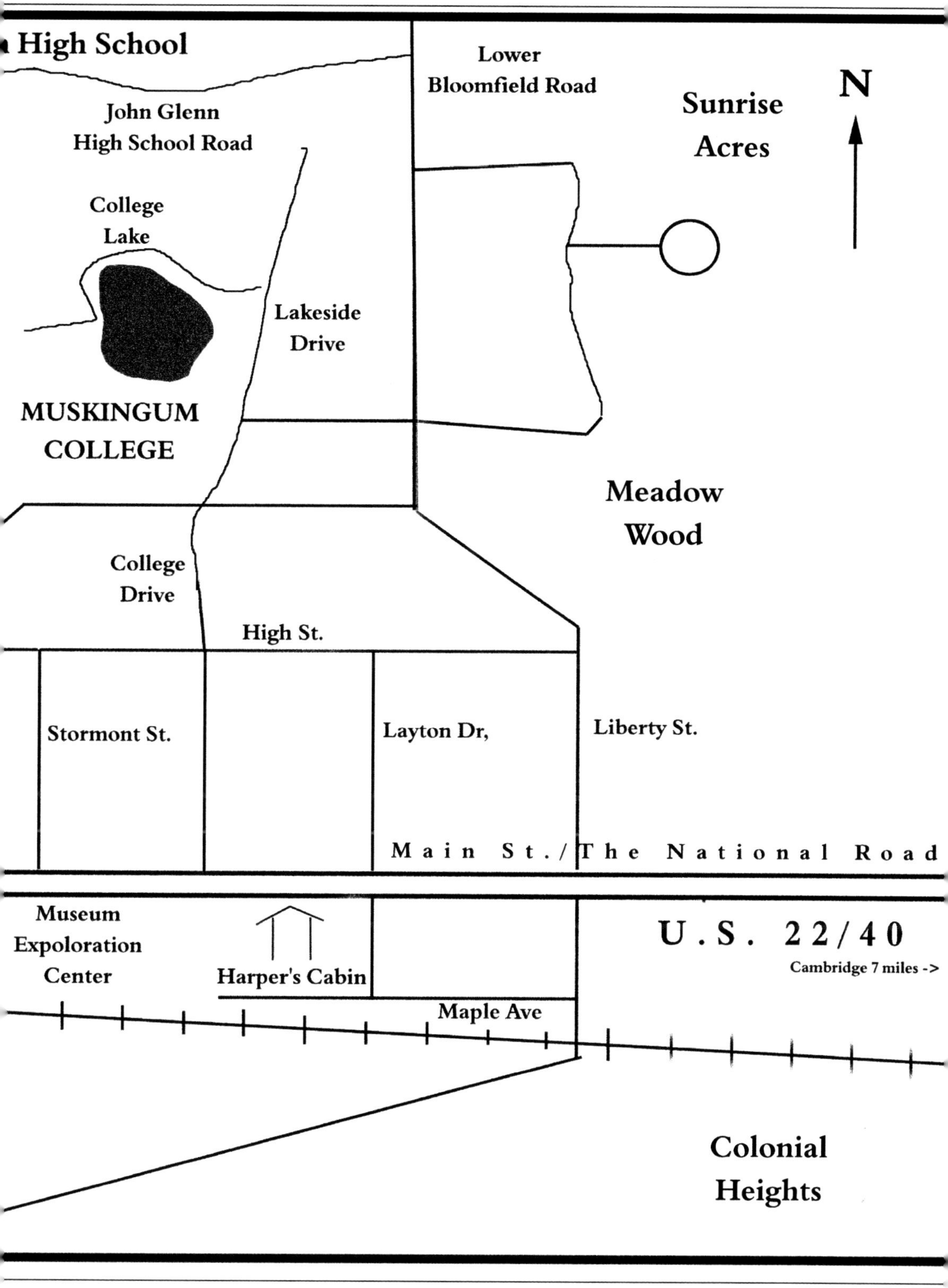
High School
Lower Bloomfield Road
Sunrise Acres
N
John Glenn High School Road
College Lake
Lakeside Drive
MUSKINGUM COLLEGE
Meadow Wood
College Drive
High St.
Stormont St.
Layton Dr,
Liberty St.
Main St./The National Road
Museum Expoloration Center
Harper's Cabin
U.S. 22/40
Cambridge 7 miles ->
Maple Ave
Colonial Heights

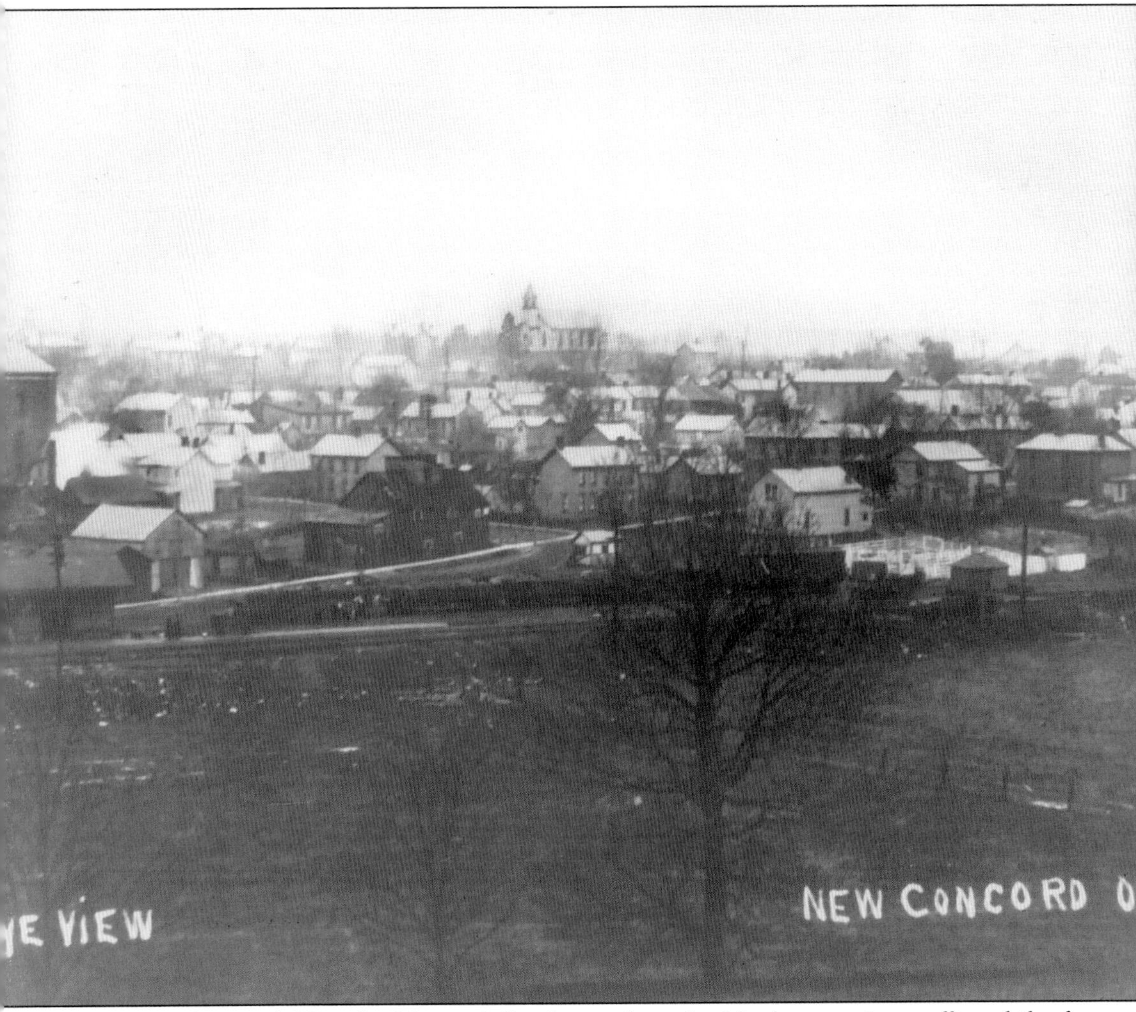

During the Civil War, the National Road was clogged with slow moving traffic, while the railroad ferried supplies and troops to the western theater of war and brought veterans, invalids, and coffins home. The railroad support system grew rapidly. Maple Avenue south to the railroad developed as housing for railroad crews and "drovers" (cattle men). Feed pens lined the back yards. In this photo (c. 1910), the railroad tracks run east to west in the center of the photo, just below the feed pens and the laundry line (right). Upper left is the Village Hall (razed in 1957). The Feed Mill (razed in the 1980s) is the dark building in center left. Westminister Presbyterian Church crowns the hill center top.

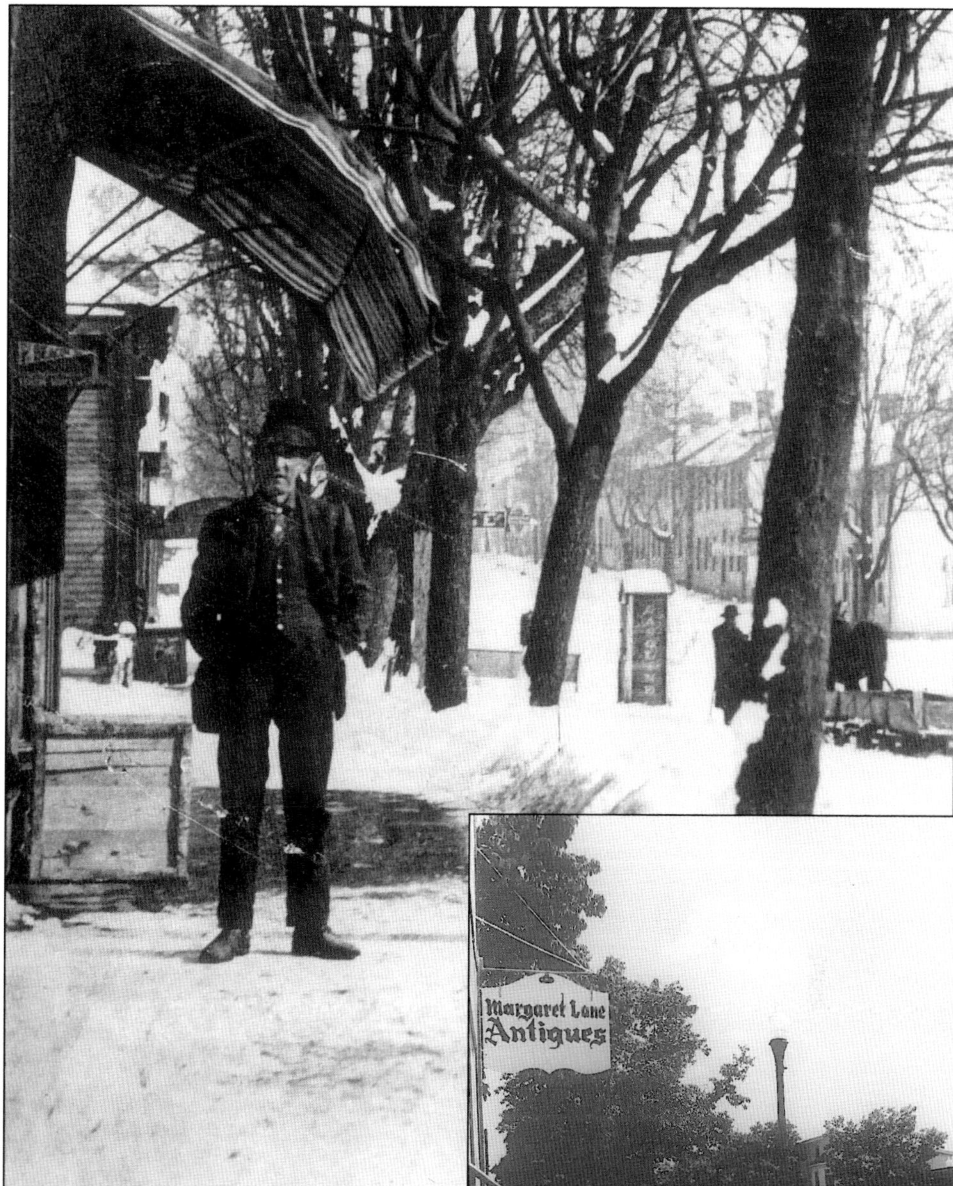

In this photo (c. 1910), dry-goods shop owner Sam Noble stands beside his store at 2 East Main Street (corner of Main Street and Layton Drive). Looking eastward, over his shoulder, the Federal-style houses which once lined the National Road can be seen. Note the gas pump beside the man and horse pulling a delivery sled.

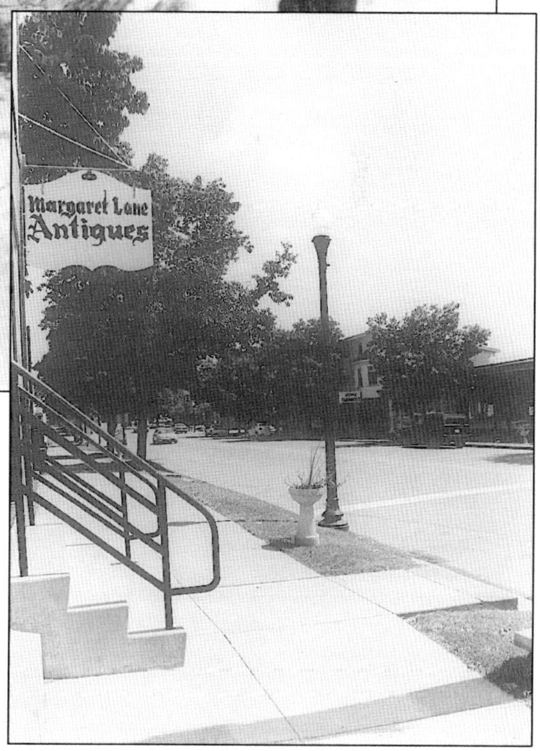

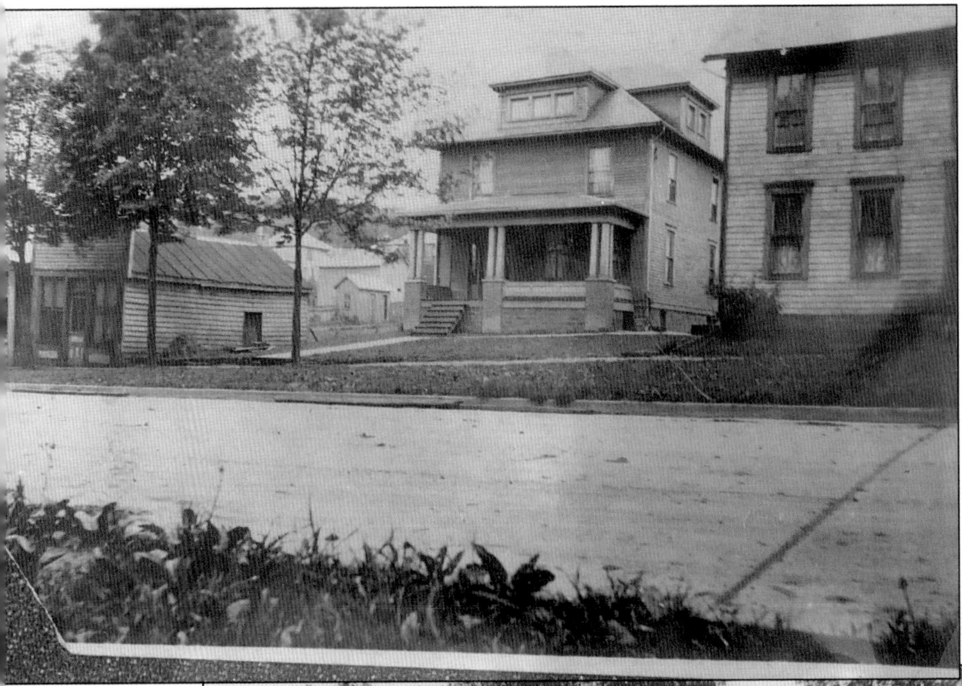

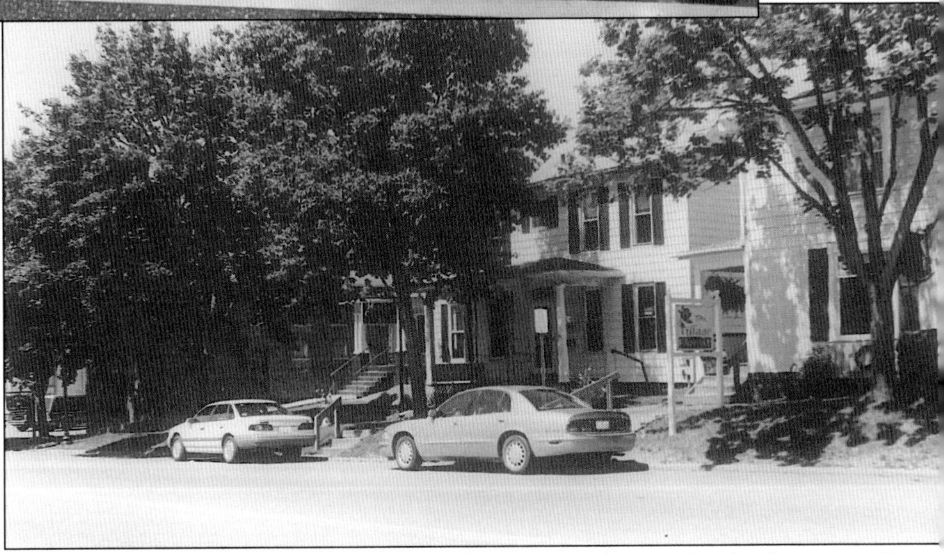

National Road architecture reflected three styles: low "Pennsylvania-Maryland cottages," two-story "Federal-style" houses, and "shotgun" houses—so named because you could fire a shotgun through the front door and hit a target out the open back door. These shotgun-style businesses once checkered the street. The second of these buildings from the left was widowed Mary Ann Hughs' grocery during the Civil War.

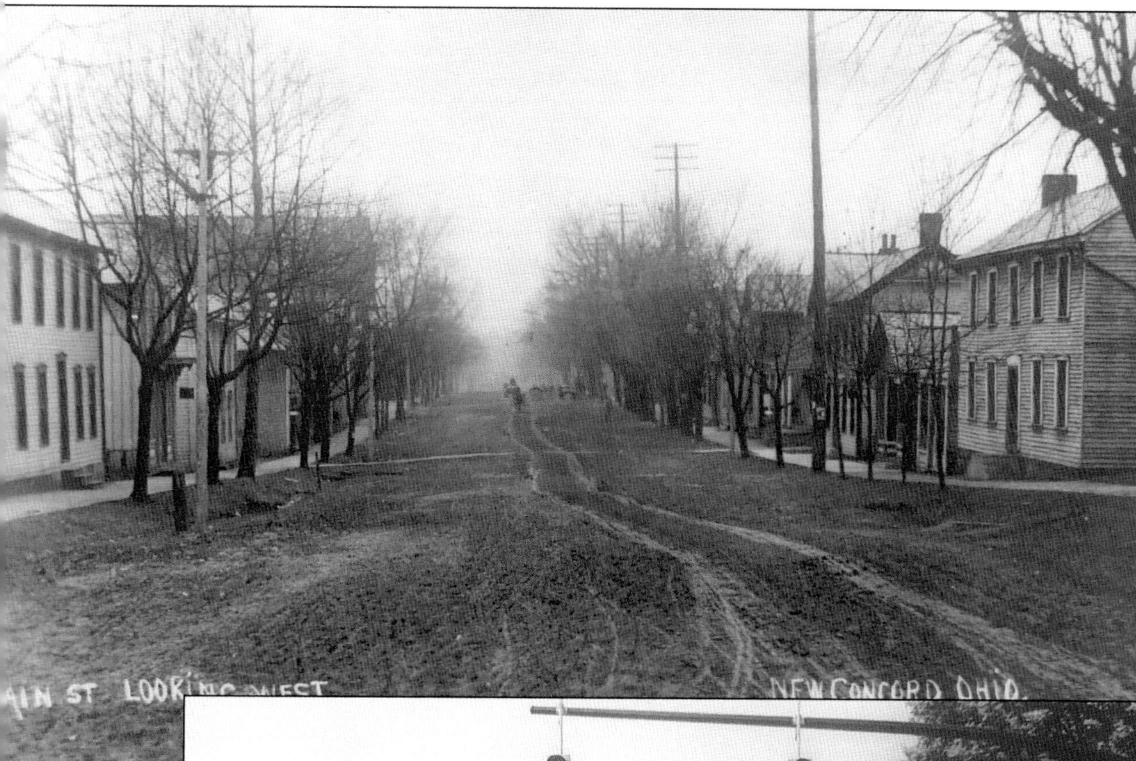

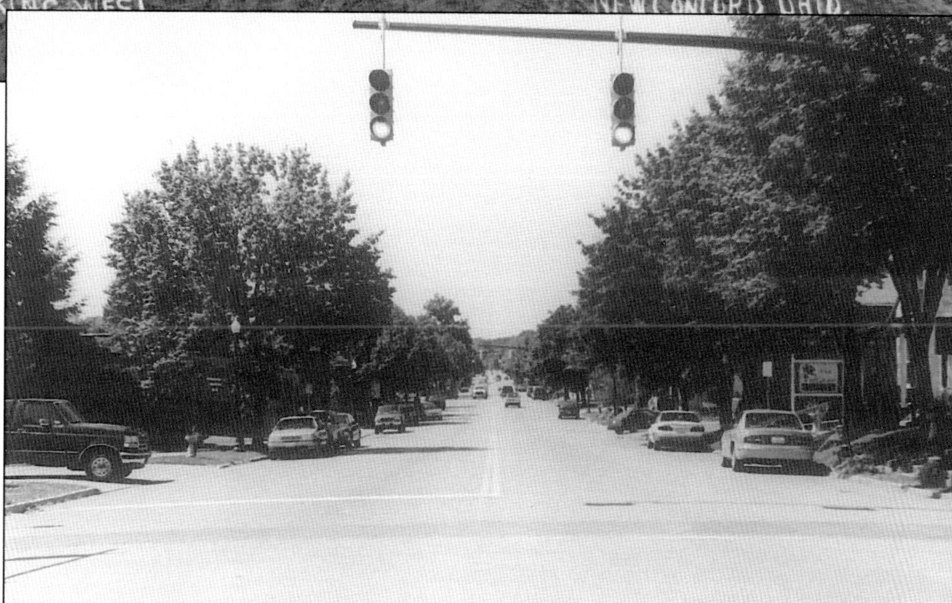

In the top photo (c. 1910), Main Street looking west from Liberty is documented. Note the telegraph poles. At this stage, the National Road had become less important than the railroad, and little was spent on its maintenance. It was frequently a river of mud. The building to the right was replaced by one that would later house the Glenn Plumbing store. The American House Hotel operated in the building to the left.

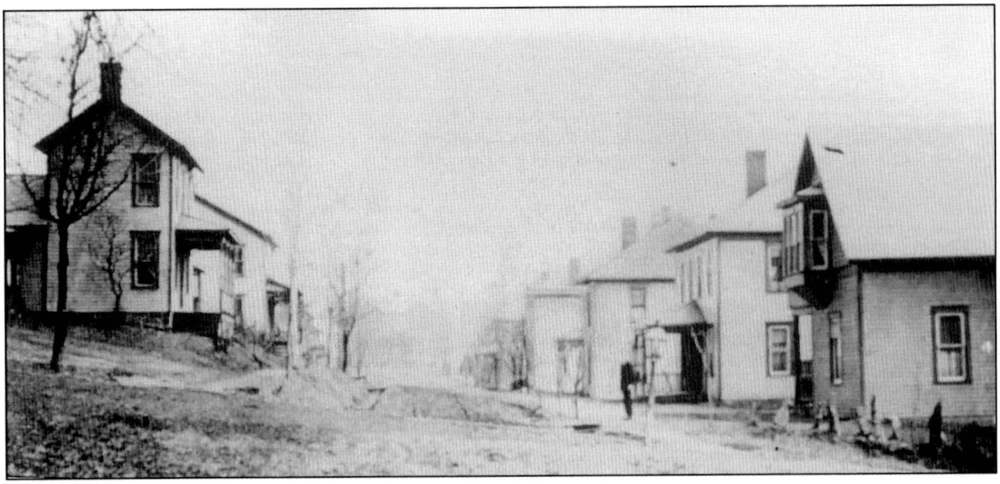

In the early 1900s, New Concord's position in the center of a rich farm community with access to the National Road and the railroad encouraged more development. High Street east of College Drive boasted houses which straddled a muddy side street. The top photo (c. 1900) shows East High Street looking east from Layton Drive. Note the gas light. The second photo is distinguished by telephone poles, but the street remained a muddy avenue. Wooden sidewalks enabled pedestrians to travel more conveniently than did the mud-caked wheels of carts and automobiles.

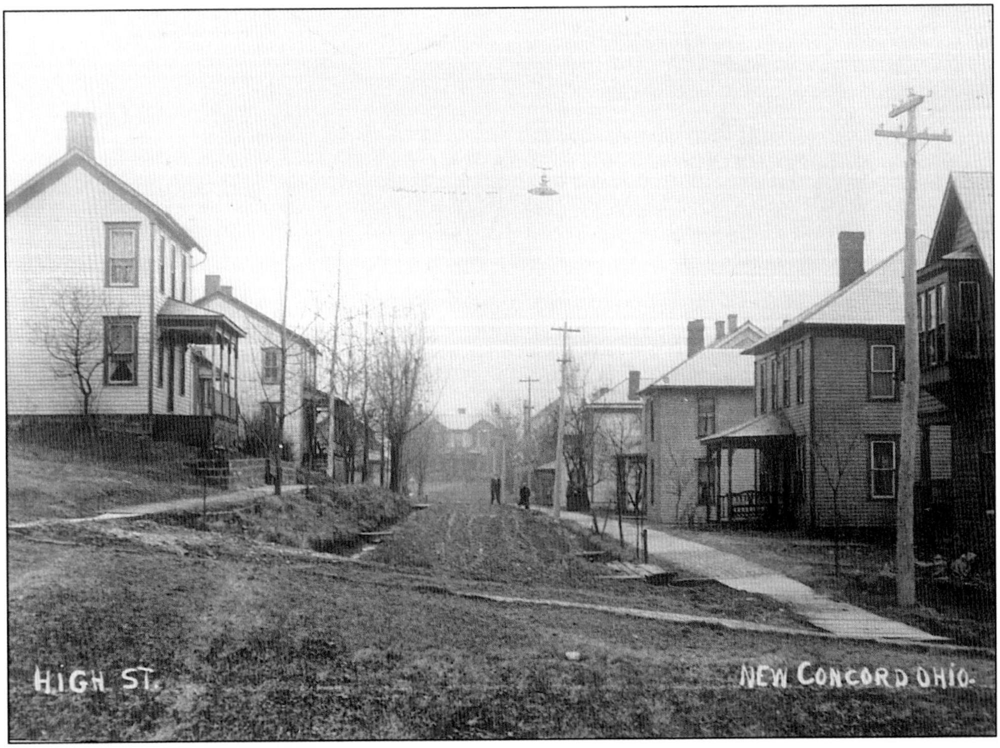

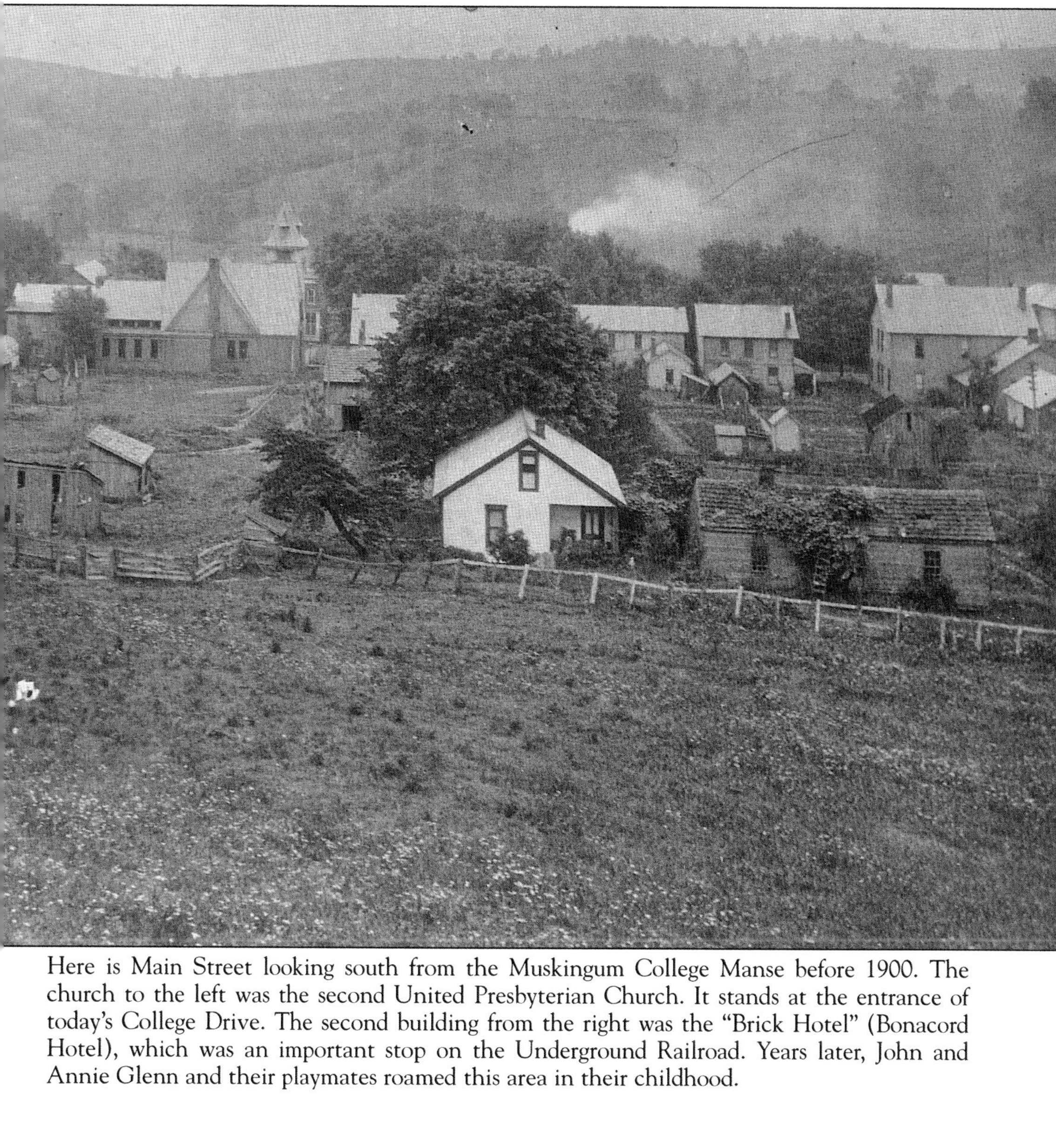

Here is Main Street looking south from the Muskingum College Manse before 1900. The church to the left was the second United Presbyterian Church. It stands at the entrance of today's College Drive. The second building from the right was the "Brick Hotel" (Bonacord Hotel), which was an important stop on the Underground Railroad. Years later, John and Annie Glenn and their playmates roamed this area in their childhood.

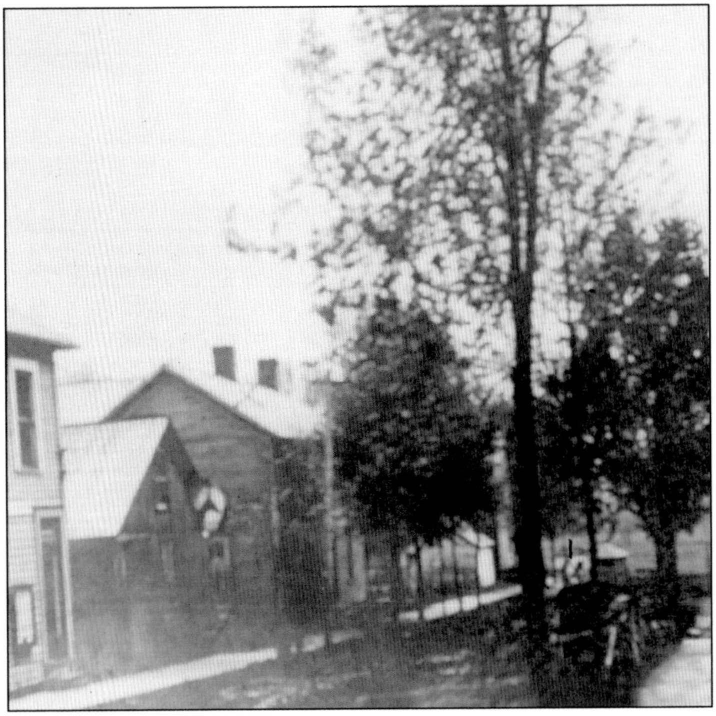

New Concord had its full share of blacksmiths. Joseph McKinney was the pioneer blacksmith—moving his forge from the Zane's Trace to New Concord as soon as Judge Findley platted the village. Unfortunately, only artists' representations can be had for the earliest shops. However, three smiths operated here in the early 1900s, and at least one, J.R. Roon, continued through the 1940s. His son Rex and John Glenn Jr. were staunch childhood friends.

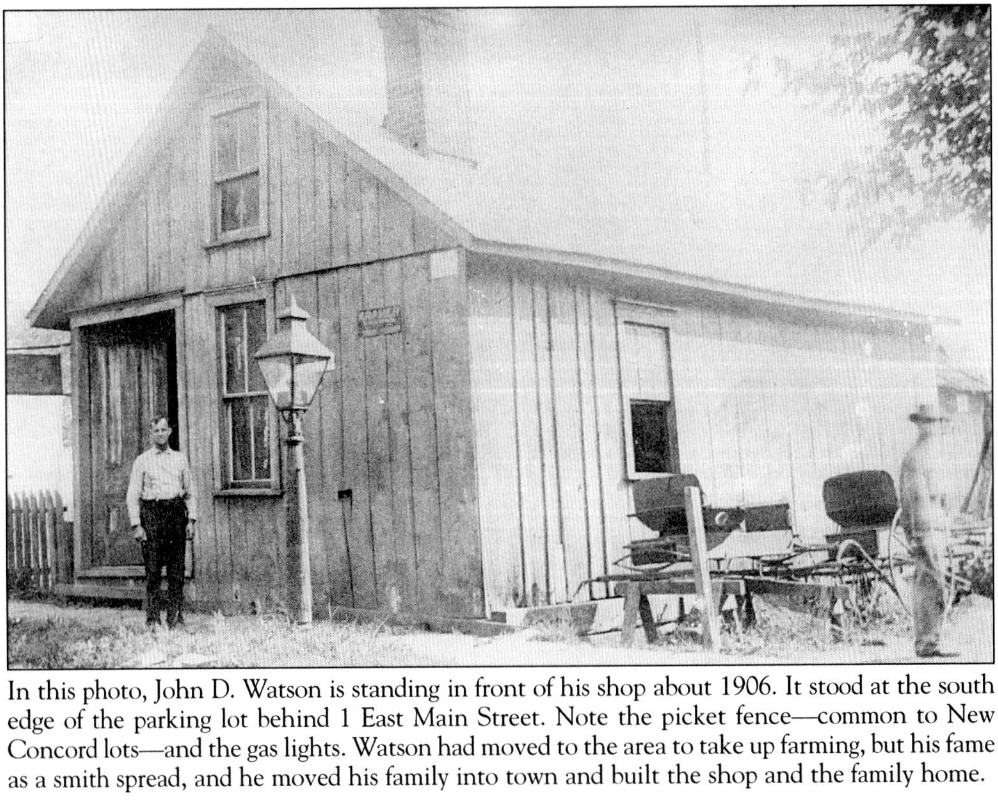

In this photo, John D. Watson is standing in front of his shop about 1906. It stood at the south edge of the parking lot behind 1 East Main Street. Note the picket fence—common to New Concord lots—and the gas lights. Watson had moved to the area to take up farming, but his fame as a smith spread, and he moved his family into town and built the shop and the family home.

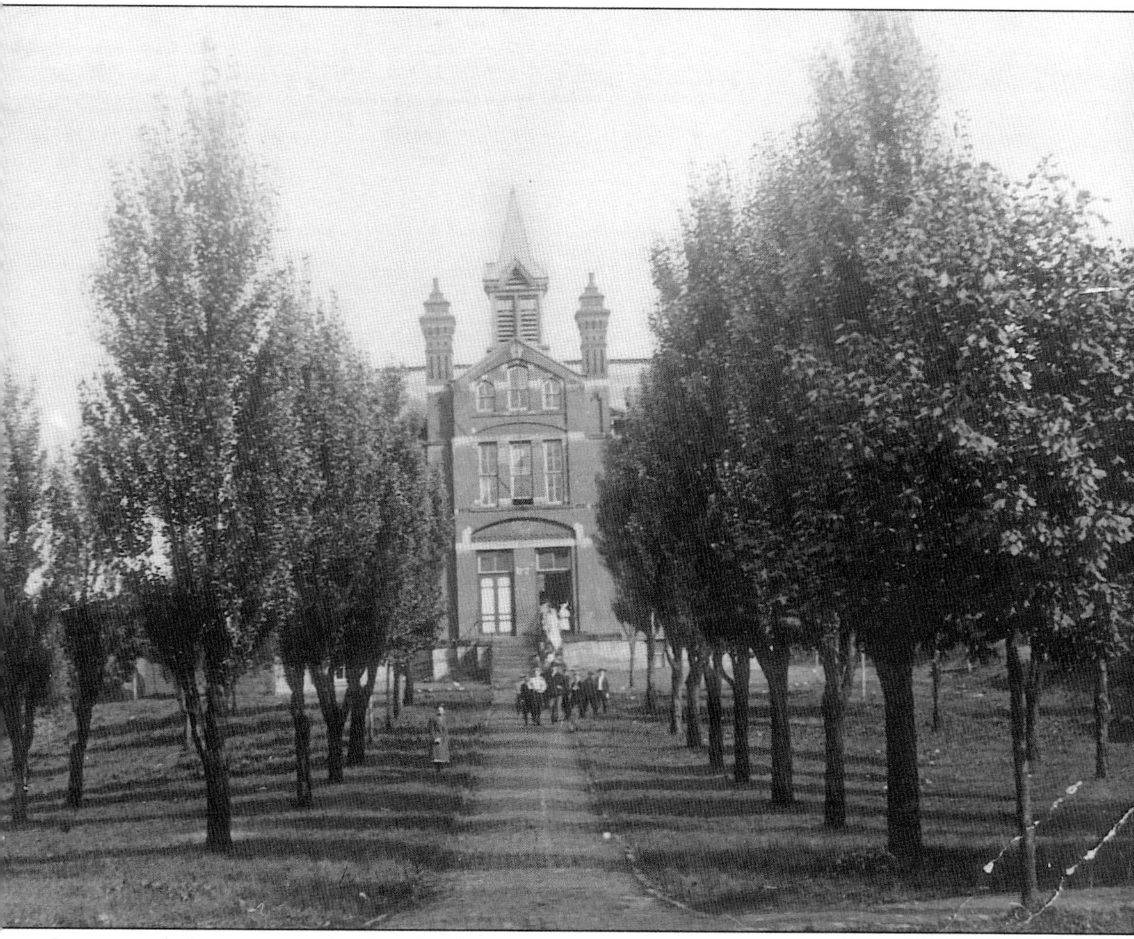

Prosperity led to a spate of public building. Particularly important was the elementary school built on East High Street and facing Main Street. This beautiful building, erected in 1874, served until 1931. The village high school was organized in 1887 and continued until 1908. Then the New Concord Academy, which met in Muskingum College's Paul Hall, functioned from 1908–1931.

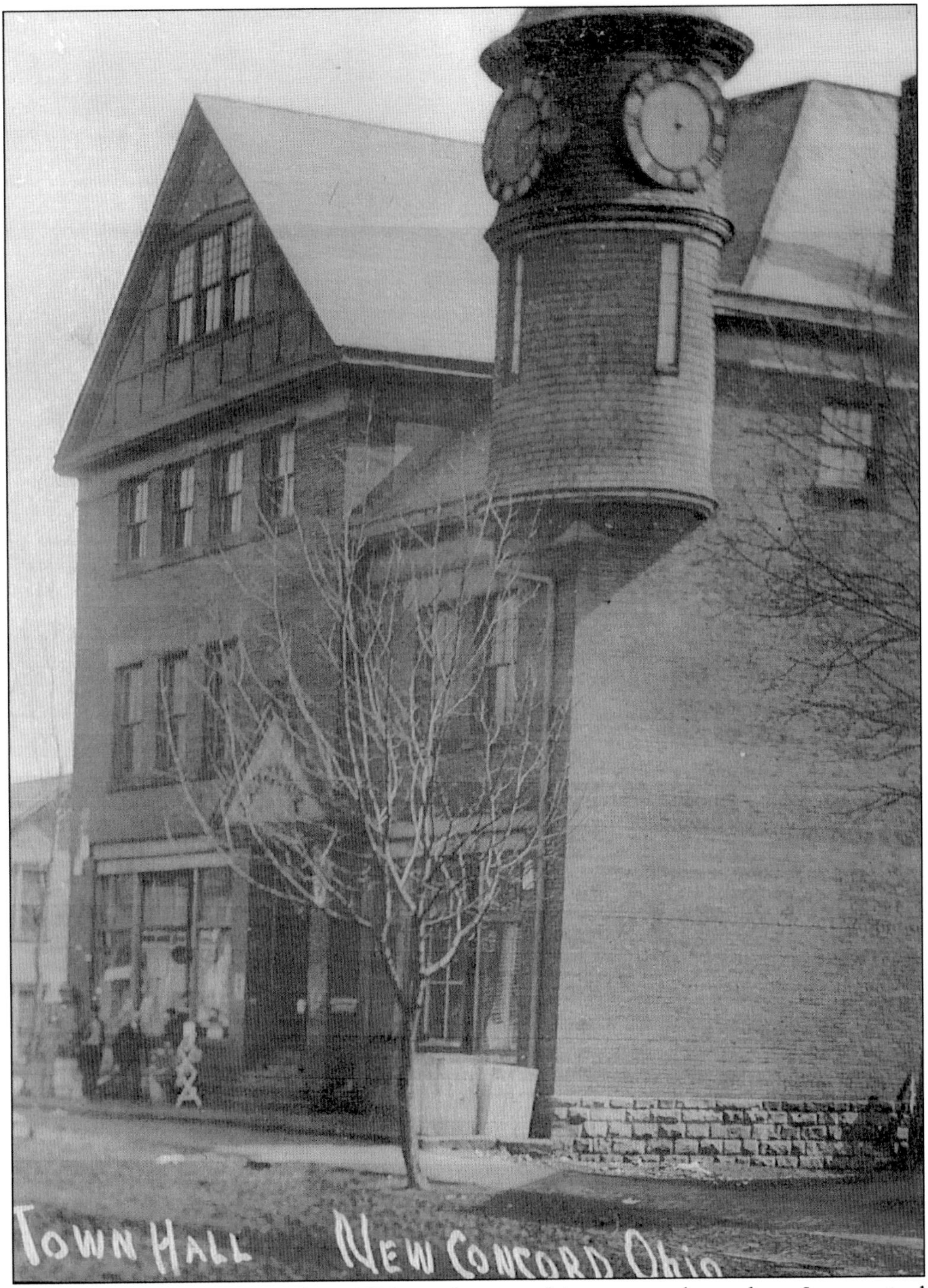

The Village Hall was erected in 1888 on the site of its current descendent. It contained government offices, a grocery, a dentist's office, a bowling alley, the Masonic Hall, and the Roy Theatre. It also boasted a splendid clock tower. The building fell victim to "progress" in 1959.

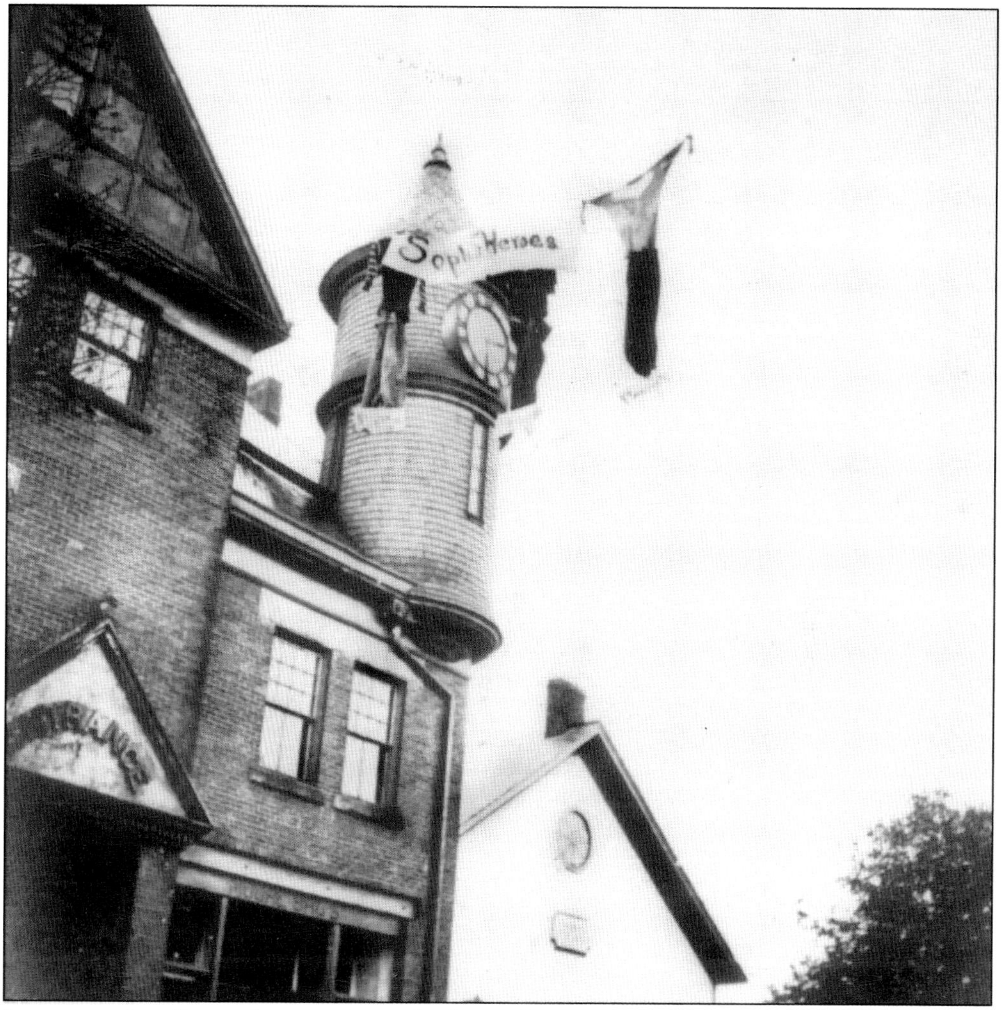

In a town that frowned on smoking, drinking, dancing, and card playing, pranksterism was developed to a high art. Here, the Muskingum College sophomore class has successfully circumvented security to hang "long johns" from the flag pole. (The Reformed Presbyterian Church is seen to the right of Village Hall.) After one too many such college pranks, the "town fathers" dismantled the clock tower.

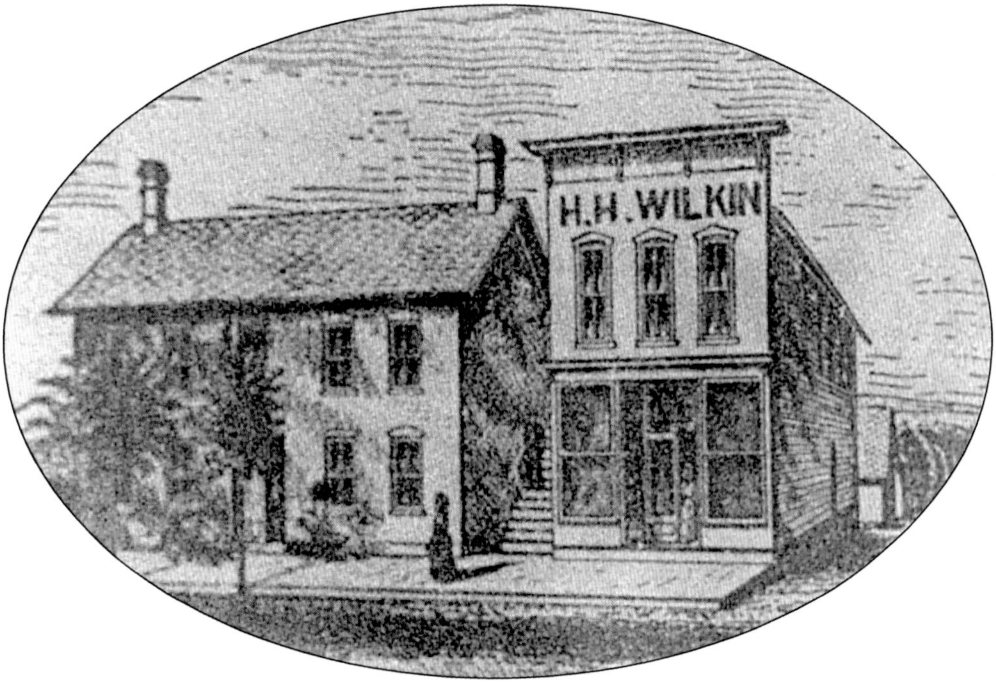

Railroad prosperity produced glory days for the New Concord area. Much of the village business centered around transportation. Blacksmith shops, hardware stores, and farm implement manufacturing dominated East Main Street's business section. These buildings stood at the corner of Liberty and Main Street until the 1970s.

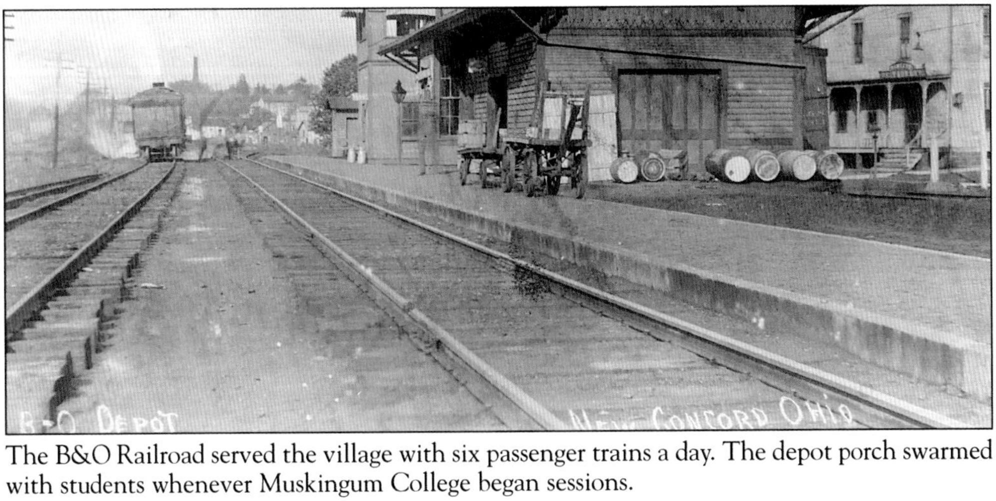

The B&O Railroad served the village with six passenger trains a day. The depot porch swarmed with students whenever Muskingum College began sessions.

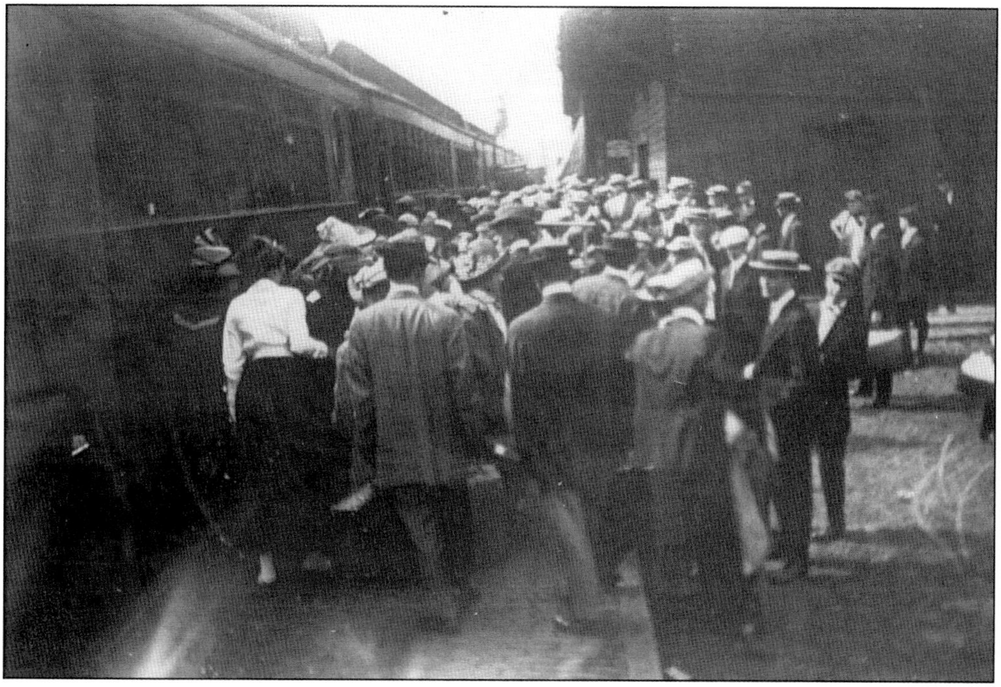

Muskingum College students came to New Concord on one of the six passenger trains which stopped daily in the village. They were drawn from the Scotch-Irish/Presbyterian areas of Pennsylvania, Ohio, and North Carolina. There was a homogeneity to the college and the community. The railroad conductors jokingly referred to the area as "Saints Rest."

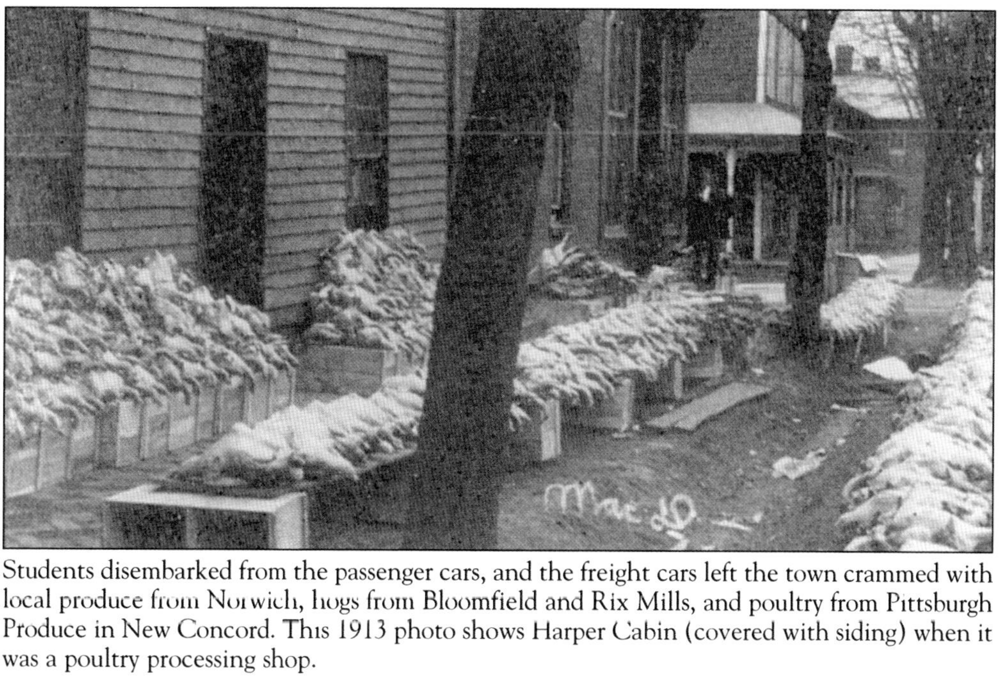

Students disembarked from the passenger cars, and the freight cars left the town crammed with local produce from Norwich, hogs from Bloomfield and Rix Mills, and poultry from Pittsburgh Produce in New Concord. This 1913 photo shows Harper Cabin (covered with siding) when it was a poultry processing shop.

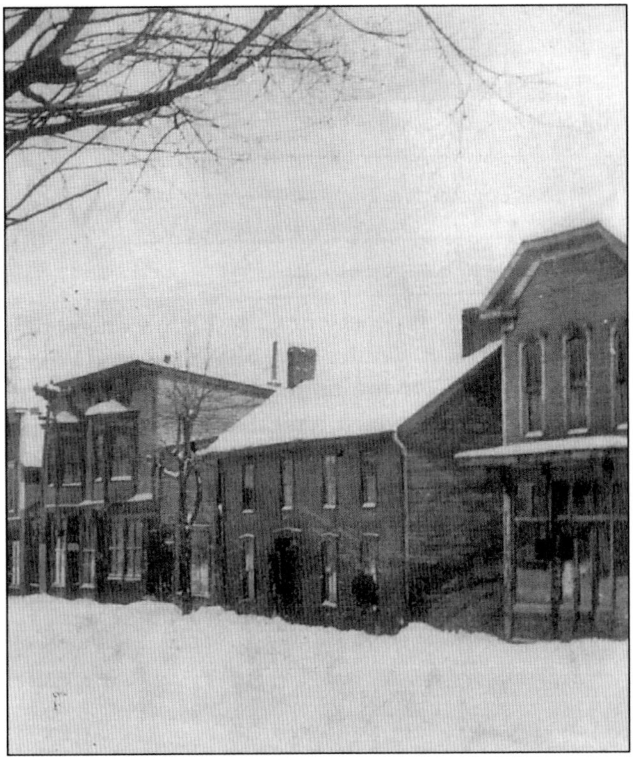

Although New Concord was connected to the world through its transportation arteries, the village had a self-sustained economy with many shops and restaurants. This central block of East Main Street featured the Mecca Restaurant.

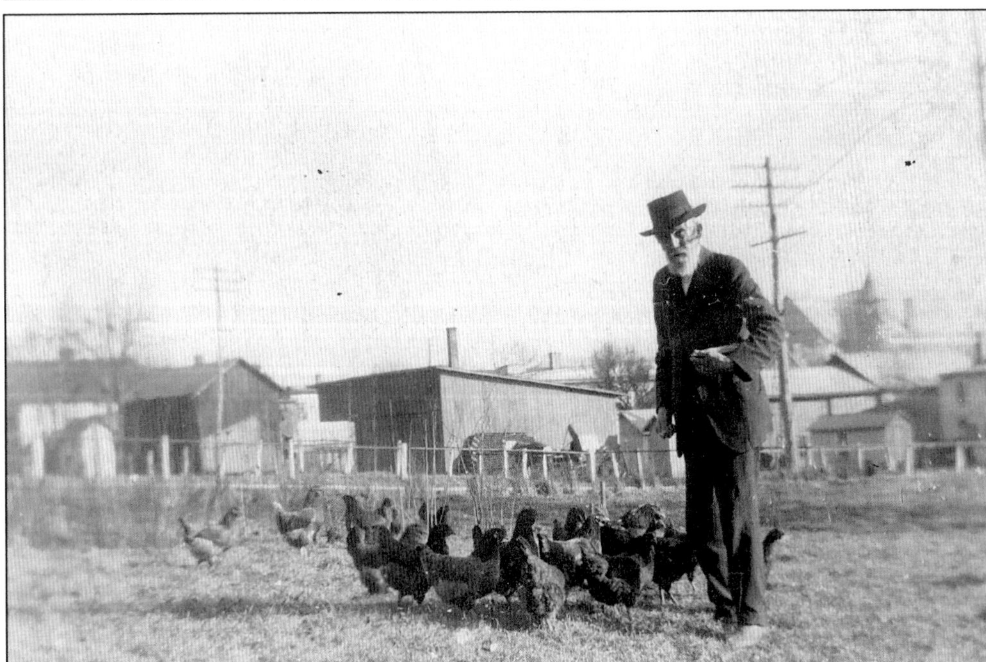

In its self-containment, chickens, goats, and cows were kept in the village until after World War II. Dr. Henry McCreary is pictured with a flock of chickens which provided eggs for his daughter Helen Garrison's "fort" (college eating club). The Village Hall can be seen to his right.

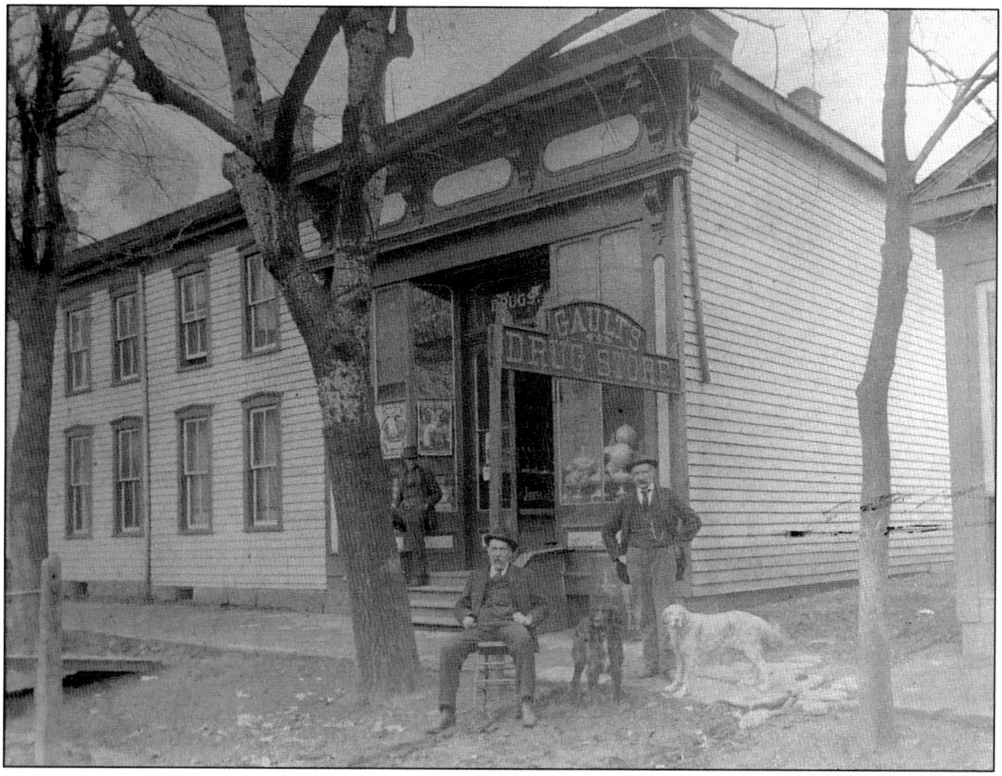

Jack Gault's Pharmacy served the needs of citizens who were tended by two doctors and two dentists. Gault's stood cheek-to-jowl with National Road houses on Main Street.

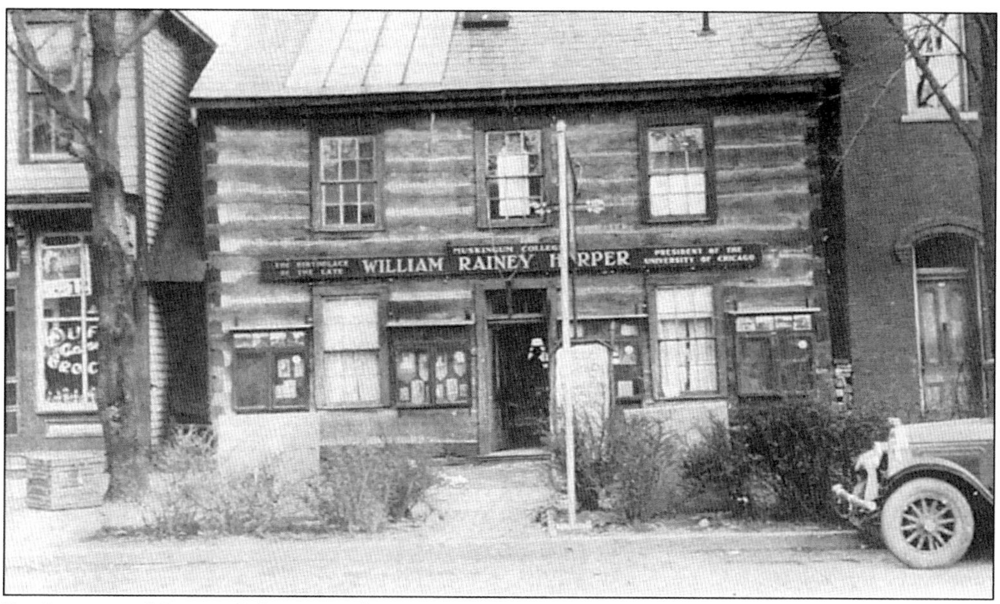

By this time, Harper Cabin served as tea room and photographer's studio. Its neighbor to the east was Duff's Cash Grocery, one of a half dozen in the village.

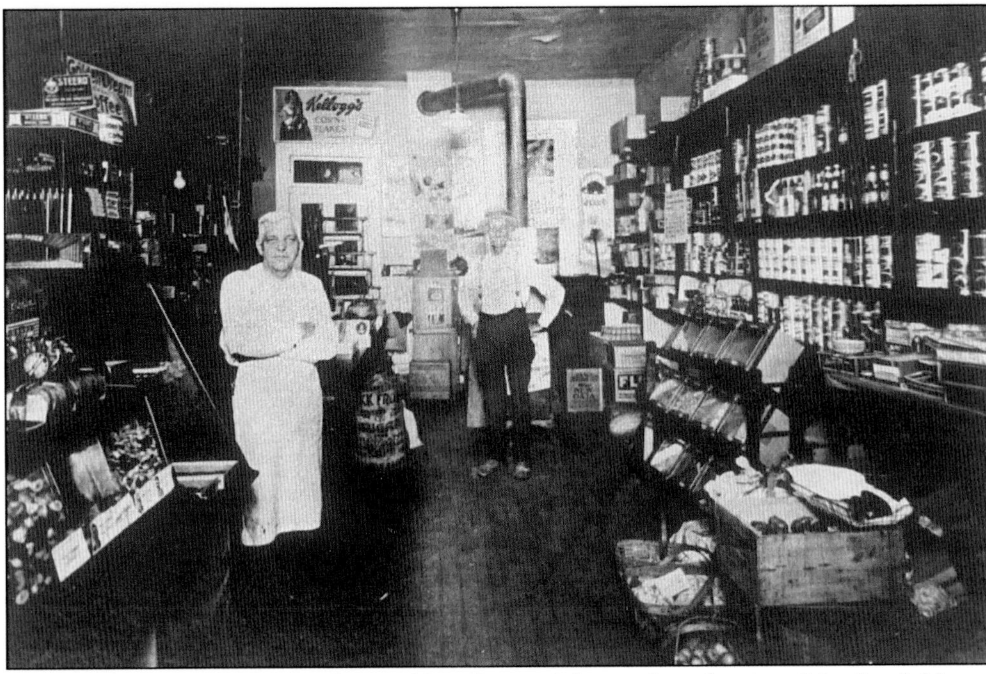

Duff's Cash Grocery was one of six in New Concord. It stood on the site of the Frank Harper Garden. It burned in the 1930s. Threats of fire made the Volunteer Fire Department (founded in 1845) a crucial part of village life.

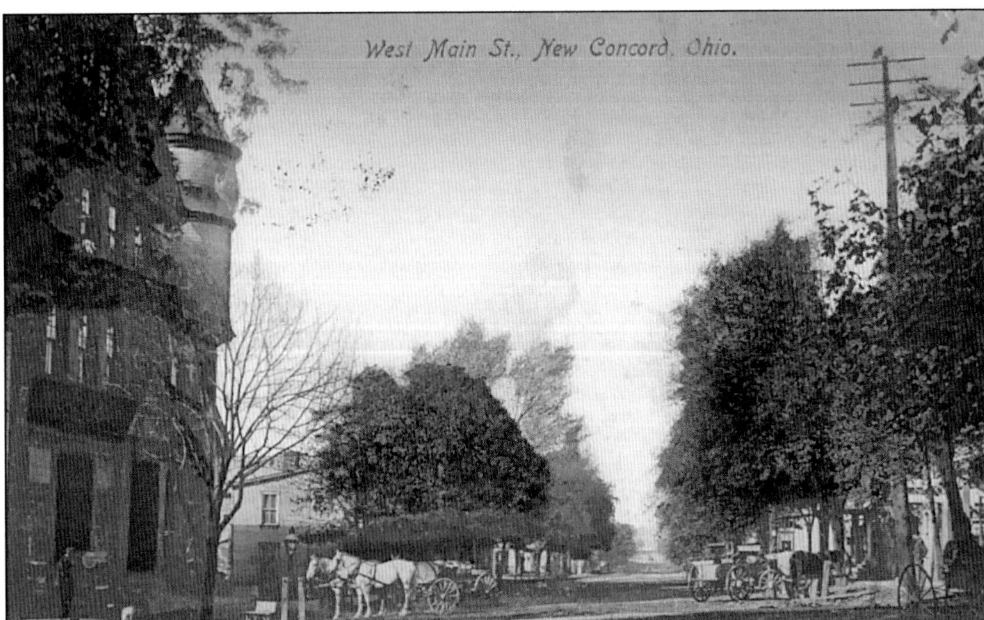

New Concord in 1910 was a prosperous agricultural market town, served by the National Road and the B&O Railroad. Its added attraction was a small but promising academic institution. Both New Concord and Muskingum College would blossom in the next two decades.

Three

"The Social Gospel"

Republican New Concord reveled in the election of Democrat Woodrow Wilson as president in 1912. The Scotch-Irish Wilson was the son of a Presbyterian minister and President of Presbyterian Yale University. His co-religionists fully expected the dawn of a new age of government dominated by the Social Gospel. This move to infuse Christian principles into government policy was widely shared by America's mainstream Protestant denominations.

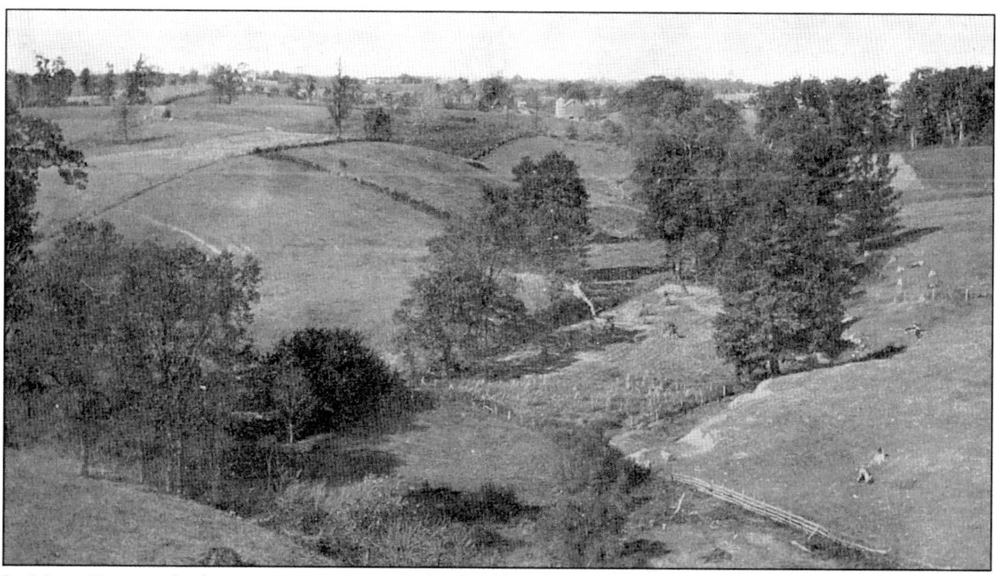

In New Concord, the movement was embodied by the energetic Muskingum College President John Knox Montgomery, who turned to the north of his small campus—then only Paul Hall and Johnson Hall—and built Brown Chapel, the College Lake, Lakeside Drive, Montgomery Hall, and Cambridge Hall on land that had been hilly pastures and strawberry farms. This photo shows the terrain which President Montgomery would transform by 1929.

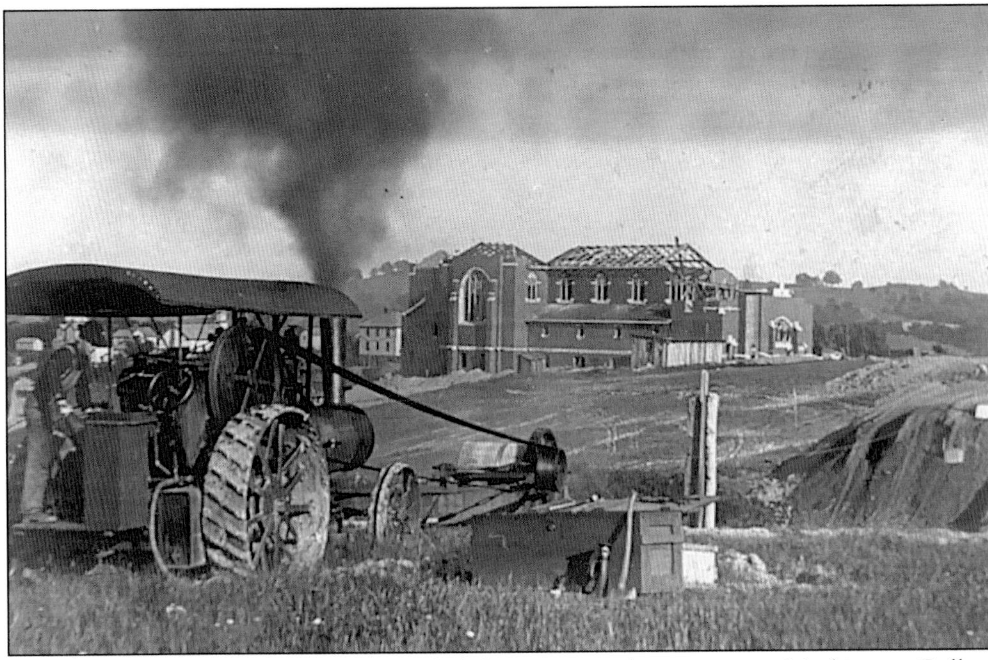

Basking in prosperity, the local area exploded in a wave of construction. Muskingum College built Brown Chapel in 1912. Local men, working with pick and shovel and steam engines, dug out the Muskingum College Lake in 1914. The college power plant, financed by fines paid by an illegal liquor operation in Zanesville, supplied electricity to the entire community until 1947.

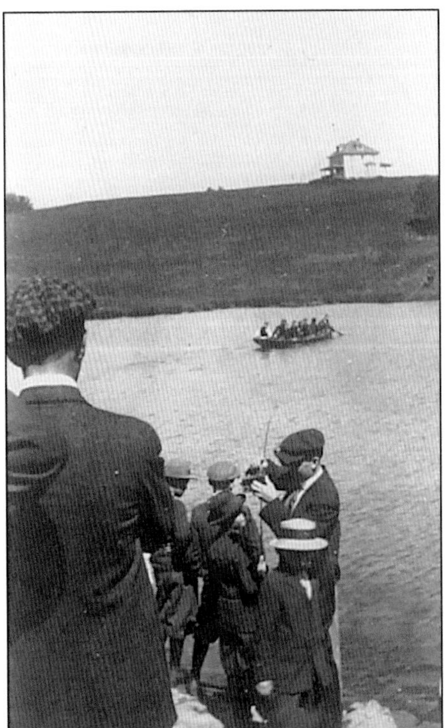

Houses began to sprout on Lakeside Drive. First one . . .

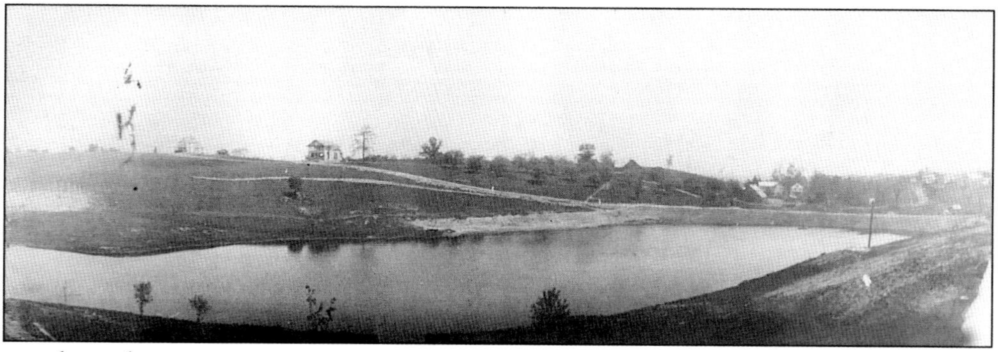

. . . then others.

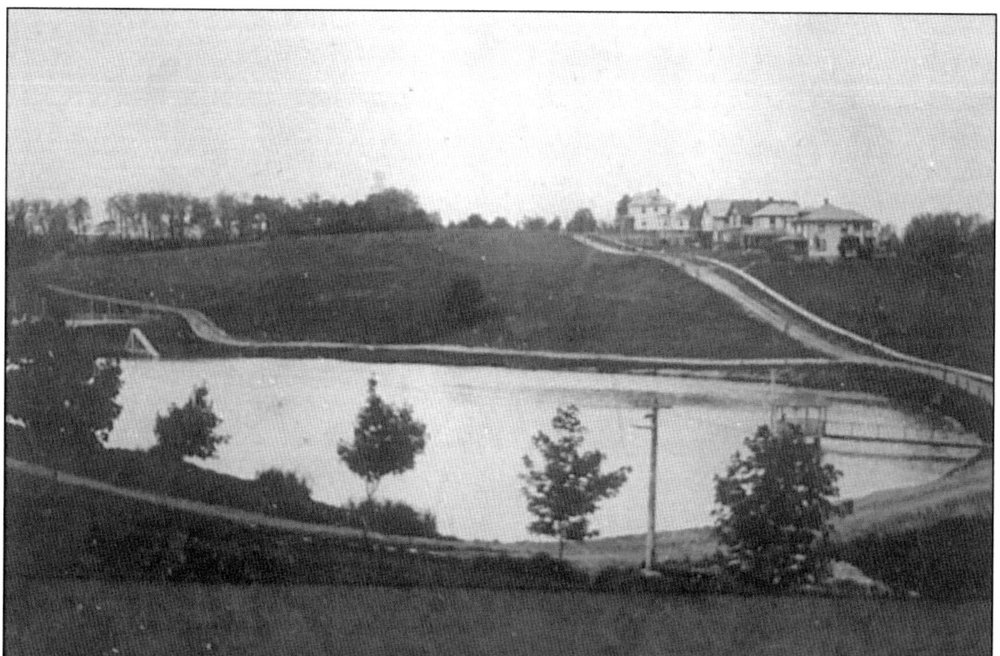

The Lakeside Drive houses were residences for Presbyterian ministerial families on sabbaticals from foreign missions. Their presence added a cosmopolitan flavor to Muskingum College and the village.

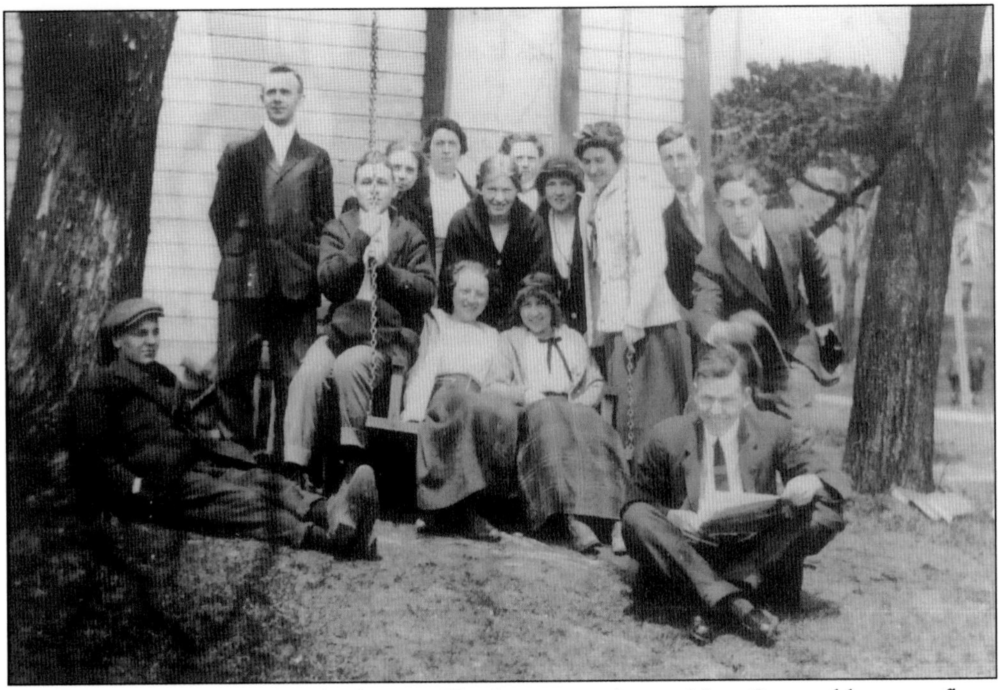

Muskingum College's student body grew. The large size of many New Concord homes reflects their use as boarding houses for New Concord Academy and Muskingum College students. The college's first dormitory (Patton Hall) was not built until 1922. This was Garrison's Fort at West High and College Drive opposite the United Presbyterian Church.

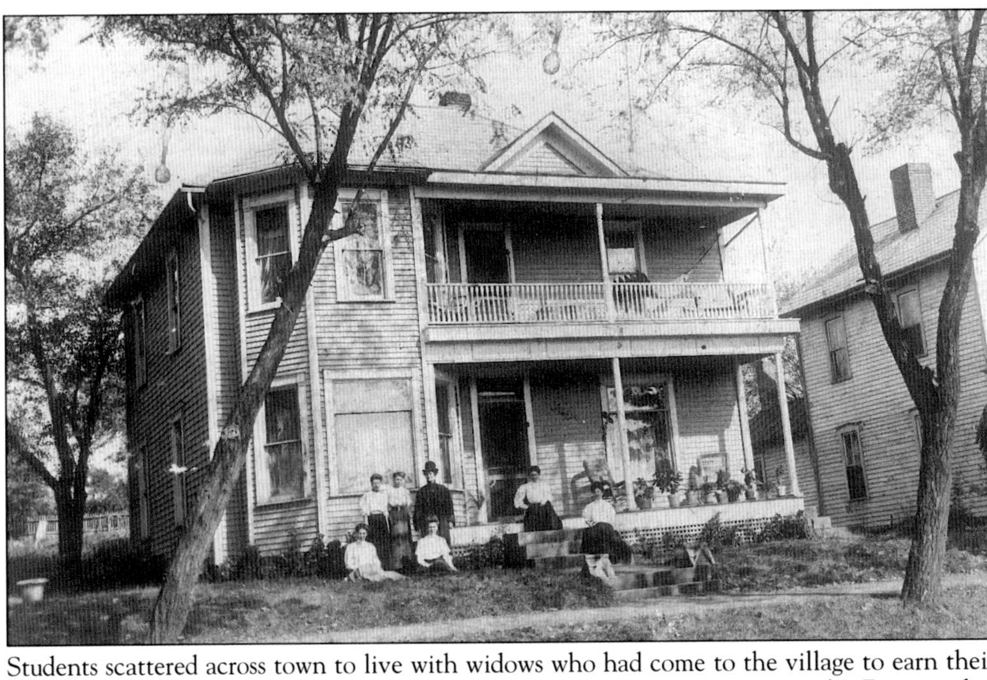

Students scattered across town to live with widows who had come to the village to earn their living as rooming house owners or to operate dining clubs, called "Forts." Gault's Fort stood at the northwest corner of Comin and Main Streets.

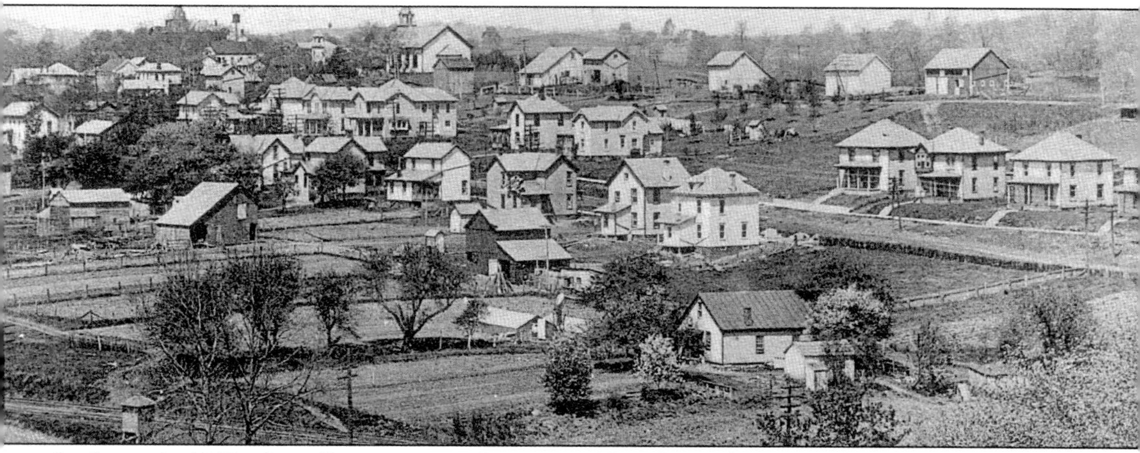

In the early 1900s the village continued to grow. This photo shows the development of the eastern edge of the village by 1915.

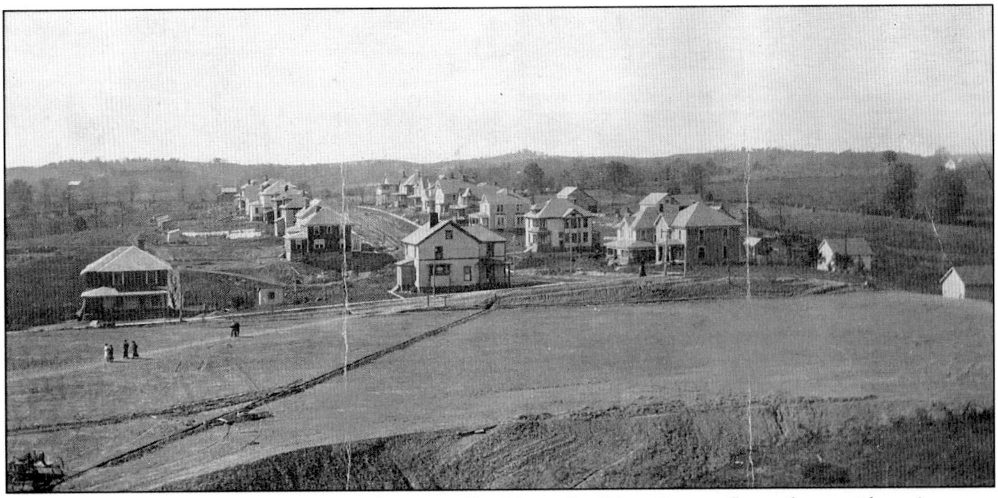

Another residential section, named originally "Lincoln Place" to reflect the residents' strong Civil War opinions, was developed between 1913 and 1920. Now known as Montgomery Boulevard, the development is shown from what would be the Muskingum College Student-Faculty Center looking west.

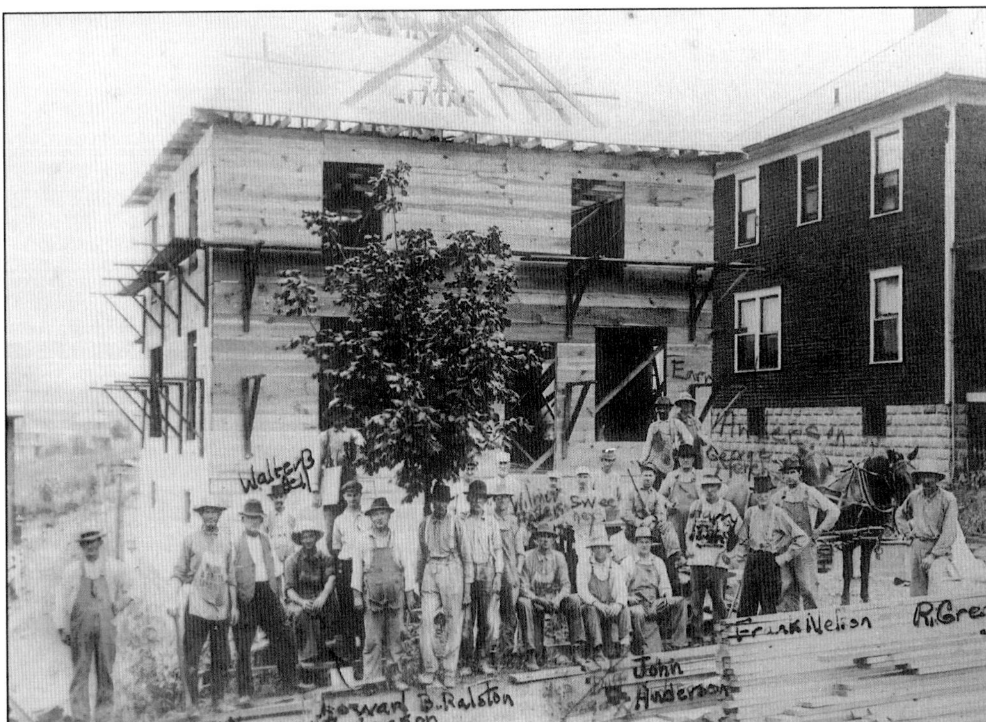

The building boom brought steady employment for local men. This building, at the corner of Comin Street and Montgomery Boulevard, has since been replaced by a brick apartment building.

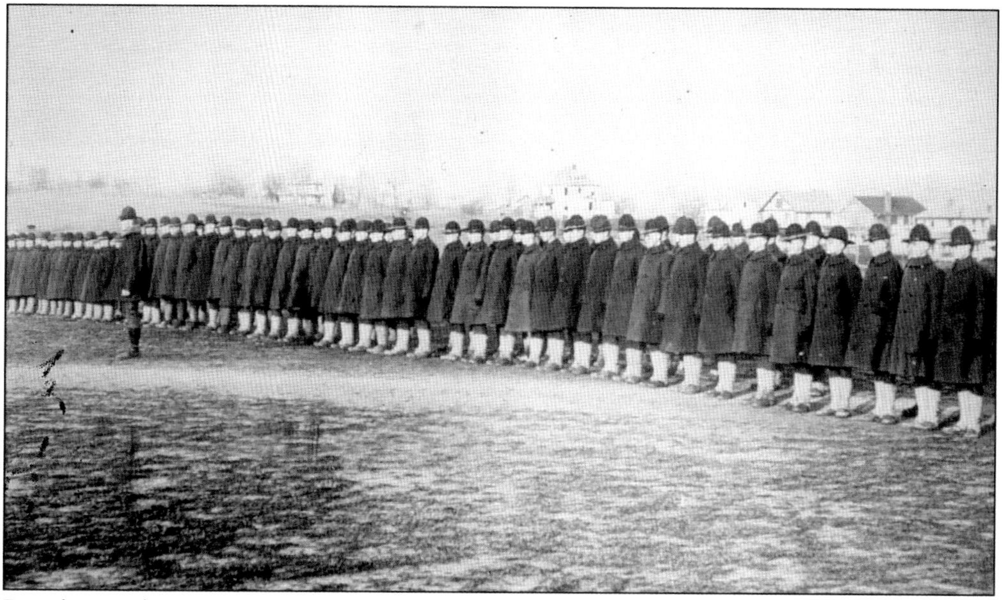

President Wilson's call-to-arms in 1917 as America entered World War I drew an enthusiastic response from church people who were determined to end evil in the world. The clarion cries of "a war to end all wars" and "a war to make the world safe for democracy" struck chords in the Social Gospel community. Not only did local men enlist to go "over there," but this army unit trained at Muskingum College.

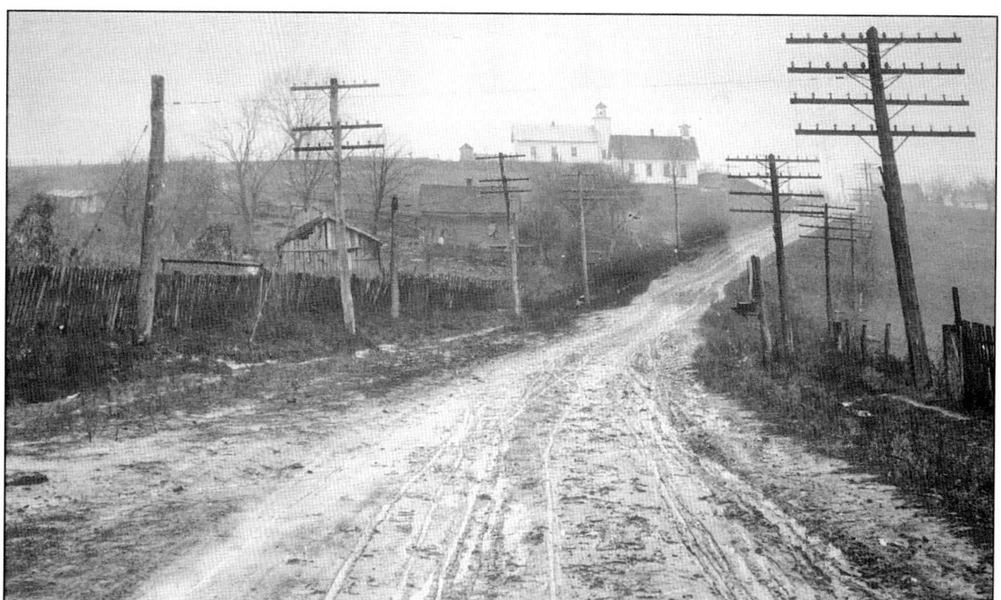

The National Road (now designated also the Old National Trail) was indeed "America's Road," but it was muddy and unimproved. World War I led to rapidly increasing traffic on the National Road and the B&O Railroad. This photo shows Hopewell, west of Zanesville.

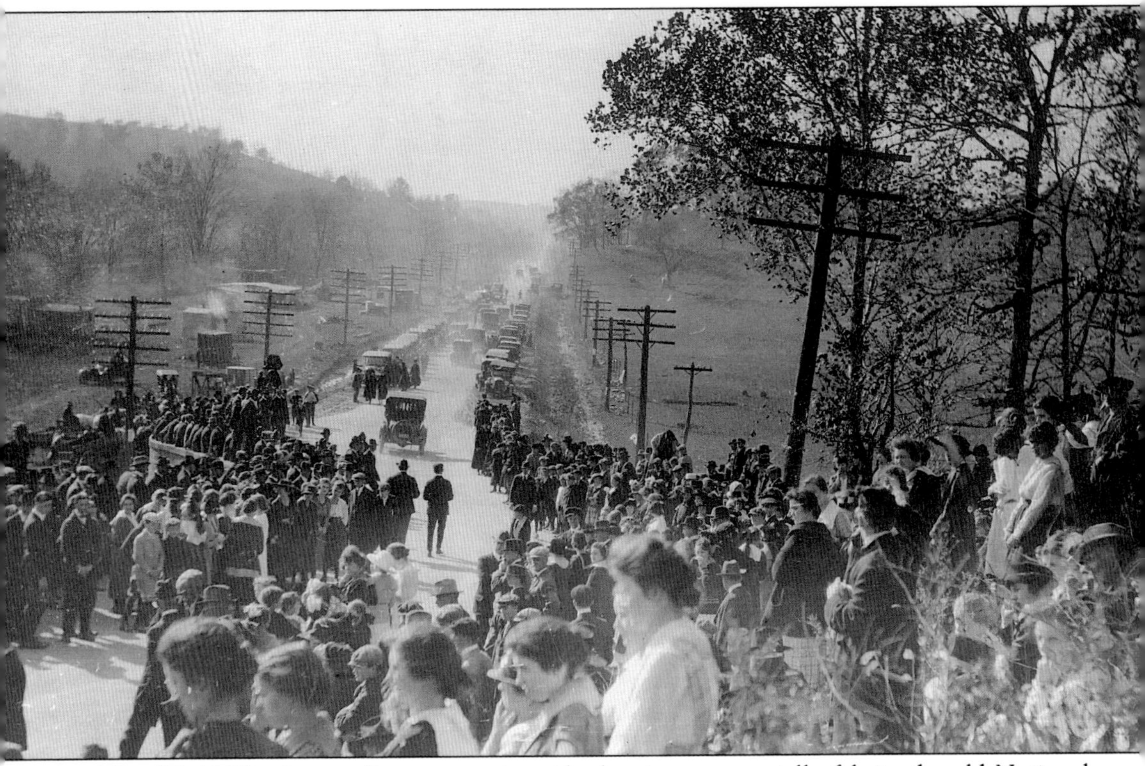

The World War I war effort was nationwide, but it was especially felt in the old National Road towns. A mighty effort was made to transform the river of mud into a fast, efficient transportation stream. The entire six-state length of the National Road was cemented or bricked in an attempt to relieve the clogged railroad traffic. In 1918, the work was completed and the final brick for the entire project was set in the center of New Concord's Crooked Creek "S" Bridge by Ohio Governor James Cox. The event brought national attention to the village. This photo shows the road looking west from the bridge.

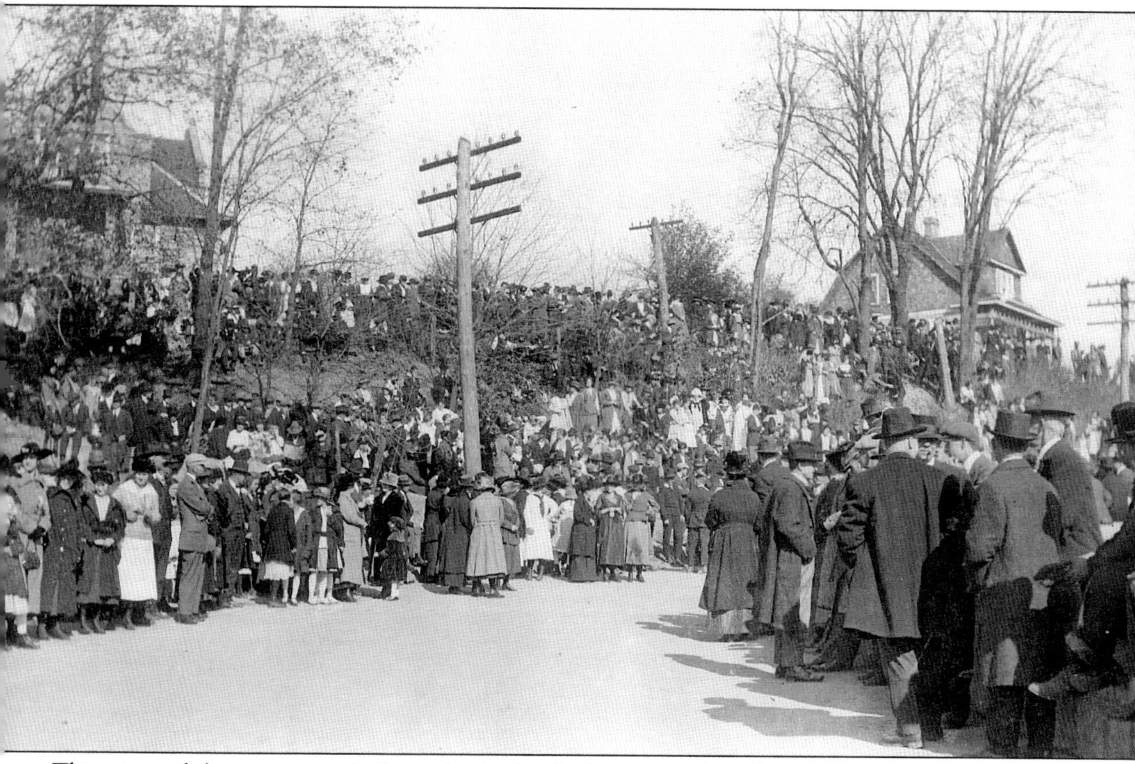

This view of the ceremony is from the bridge looking east. McCloud House is to the right. Three years later, John Herschel Glenn, a wounded World War I veteran, would move his family to New Concord from Cambridge and build their house to the right of McCloud House. The celebration included a grand parade through New Concord.

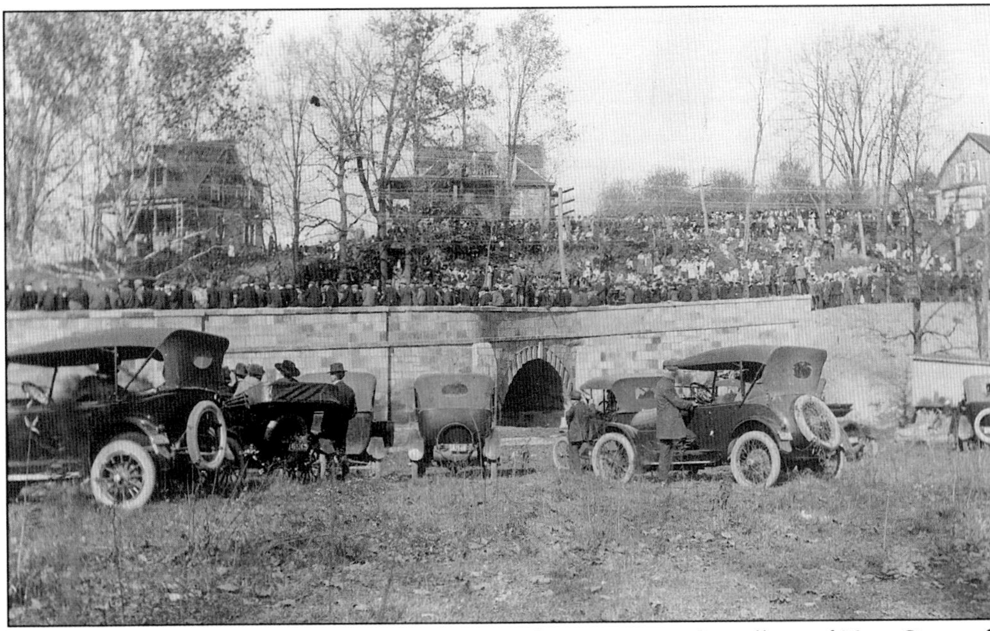

The bricking of the National Road drew national attention to the village of New Concord. Newspaper people descended on the village.

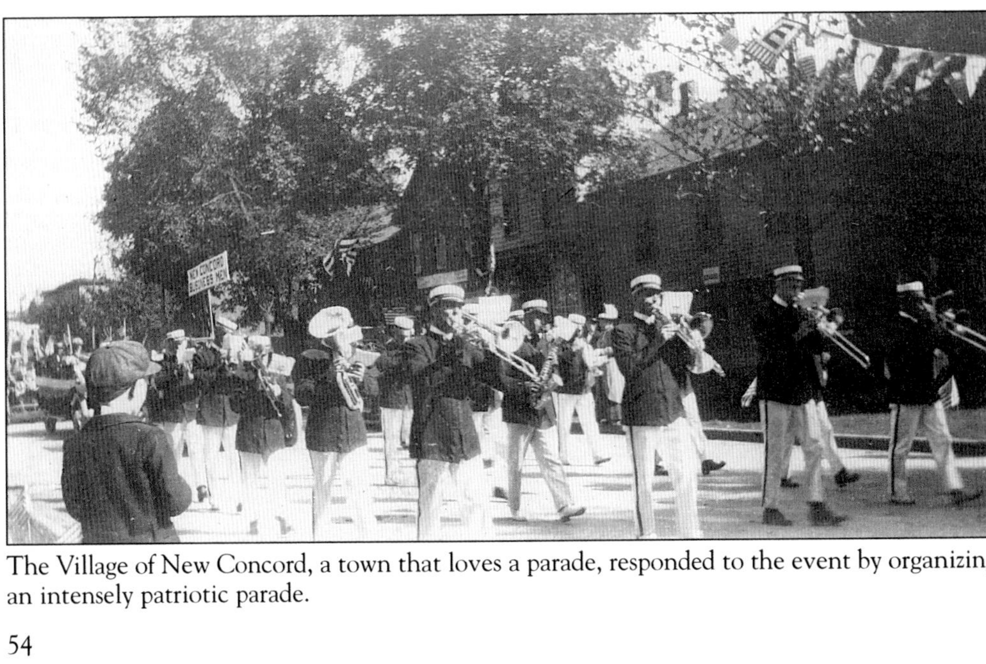

The Village of New Concord, a town that loves a parade, responded to the event by organizing an intensely patriotic parade.

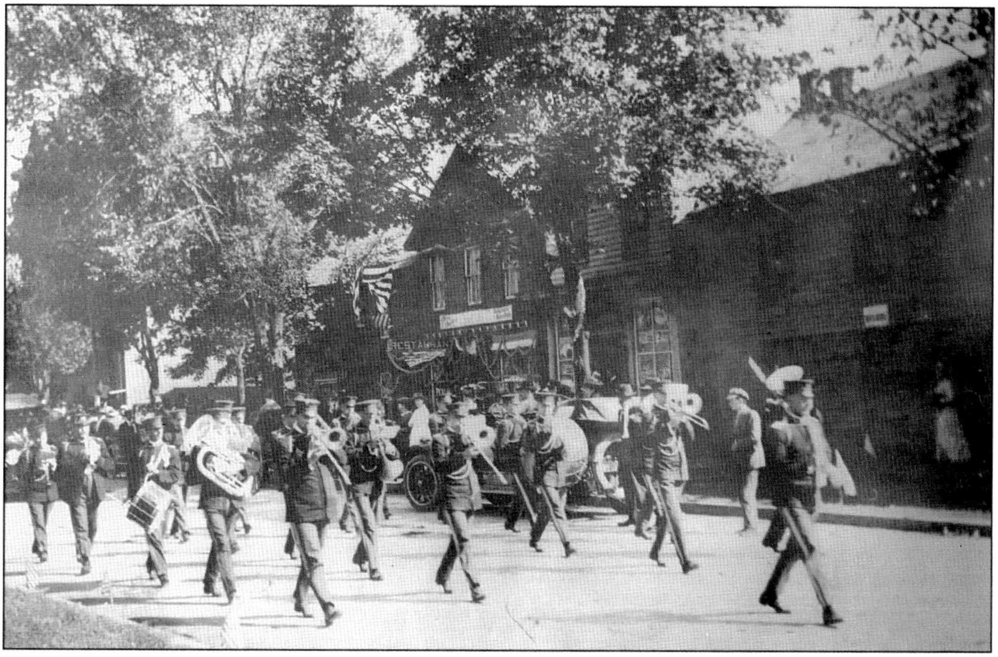

A military band parades westward on Main Street in front of Duff's Grocery and Harper Cabin.

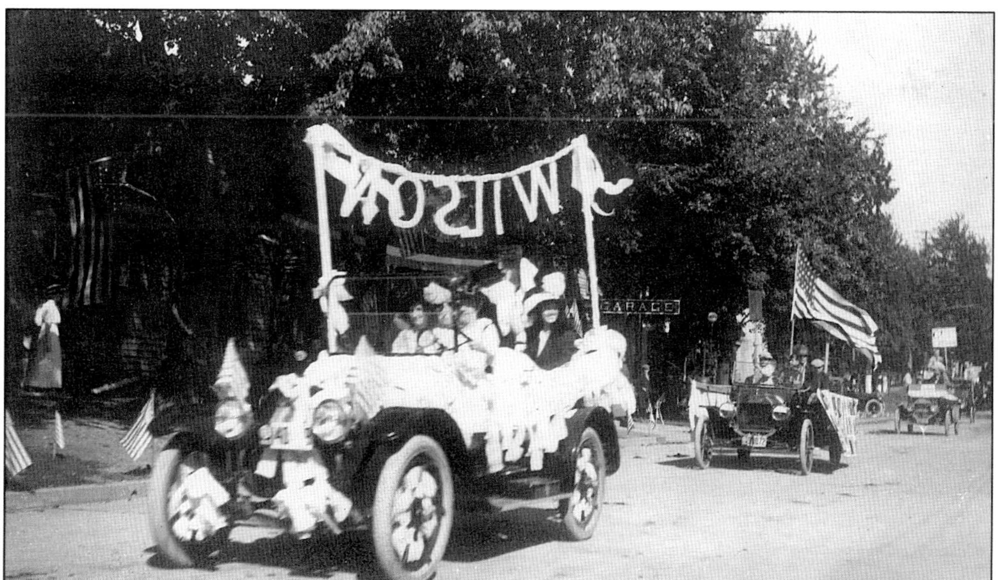

An automobile, festooned with the name of President Woodrow Wilson, leads the parade toward the "S" Bridge.

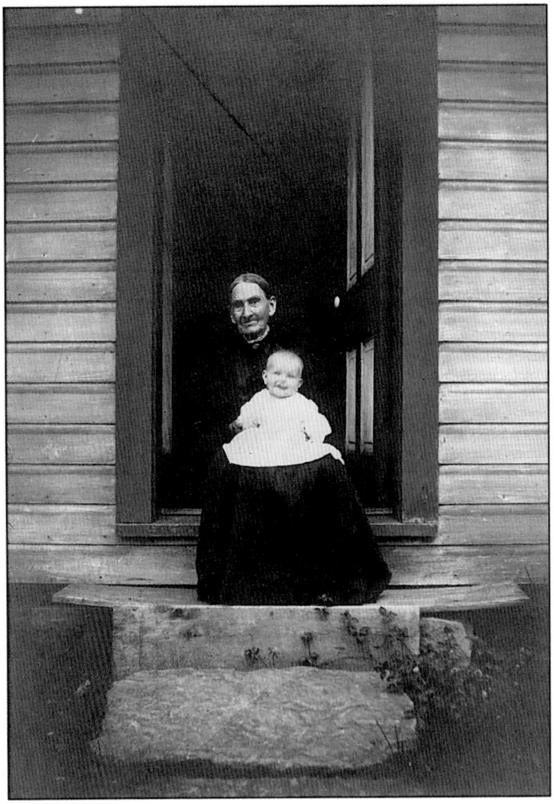

Family after family lined the National Road for the parade. Janie McCreary and her grand-niece Jane McCreary (Wilson) perch on their front stoop.

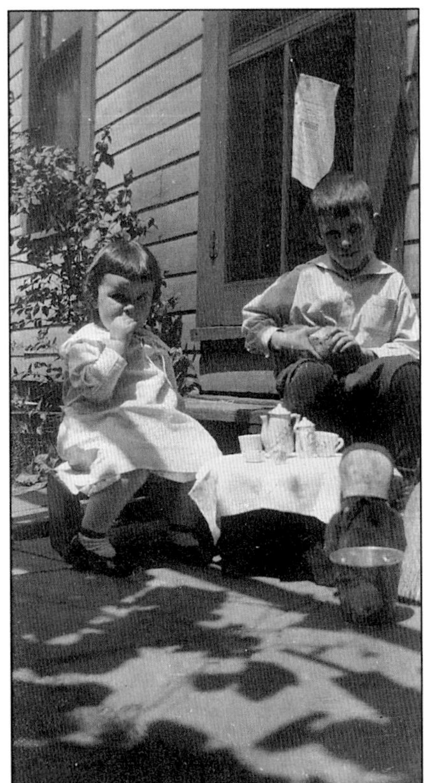

Ruth and Paul Ransom pass the time "taking tea." High spirits were enjoyed in New Concord that day. Soon the enormous impact of the automobile would change the community.

Four

A Town Set Apart

Even sedate New Concord responded eagerly to the "new-fangled machine"—the automobile. The "horseless buggies" manufactured in Detroit revolutionized American life. In 1910, fewer than 5 million narrow-tired "Tin Lizzies" moved on American roads; in 1920 more than 9 million churned through the muddy avenues. That figure would leap to 26.5 million in 1930. Standardized parts and efficient management in the new industry soon transformed America from a sleepy agricultural society to an industrial giant. The Great Bull Market of the 1920s was fueled by such industry and the investment returns it promised. The phenomenal popularity of the automobile led to the redesignation of the National Road into U.S. 40 in 1926.

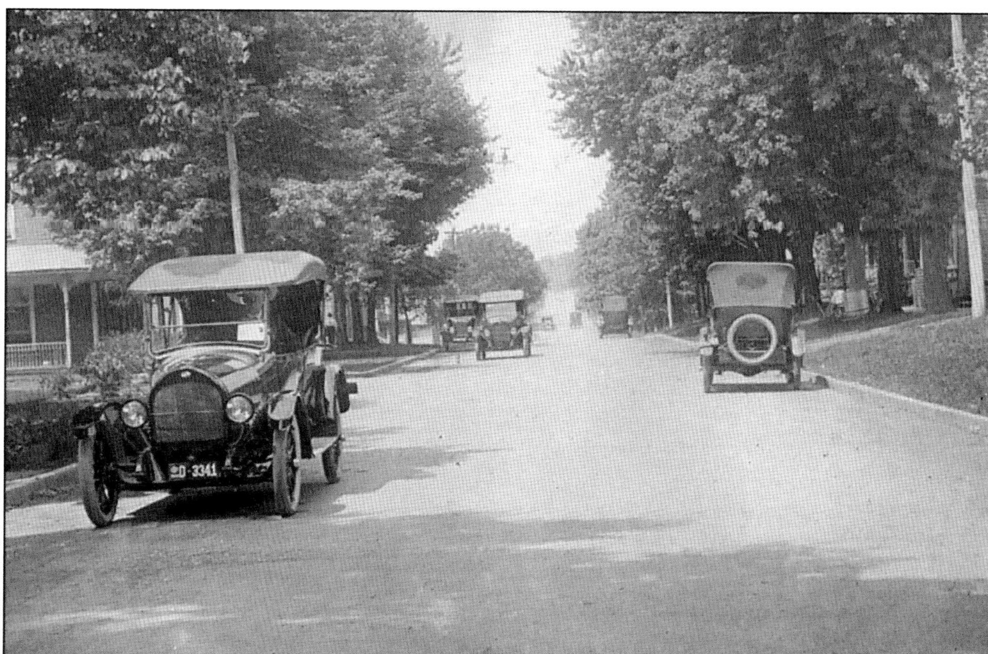

This photo captures the National Road in 1919. The improved driving conditions stimulated great interest in automobiles. Within the decade, four auto dealerships appeared in New Concord. They usually stocked one car apiece and drove to Cincinnati to replace it if it sold.

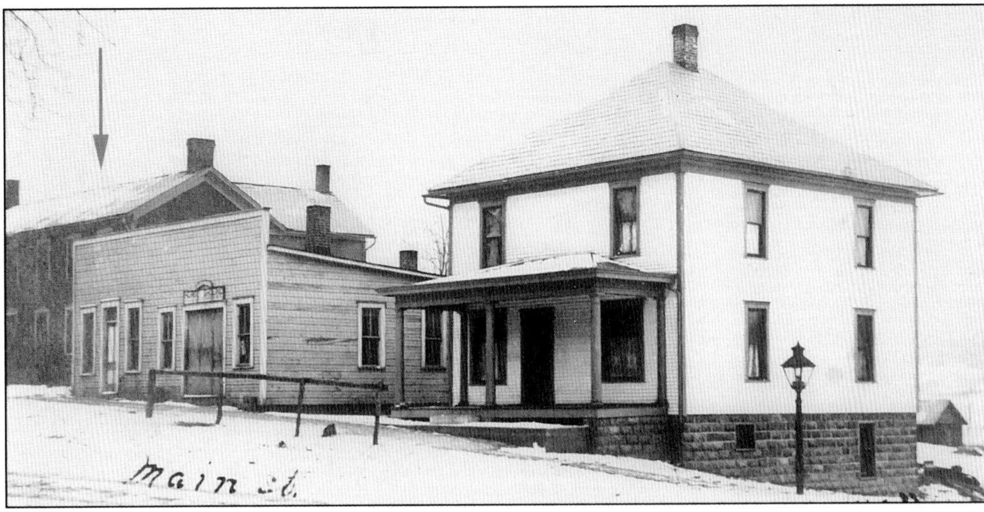

Cashing in on the "auto" craze, John Parks built a house and a garage on Main Street. It also served as a Ford dealership. The Glenn Home-Museum site is to the left in this photo, under the "1905" arrow. The National Road Federal-style house was razed in the 1940s. The second photo is c. 1920. The popularity of the automobile damaged the railroad's business. It also facilitated social change. It made possible "commuting" to work and the consolidation of schools. Rapidly seen as a necessity, the automobile (available for $260 in the late 1920s) fed streaks of independence in people and made possible the hankering for "the other side of the hill." Americans began to glory in mobility. The automobile—more than any other factor—led to the demise of small towns. New Concord, unlike many small villages, would survive, largely because of the presence of Muskingum College.

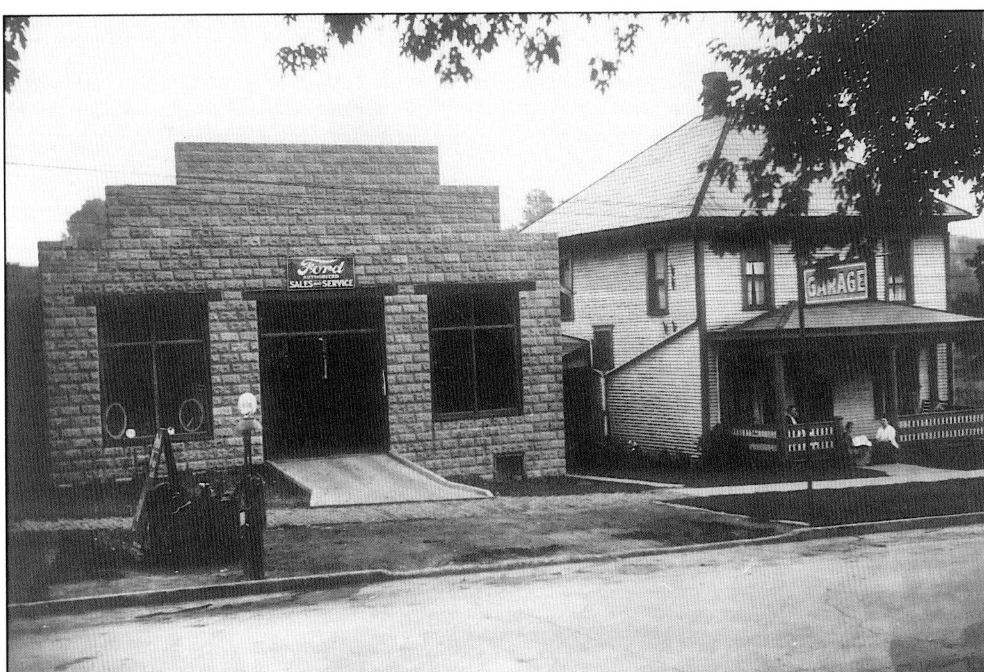

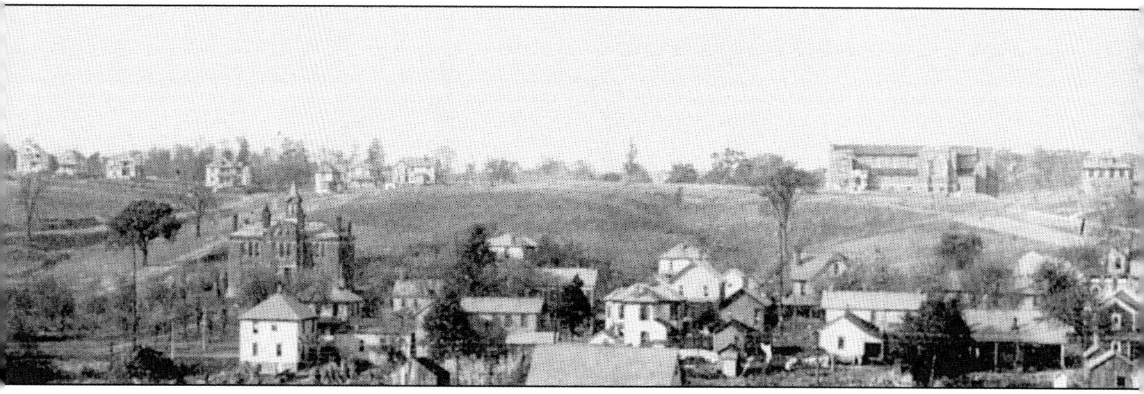

New Concord's prosperity, and its Scotch-Irishness, drew Herschel and Clara Glenn (Senator Glenn's parents) to the community.

Herschel Glenn and Clara Sproat married at Camp Sheridan in Montgomery, Alabama, shortly before Herschel was shipped overseas during World War I. As a member of the 37th "Buckeye" Division—a unit the German General staff rated one of the five best American divisions—he participated in the battles of Verdun and St. Mihiel. Glenn was rendered partially deaf from his wounds.

Herschel had worked on the B&O Railroad and apprenticed as a plumber. Clara, who was a teacher, had been educated at Muskingum College. Their son, John, was born in Cambridge, Ohio, in 1921. The family moved to the house built for them in New Concord in 1923. Herschel opened his plumbing business on Main Street and eventually stocked a display model Chevrolet for sale. Clara "minded the store" and put baby John to sleep on blankets laid out in a porcelain tub.

The Glenns quickly became friends with Dr. Homer Castor, a village dentist and son of a village undertaker, and his wife Margaret Alley Castor. The couples were part of a social group called "the Twice Fives." John and Annie first met as toddlers in a playpen at one of the group's carry-in dinners.

This photo shows the Village of New Concord when the Glenn family settled there. At the top left is Thompson Avenue. The large white house at bottom left (103 West Main Street) was the Stormont farmhouse (the farm was the vacant land to the north). The village elementary school dominated the center left, and Muskingum College crowned the hill to the right. The Glenn home stood three blocks to the west of Stormont House.

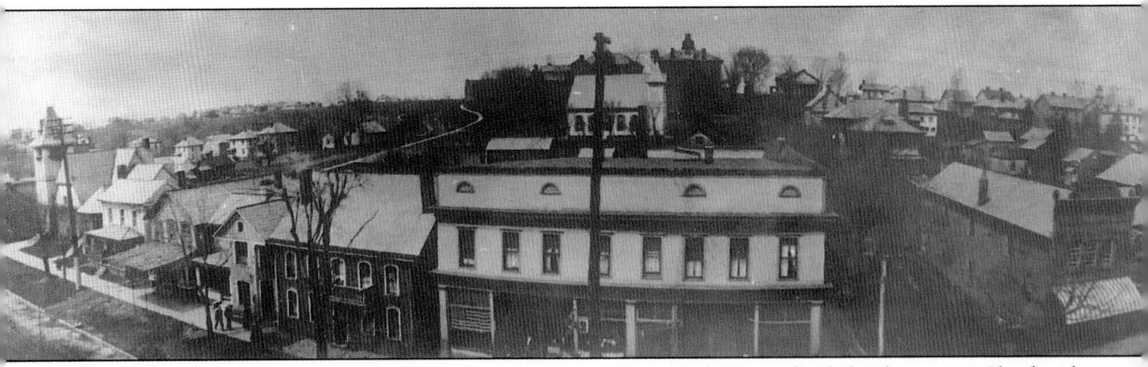

Large houses were built to house college students. Herschel Glenn built his house on Shadyside Terrace with the intent of renting to students. Muskingum College built its first dormitory (Patton Hall) that very year, so the Glenns rented rooms to tourists instead. John and his chums sat on the front porch swing and watched the United States pass below on the National Road.

The Senator recalls an idyllic childhood . . . in "a real life *Music Man* town." He referred to the popular 1960s musical by Meredith Wilson, which captured life in a small Iowa village in the 1910s.

John Glenn Jr. (or "Bud" as he was known around town) and his pals had the run of the village. They fished in the creeks, hunted in the woods, and bunked at their own self-built "Ohio Rangers" camp. Happily joining the girls, they picked strawberries at the village's two strawberry farms, and enjoyed ice skating and sledding. They played checkers and baseball, popped popcorn and pulled taffy, saw an occasional movie, and enjoyed listening to the radio.

This "fisheye" photo captures Main Street in the 1920s. The second United Presbyterian Church anchors the left; Muskingum House, a popular restaurant, dominates the center with the first United Presbyterian Church and Paul Hall of Muskingum College above it.

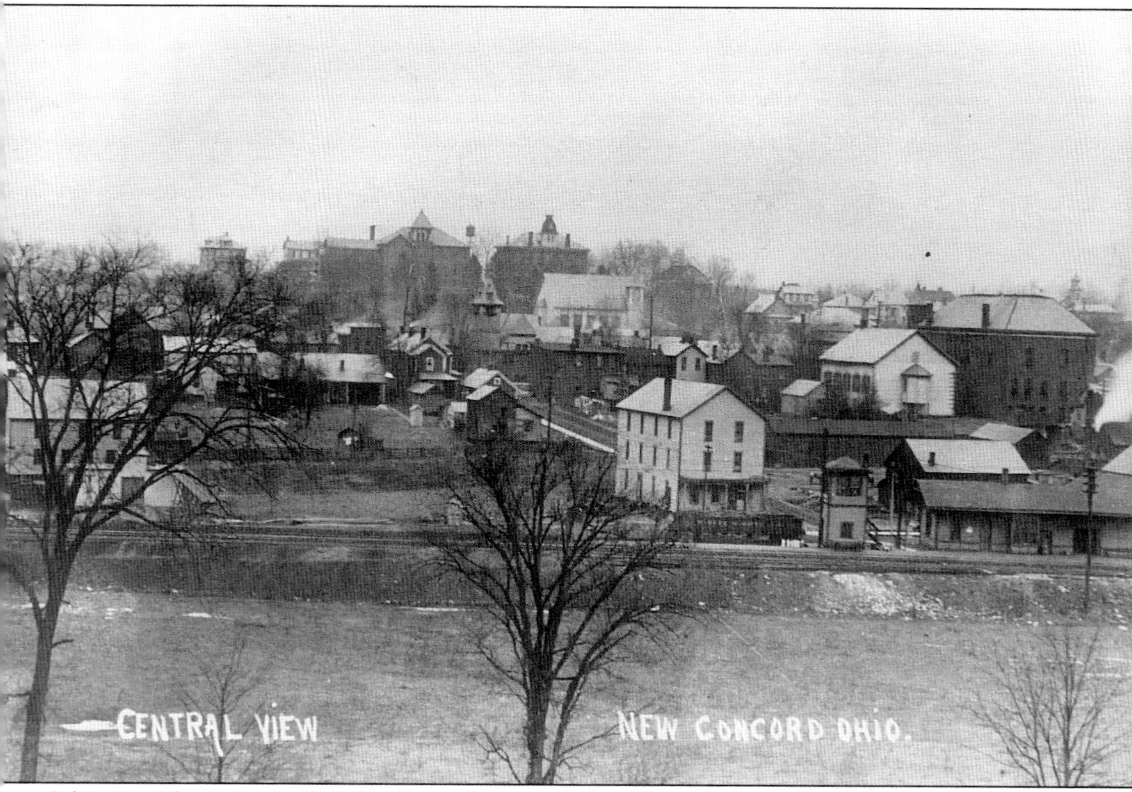

John H. Glenn Jr. (called "Bud" to distinguish him from his popular father) was always fascinated with engines—his friend Ed Houk once drove a car with Bud hanging over the side as he observed a new suspension system.

Bud loved the adventure of "Steve Canyon" and "Jack Armstrong—All American Boy" on the radio. Lying in his bed in tiny New Concord, his imagination soared to the stars.

Bud wheedled Fred Finley, the telegraph man, into letting him catch the messages from the train as it whizzed by. It was, at ten, his first experience at forcing himself to stand his ground and conquer personal fear. He also climbed to the top of one of the village's huge sycamore trees—to prove to himself he could do it.

This photo of New Concord is dominated by the Muskingum College buildings in the center. The large structure at the right is Village Hall. Fred Finley's telegraph office stands beside the B&O Railroad Depot, center right.

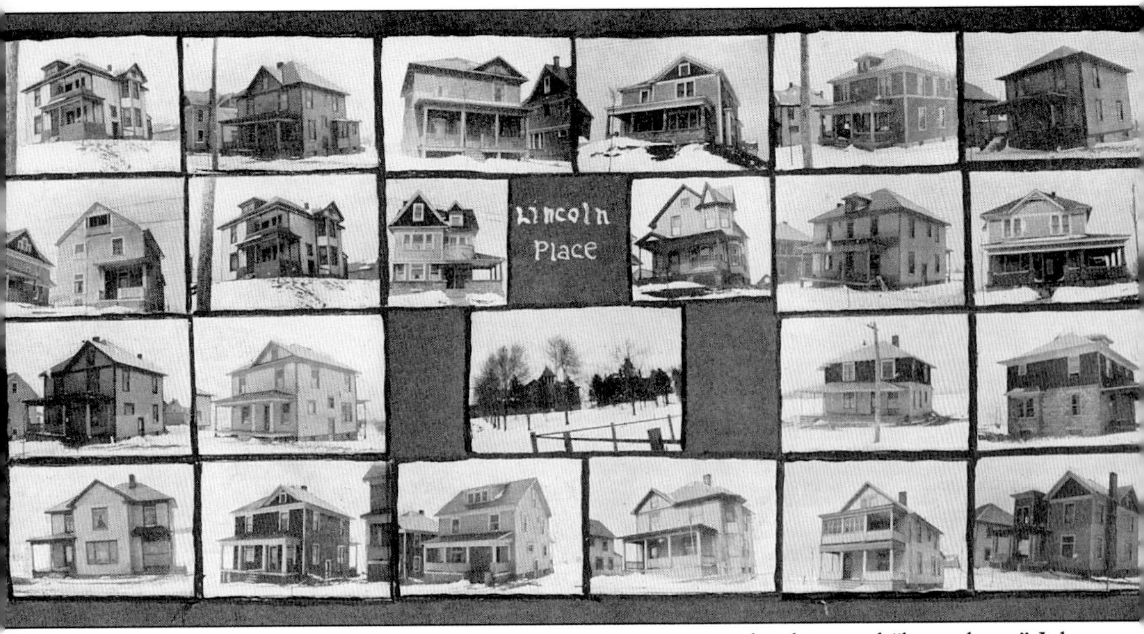

Village boys happily roamed the streets, eating ice cream at the dairy and "being boys." John Glenn Jr. had a paper route, which took him all across town each day. Women who baked their bread daily were likely to hand out bread and jam to any hungry child, and he was no exception. The immediate area around town was "stomping grounds" for the children. The Christmas tree farm and the sorghum molasses mill on Patch Road east of town were fascinating hikes. Maple Brook Grove to the west was the site of picnics. Montgomery Boulevard (Lincoln Place) is shown as it was when John H. Glenn Jr. delivered newspapers in the village of New Concord.

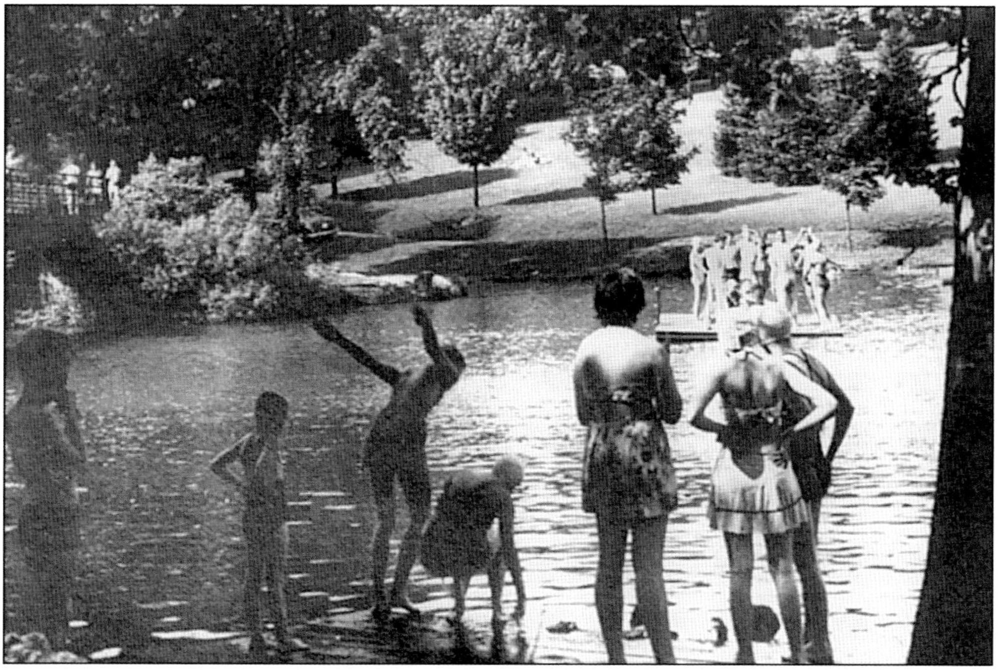

The Muskingum College Lake was a favored "swimming hole" for students and villagers alike. Boating was a popular leisure time event. Particularly on the Sabbath, when all other activity in the community came to a halt, strolls around the lake were prized. The "spoonholder"—the signature structure on the lake—was constructed and was a traditional site to announce engagements.

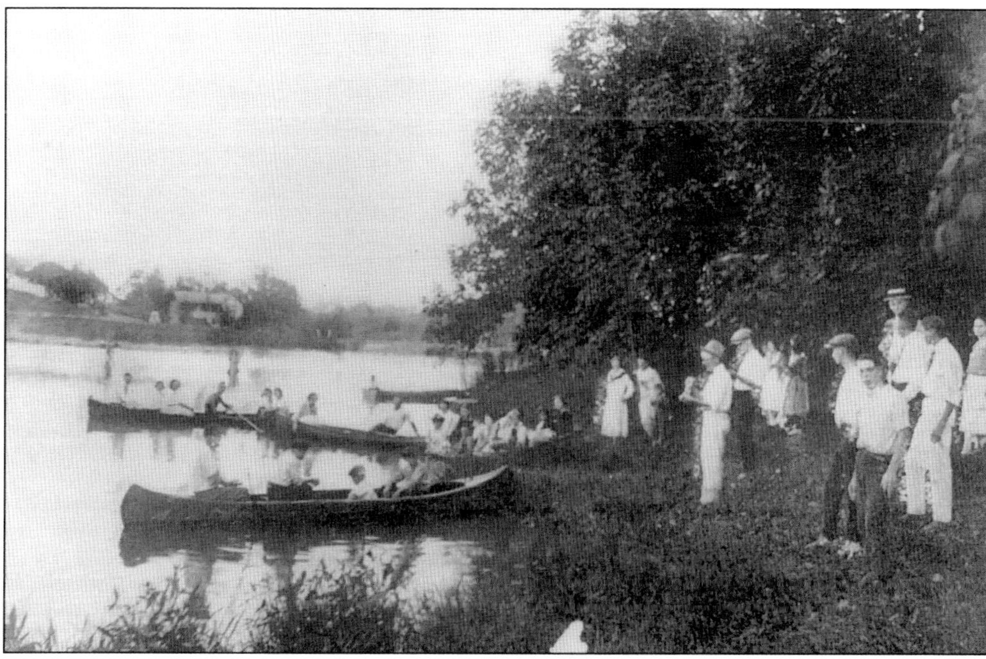

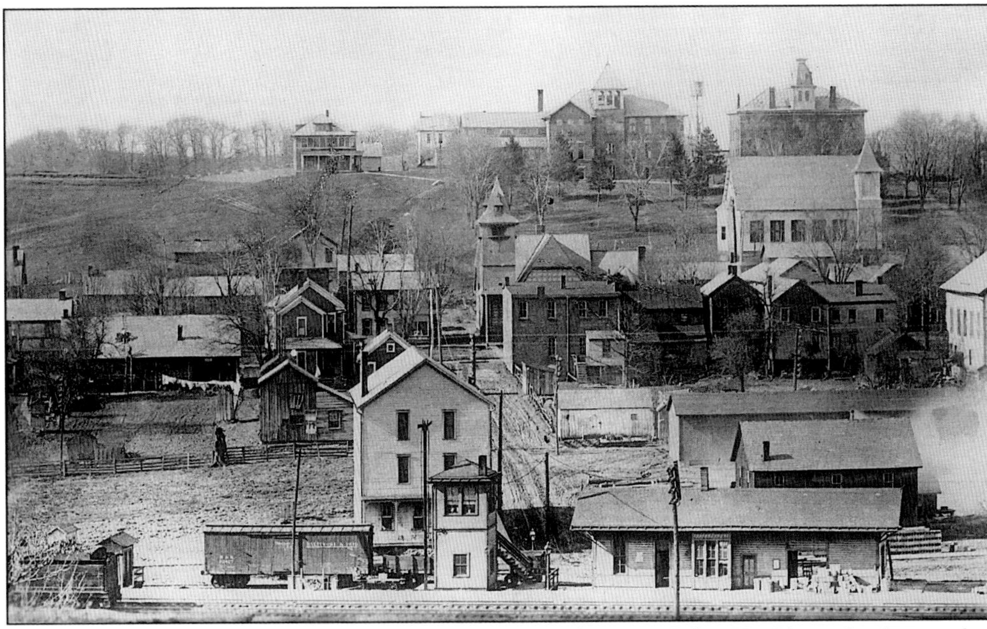

While his friends dreamed of becoming cowboys or firemen, John H. Glenn Jr. dreamed of flight. Eighteen years before Glenn's birth, the Wright Brothers flew at Kitty Hawk (remaining in the air 12 seconds). When Glenn was six, Charles A. Lindberg flew *The Spirit of St. Louis* from New York to Paris in 33 hours; when he was ten, Glenn's father treated him to an aircraft ride offered by a traveling flyer (a "barnstormer").

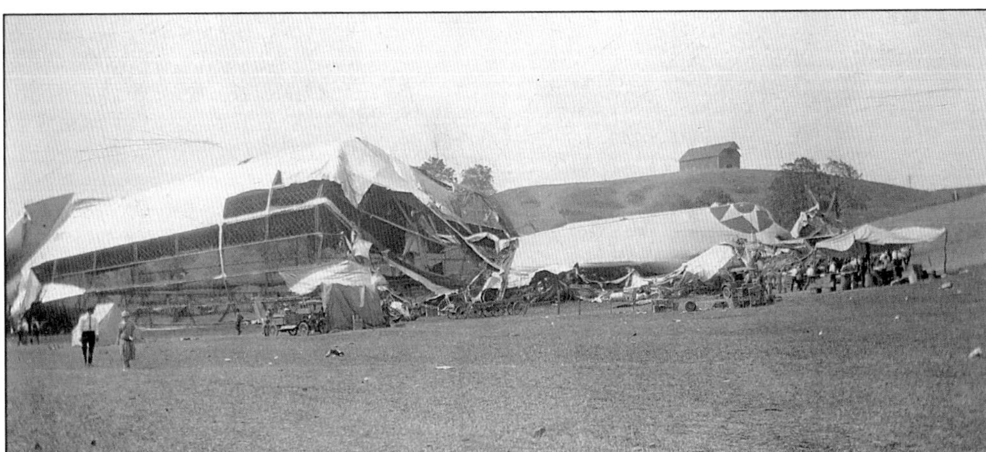

John H. Glenn Jr., sitting at his desk in tiny New Concord, built model planes and devoured books about aviation—and his spirit soared. For Glenn, his world's boundaries would be much larger than the National Road and the Baltimore and Ohio Railroad tracks. He wanted to fly. Glenn's parents tolerated his fondness for "Steve Canyon" and "Jack Armstrong—the All American Boy," but they were apprehensive about his dream of flight—aircrafts were too often "flying coffins," a fact Herschel realized from his World War I service. Mortality came home early in Glenn's life, when in 1925, 30 miles south of New Concord, the great American zeppelin, the *U.S.S. Shenandoah*, crashed in a storm, killing Lt. Commander Zachary Lansdowne and 13 of his crew. A career in flight was not something the elder Glenns' wanted for their young son. First would come school and college, perhaps time to cool his love for speed and flight.

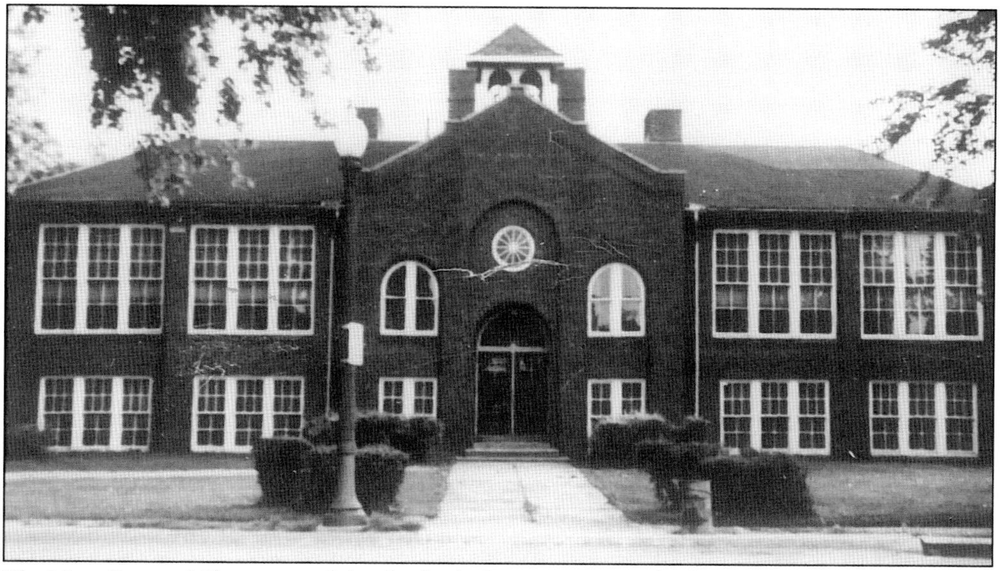

The New Concord Elementary School, which Annie Castor and John H. Glenn Jr. attended, was razed in 1979. The Village Library now sits on this site. In 1930, the high schools in the nearby villages were closed, and young people from Bloomfield, Rix Mills, and Norwich were bused to New Concord. The new high school was built in 1931.

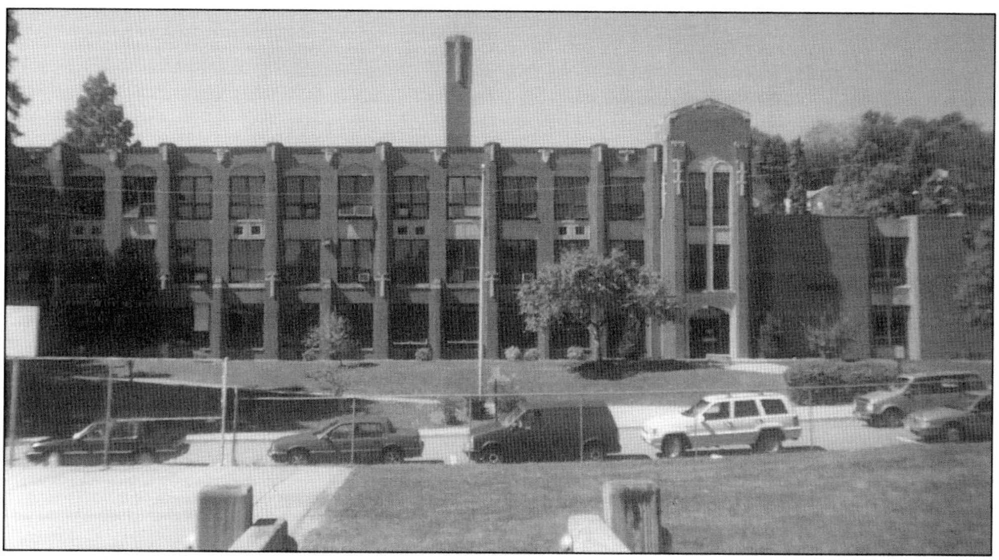

In 1930, the high schools in the nearby villages were closed, and young people from Bloomfield, Rix Mills, and Norwich were bused to New Concord. The new high school was built in 1931. (This is the current Stromont Elementary School on Stormont and Comin Streets.)

Village children remember their exceptional teachers: Grace McCreary, the geography teacher; Janey Trace, the music teacher; and Jenny Dixon, for whom generations of children learned and recited "Under the Spreading Chestnut Tree." This was a problem for Annie Castor. Dr. Homer Castor stuttered, and his daughter Annie suffered so greatly from the affliction that she never spoke in class. Friends asked questions on her behalf. John Glenn Jr. was always interested in theatre (his mother's influence) and in music (his father's influence). He sang barbershop harmony with his dad and developed his talent on the trumpet.

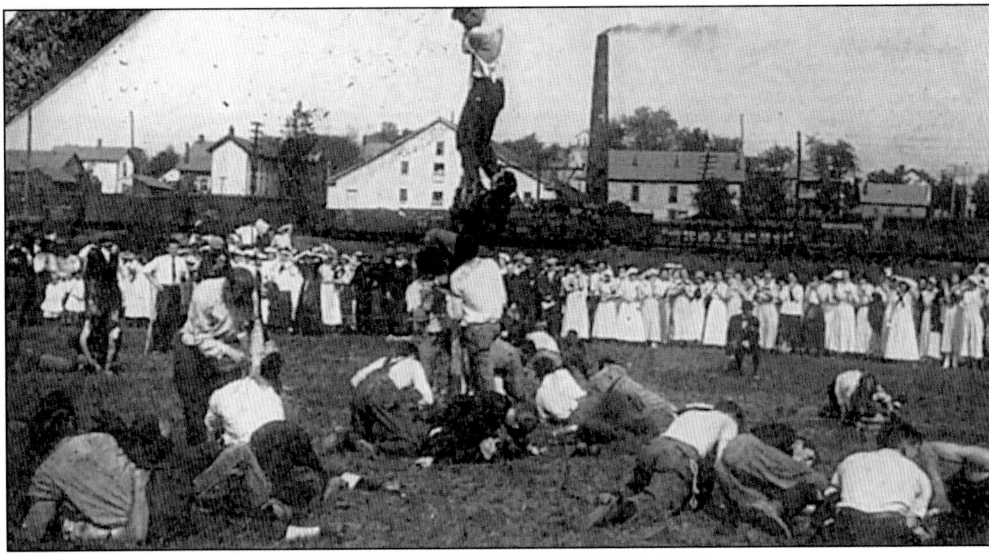

Village school children were deeply influenced by Muskingum College students, most of whom lived in villagers' homes. The Muskingum College students were part of the fabric of village life. The annual Scrap Day between sophomores and "freshies" drew a large village crowd as seen in the above photo. College "pranks" were emulated by village children, many of whom would automatically go to Muskingum College. Below, the annual Halloween hijinks resulted in the blockading of Muskingum House with wagons, crates, and even a relocated "privy." The Muskingum College Junior Class warns its Senior rivals of their fate during the annual "Scrap Day" competition.

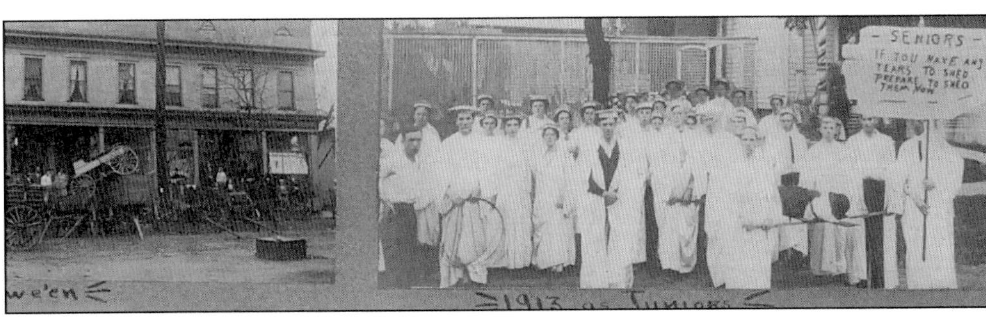

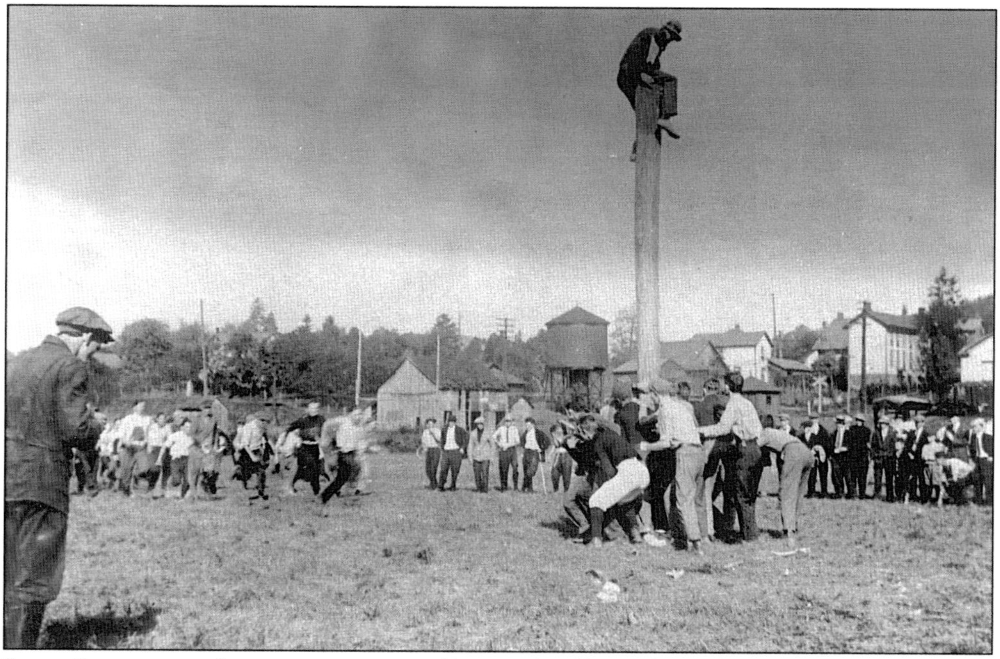

Scrap Day generated excitement in a village and college where there was no drinking, no dancing, and no smoking.

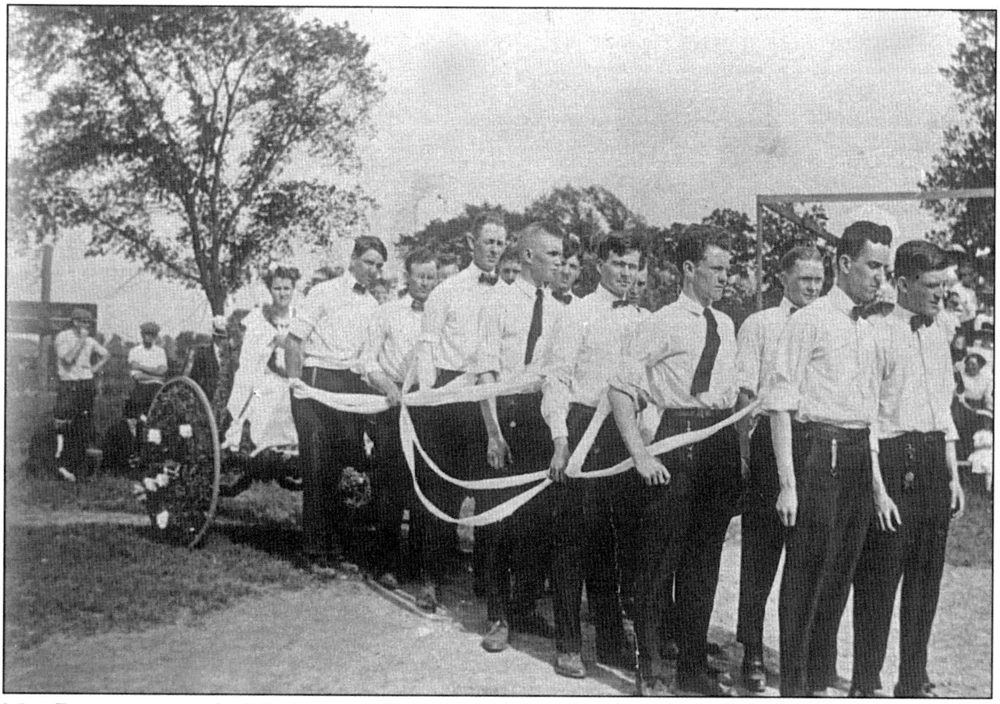

May Day was a popular Muskingum College tradition that lasted until the mid-1960s. Here the Queen of May is drawn across campus by an escort of Muskie "horses." Sometimes she arrived at "court" on a swan boat which glided across the Muskingum College Lake. Such events drew huge college and village audiences.

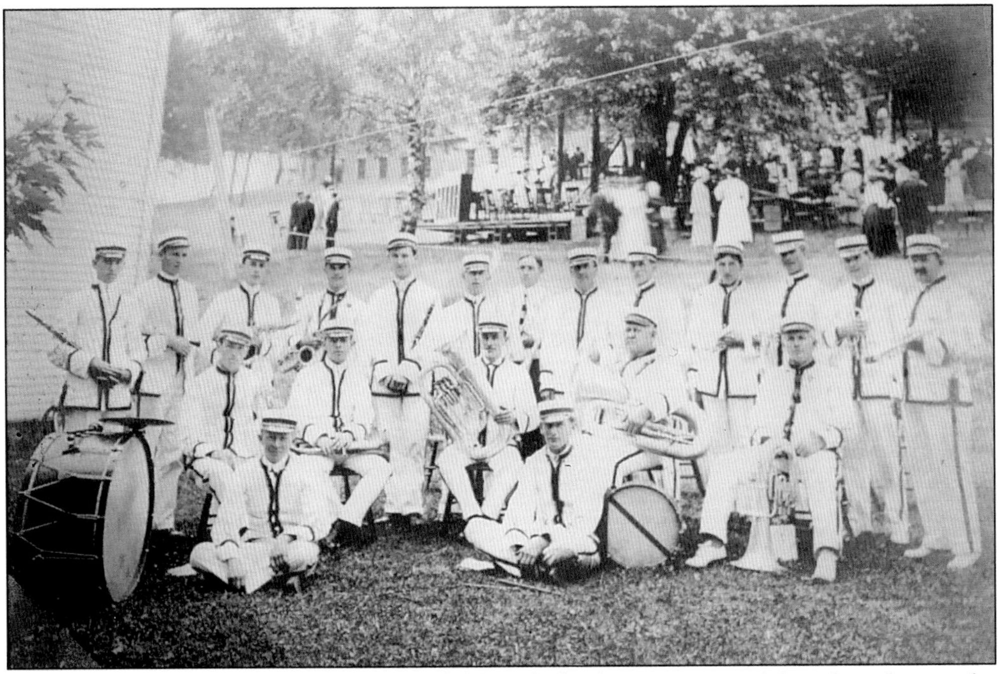

Music was a highlight of Scotch-Irish life (although the denominations debated its place in the sacred realm). William Rainey Harper founded the village's Silver Cornet Band, which was the forerunner of the strong music programs in the East Muskingum Schools and at Muskingum College—which continue to this day. This 1880s photo captures the Silver Cornet Band at the United Presbyterian Church. Paul Hall is in the background.

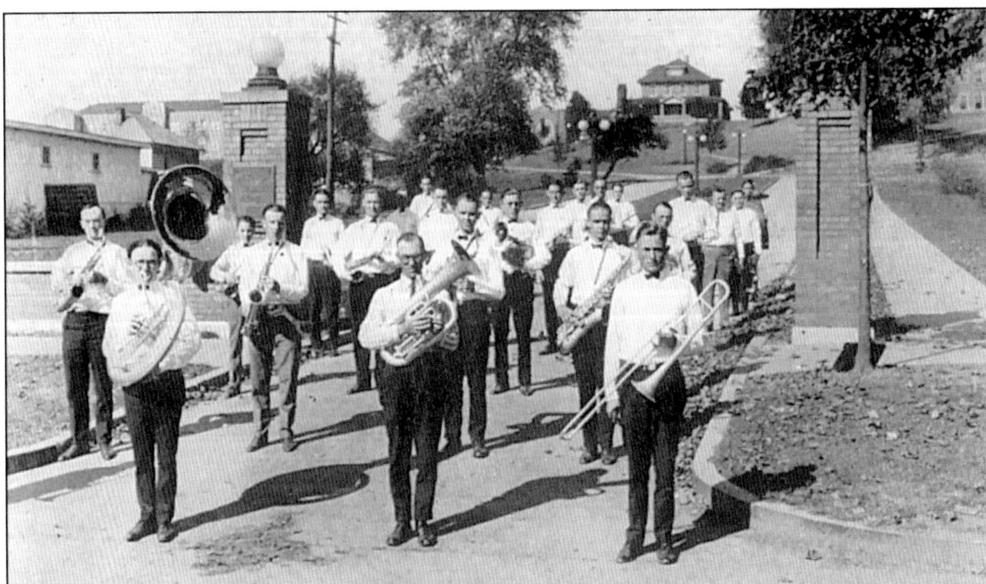

This photo shows the Muskingum College Band in 1925. The Conservatory of Music was quite strong and provided musical entertainment for the village; particularly popular was the annual violin concert. Annie Castor was a gifted musician adept at trombone and organ. She majored in music at Muskingum College. John played trumpet. Both of them played in the village band.

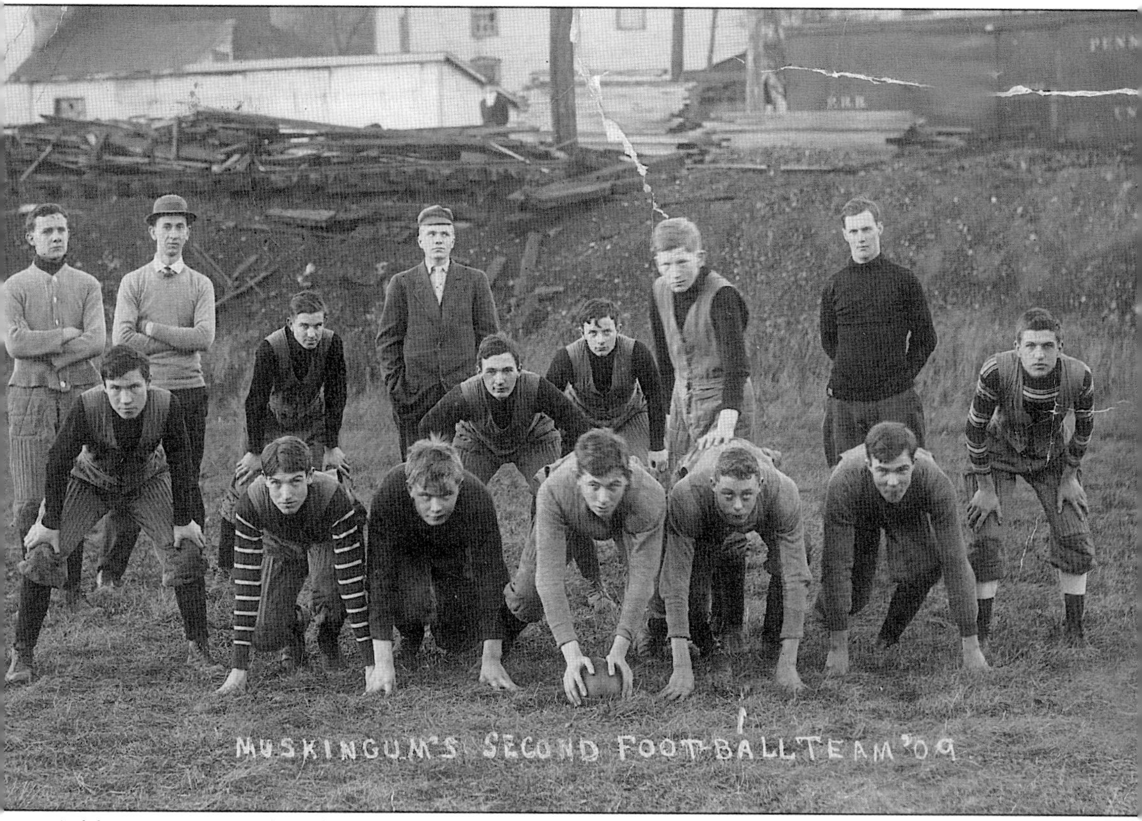

Athletics were another dominant feature of village/college life, and they remain so today. Football, basketball, baseball, and recently track and soccer have avid followings. In the 1990s, women's athletics earned an equal place with the male sports. John Glenn Jr. would later credit the teamwork and sense of competition he learned in sports with making him a successful marine. In this image, Muskingum College's second football team (1909) poses for a picture.

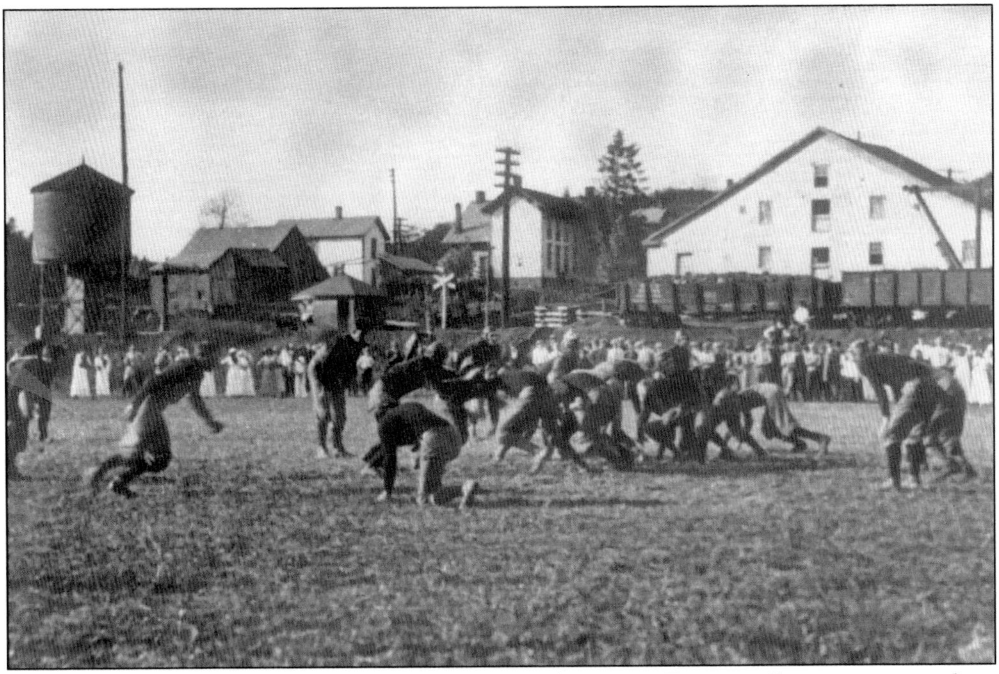

Early in the century, football mania took America by storm. Even small institutions such as Muskingum College fielded teams. In the early 1920s, Muskingum College's team played on a leveled field south of the railroad tracks. This photo shows Speer Warehouse (at the south corner of State Route 83 and U.S. 40). The railroad water tower stands in the line of the Route 83 access to Interstate 70, which was built in the 1960s.

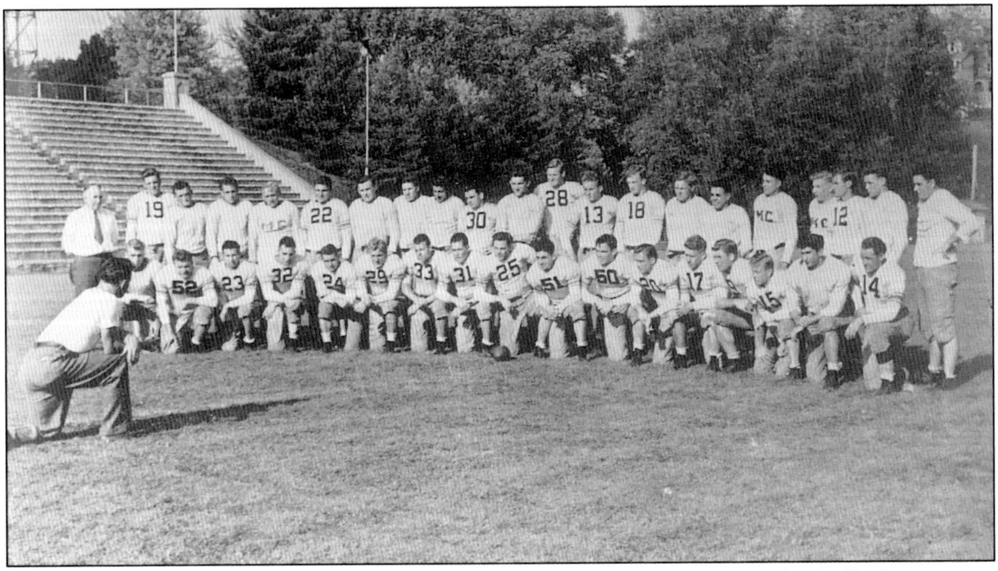

In high school, John Glenn Jr. lettered in three sports—four times in football, three times in basketball, and three times in tennis. His freshman year at Muskingum College, he was the substitute center on the football team. Annie Castor was a standout in volleyball and in swimming. Pictured is the Muskingum College football team, 1939. John Glenn Jr. is seventh from right, in the standing row.

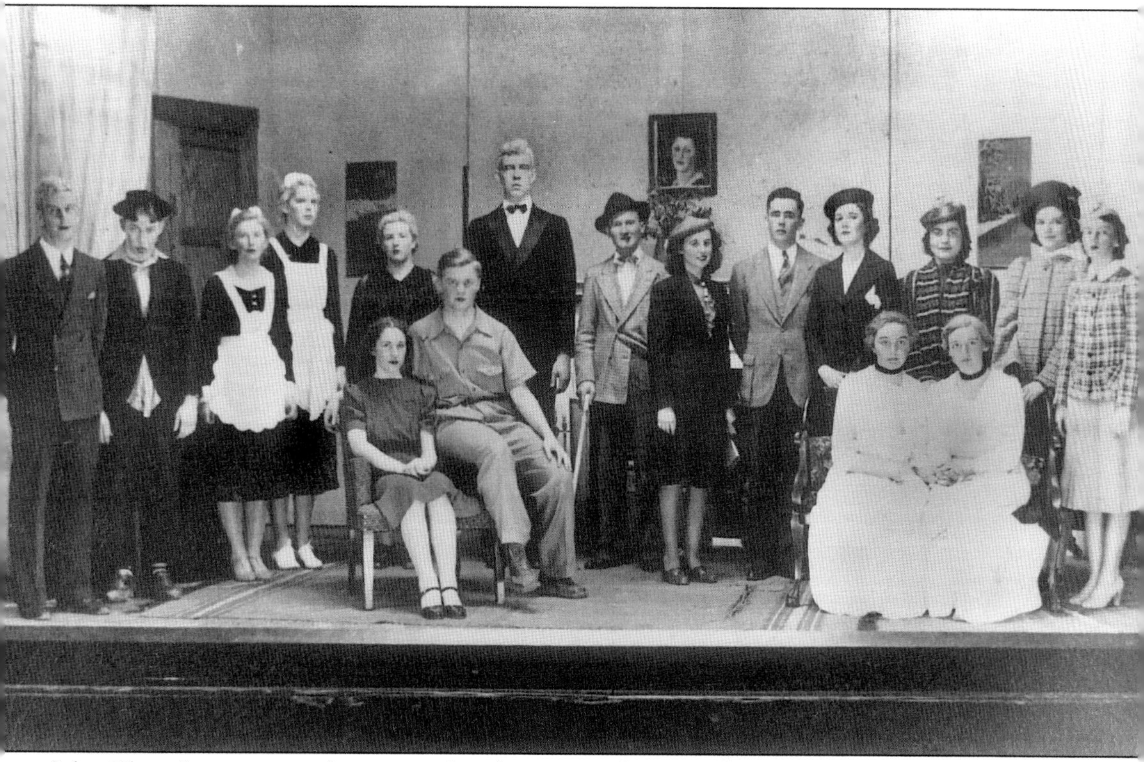

John Glenn Jr. was intensely interested in theatre, a reflection of his mother's passion. He wrote skits in grammar school, devised a Homecoming Banquet with an aviation theme, and played the lead in his senior play, *Fannie and Her Servant Problem*. Shirley Moore and John Glenn played the leading roles with talented support from Wava Buchanan, Helen Busche, Walter Chess, Ted Atkinson, Elizabeth Patton, Paul Mock, Isabel Roy, Fred Booth, Martha Patterson, Mae Scott, Goldine Addis, Dorothy Bates, Mary Wycoff, Dalka Gibson, and Elizabeth Davis. The cast was chosen from the honor students of the class and directed by Miss Grace Finley, assisted by Mrs. Winfred Conley. (Courtesy of Ohio State University Archive, John Glenn Collection.)

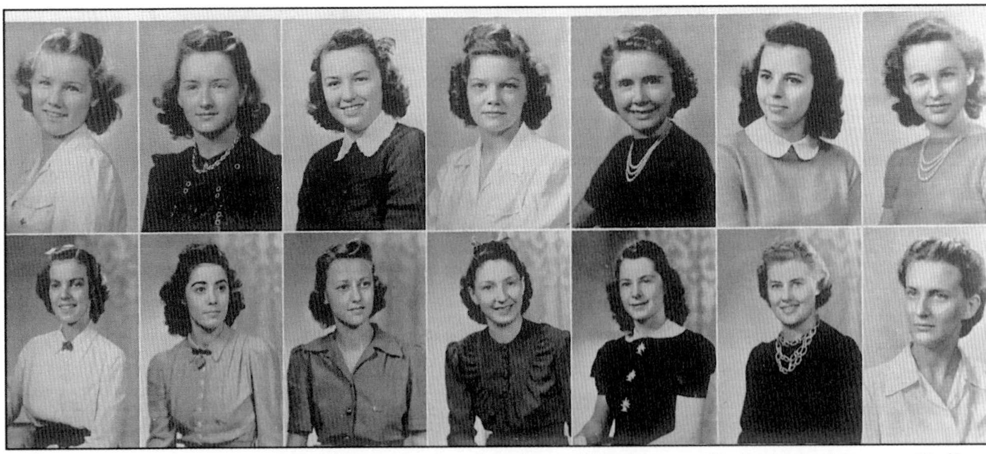

When John Glenn Jr. graduated from high school in 1939, he enrolled in Muskingum College to join Annie Castor. He also believed that at Muskingum College "character was part of its offerings." That "character" building had already been tested by the trauma of the Great Depression. It would be further tested by the worst war in recorded history. Anna Margaret Castor is pictured second from left, bottom row, in her junior year at Muskingum College.

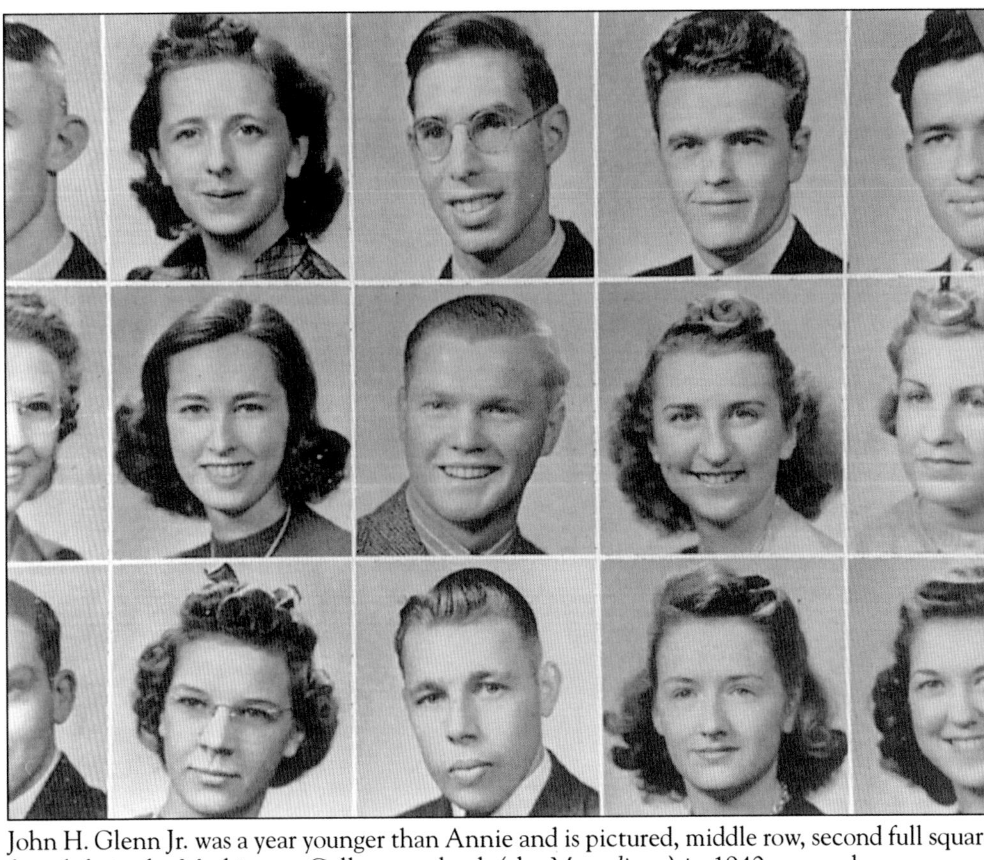

John H. Glenn Jr. was a year younger than Annie and is pictured, middle row, second full square from left, in the Muskingum College yearbook (the *Muscoljuan*) in 1940 as a sophomore.

Five

DEPRESSION AND WAR

The giddy years of prosperity in the 1920s came to an end with the Great Stock Market Crash in October 1929. This triggered a business depression which devastated American and world economies. Within a year, 7 million United States workers were jobless, and by 1932 the figure doubled. Five thousand banks collapsed as the economy malfunctioned. Farm animals were slaughtered and buried in lime pits because they brought too little at market; people went hungry.

John Glenn was eight years old when the stock market crashed in 1929. He and his contemporaries remember little of the Depression except the frugality of their parents. They kept grim news from children, though John remembers hearing his parents discuss the possibility of losing their home when, in 1932, banks began refusing to accept interest payments alone, requiring much larger payments. Children continued to enjoy a carefree existence, although all the backyards in town were turned into gardens (the Glenns had three) and produce was sold or traded. John used his prized wagon to sell rhubarb around the town.

Children remember the endless parade of "hobos" who knocked on village doors for "a handout" as they proceeded down the road and on the railroad. Annie's father was dentist. Dr. Castor took chickens and sides of beef on "barter" for services rendered in his dentistry practice. Herschel Glenn kept in business on the barter basis, supplemented by Clara's sporadic "tourist home" trade. To stretch her budget, she canned produce and rabbits trapped by John Jr.

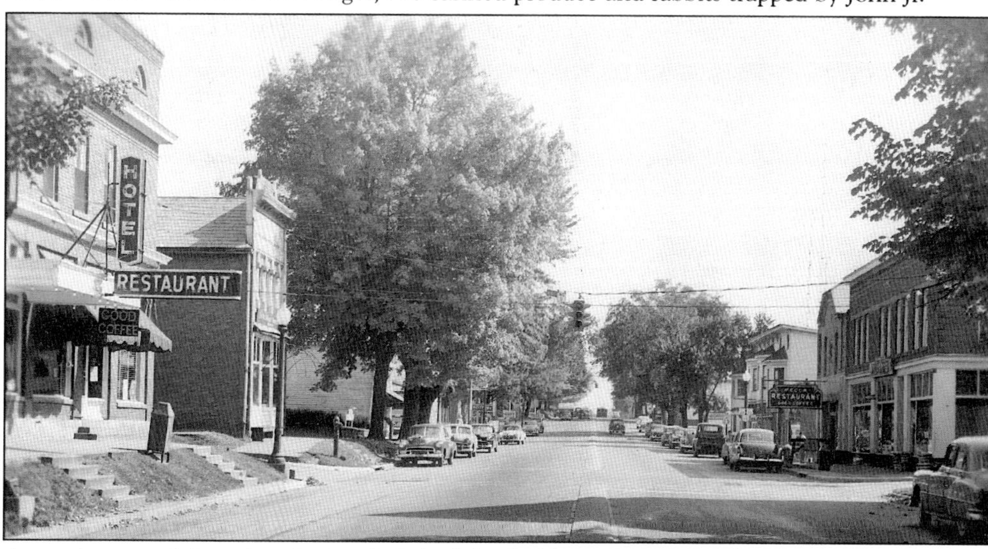

As in the rest of America, the heady life of the 1920s came to an end in New Concord. Main Street saw only a fraction of the business it had enjoyed previously.

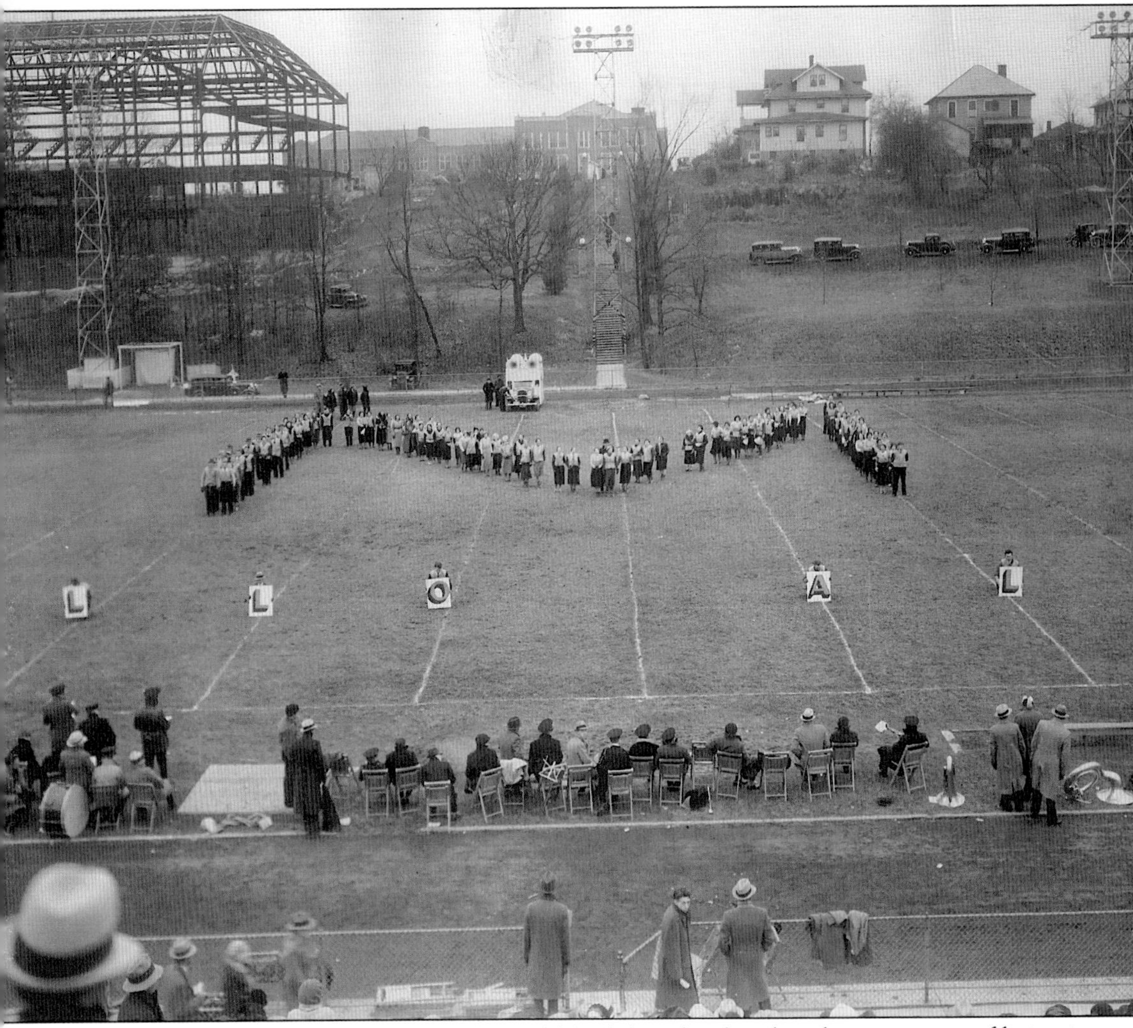

Living in a small country town, adults could feed their families, but the experience of living in a nation which had ground to a halt was frightening. Muskingum College had built Cambridge Hall in 1928, and had banked the money for Zanesville Hall (never built) and the gymnasium. The latter building, seen here at upper left, stood unfinished with its girders exposed until the Public Works Administration provided the money to complete it in 1935. The unfinished gym (where John and his buddies played on the girders without parental knowledge) was a metaphor for America at a standstill.

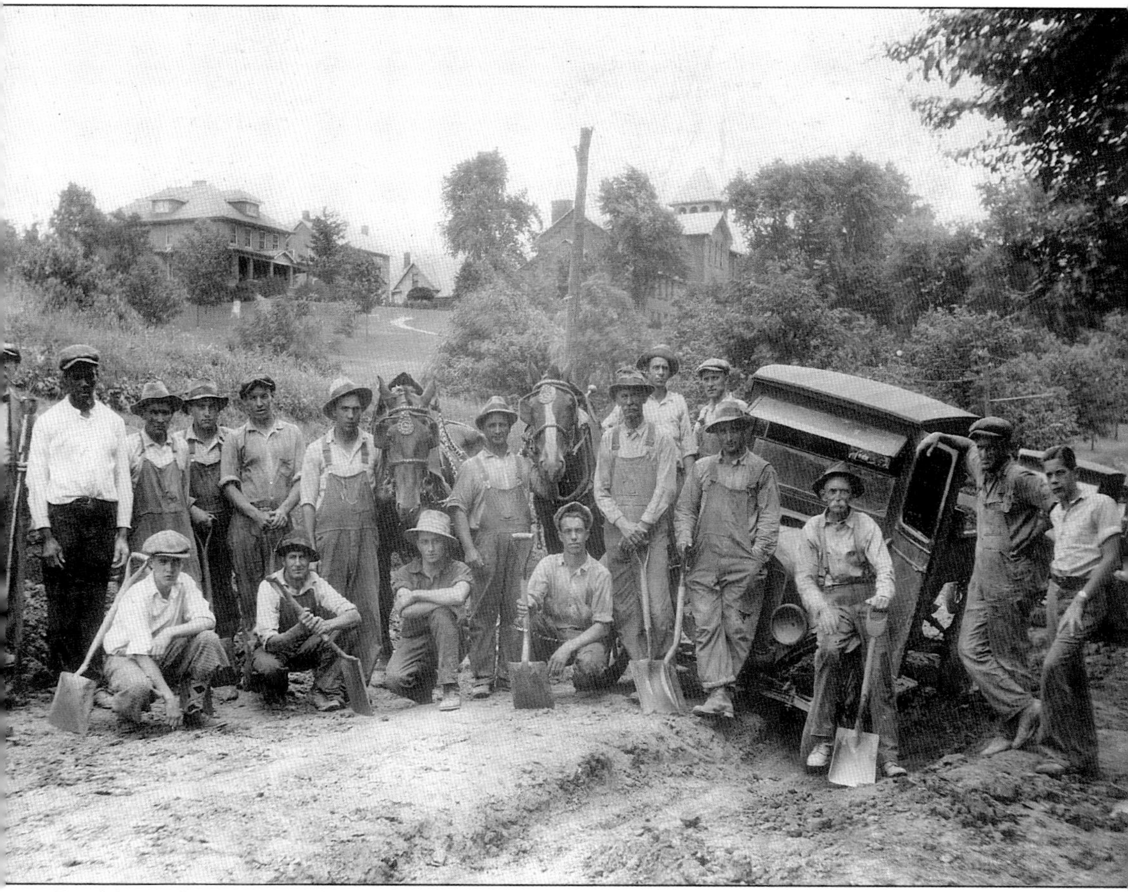

Franklin Delano Roosevelt's March 1933 inauguration sent a wave of "electrifying new hope" across the country. Although the Glenns were Democrats and believed that "Roosevelt saved America," New Concord was a staunchly Republican town, but it welcomed the life-line of renewed spirit the New Deal generated. Local men went back to work on the gym, the sewer plant, and the post office. Clyde Singer, a Malvern, Ohio, artist, moved to town to create the mural in the post office. Herschel Glenn's plumbing business began to perk up with the creation of the Rural Electrification Agency. He drove his Chevy around the county installing pumps and milking machines. This photo shows local men paving High Street in 1933. They were working on a WPA (Works Progress Administration) project. Herschel Glenn supervised such a project as it laid sewer lines in town.

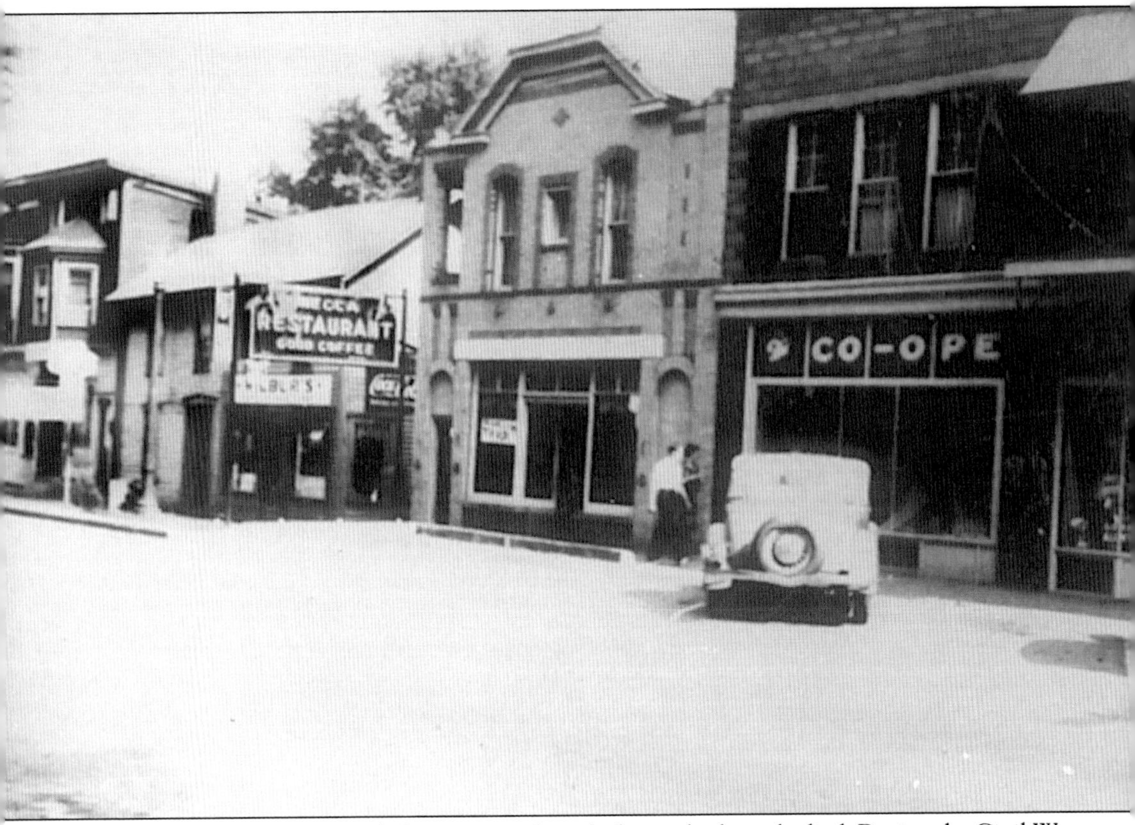

Muskingum College struggled to survive. Once before, it had nearly died. During the Civil War, so many men left to join the Union army that the college had only two seniors, both women, no juniors, and no sophomores. During the 1930s, students continued to come to college because there was no work. But even a college education was conducted on the barter system. Faculty accepted a 50 percent pay cut at Muskingum College in 1932. Tuition was paid in small installments or in produce, meat, coal, or work. As always, Muskingum College students were a constant presence in the life of the village of New Concord. Some worked odd jobs in town businesses, including the Mecca Restaurant pictured here in the center of the "Co-Op Block."

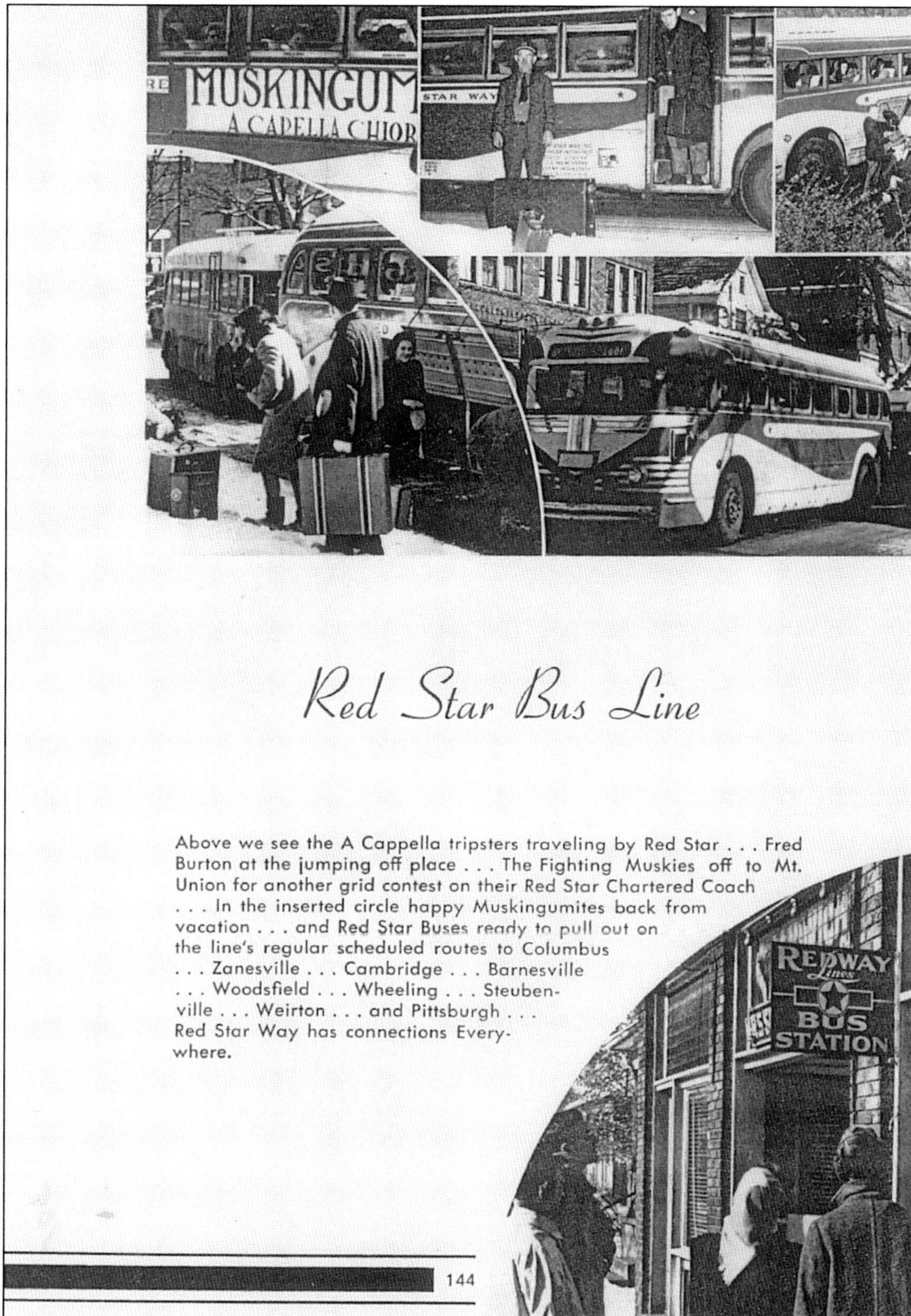

Red Star Bus Line

Above we see the A Cappella tripsters traveling by Red Star . . . Fred Burton at the jumping off place . . . The Fighting Muskies off to Mt. Union for another grid contest on their Red Star Chartered Coach . . . In the inserted circle happy Muskingumites back from vacation . . . and Red Star Buses ready to pull out on the line's regular scheduled routes to Columbus . . . Zanesville . . . Cambridge . . . Barnesville . . . Woodsfield . . . Wheeling . . . Steubenville . . . Weirton . . . and Pittsburgh . . . Red Star Way has connections Everywhere.

144

Annie Castor and John Glenn Jr. entered Muskingum College in 1939. Social life in the village and at the college were "cut to the bone." These pictures from the college yearbook, the *Muscoljuan*, catches the flavor of the Muskingum College year 1941.

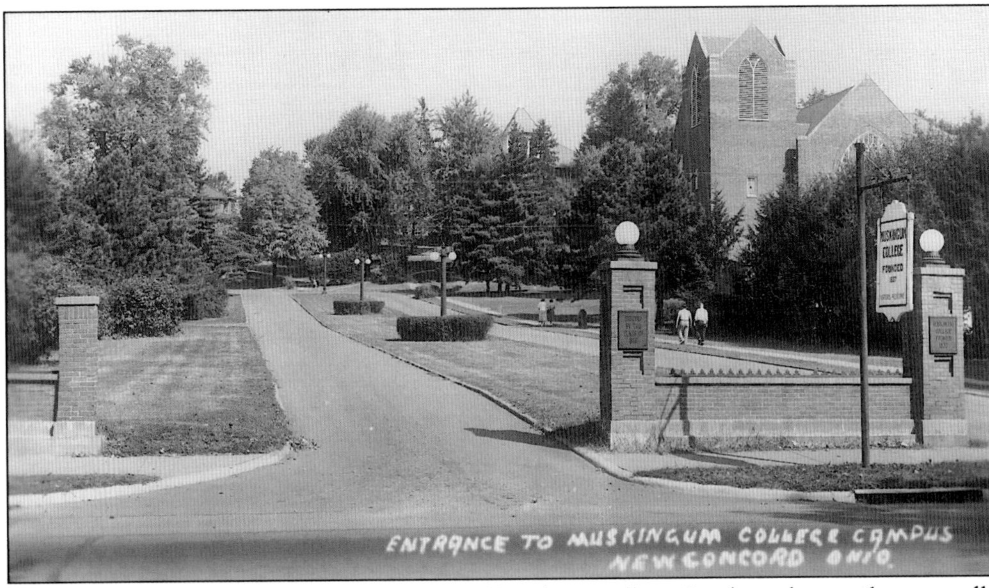

Muskingum College was a small, Presbyterian liberal-arts college. Its clientele was almost totally Presbyterian. Part of its religious and ethnic tradition was character building. Its faculty preached "The Social Gospel," a commitment to social service by bringing religious principles into the secular/political realm. To generations of "Muskies," the College Drive entrance to Muskingum College symbolized the road to public service in the ministry, in education, and other such occupations. The College Drive entrance was created for Muskingum College's Centennial in 1937. The College Drive United Presbyterian Church to the right was dedicated in 1922.

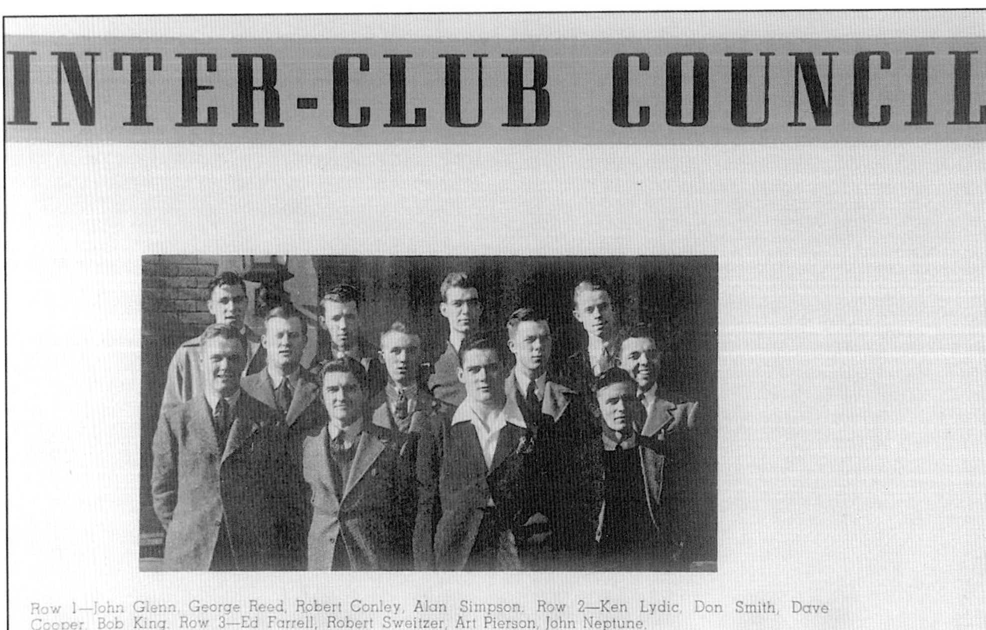

John H. Glenn Jr. (left, front row) emulated his parents in their leadership roles in the community. At Muskingum College he was elected to Inter-Club Council when a freshman. This was a rare honor for one so young.

John Glenn Jr. was a popular student at Muskingum College. He is pictured here (top center) in the 1942 *Muscoljuan.*

John Glenn Jr. and Annie Castor had been "a pair" since 8th grade. At Muskingum College, that closeness grew. Emulating other couples, they enjoyed "courting walks." On special occasions, John gave gardenias to Annie.

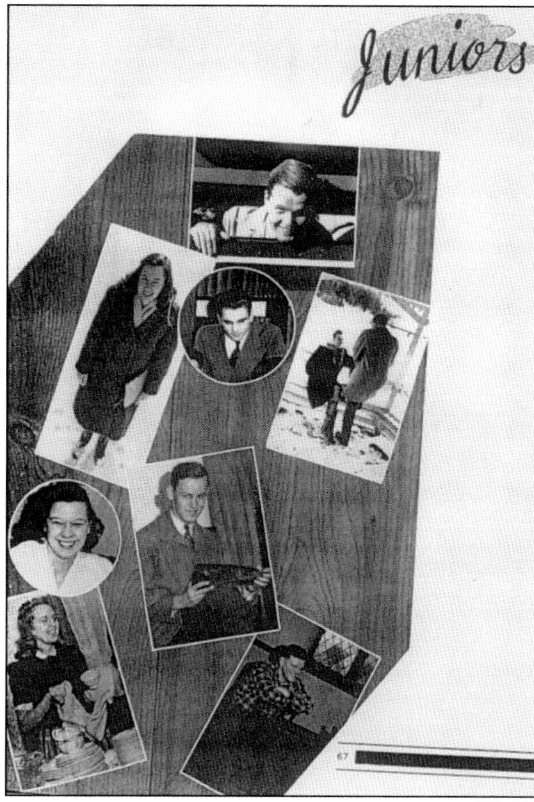

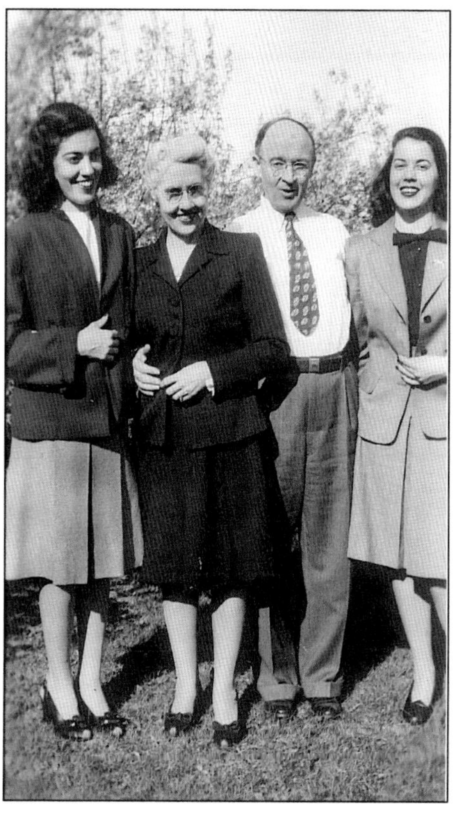

Annie Castor is shown here with her parents Margaret Alley Castor, Dr. Homer Castor, as well as her equally popular sister, Jane (Hosey). Annie was a standout athlete and a superb organist.

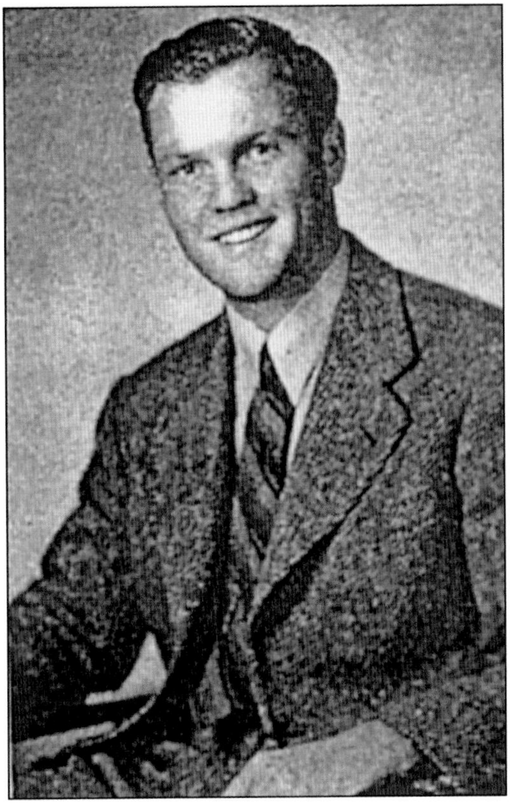

JOHN GLENN

John Glenn Jr. sat on his front porch perched high above the National Road, listened to Glenn Miller's orchestra on the radio, and watched the world pass by. New Concord was small but not isolated. The Muskingum College community had a special interest in world affairs because of the missionaries who went forth from it and who returned to campus for periodic sabbaticals.

War clouds over Europe were triggered by the Ethiopian crisis of 1936—during which Italian dictator Mussolini invaded the hapless African state. Professor Ernest Work at Muskingum College was the leading American specialist on Ethiopia, and the Emperor Haile Selassi's nephews had been educated at Muskingum.

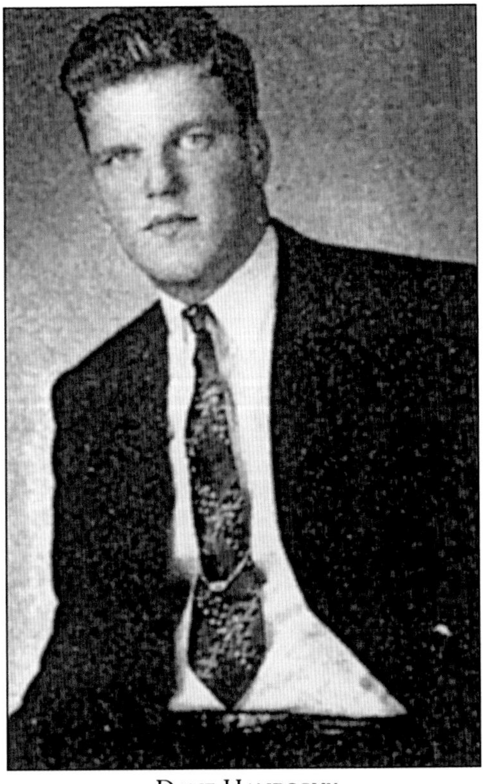

DANE HANDSCHY

Despite the Presbyterian Church's resistance to war—epitomized by this defiant slogan: "We will never be cannon fodder again!"—people knew the European war would ensnare America. John Glenn Jr. jumped at the chance to join the Civilian Pilot Program by which the government was attempting to build up its woefully inadequate Air Force. Finally convincing his fearful parents on this matter, John and three buddies, including Dane Handschy, drove to New Philadelphia for training, and John Glenn Jr., always fascinated with flight, whose heroes had been Lindberg and "Steve Canyon- types," learned to fly.

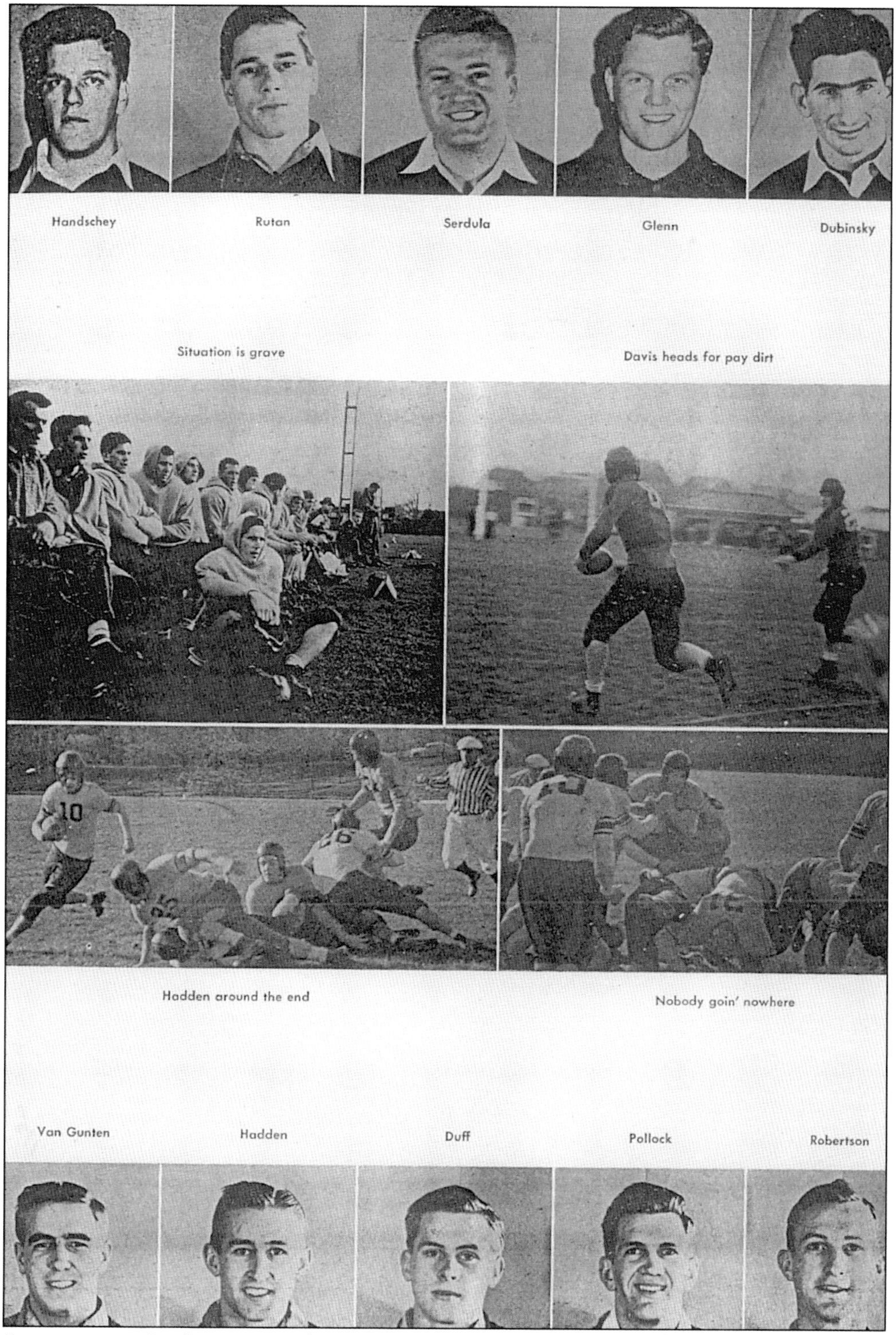

Spring training for the 1941 Muskingum College football season seemed routine. But during the next four years, most of these young men would be in uniform, and Joseph Dubinsky would die.

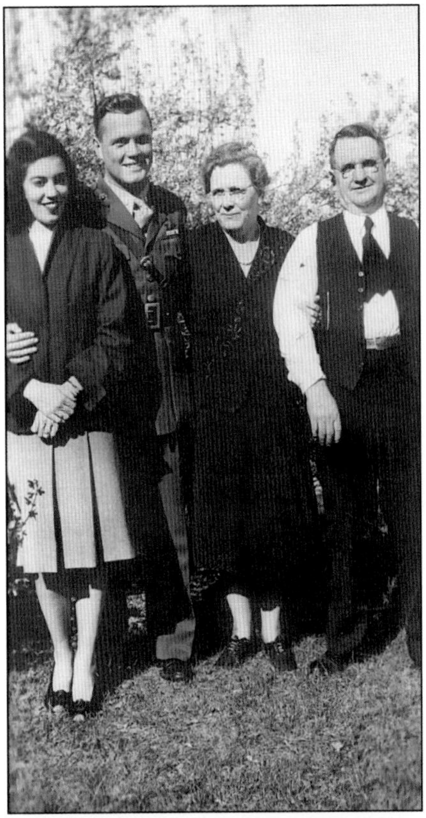

Since the 1930s, the Presbyterian Church had advocated pacifism. Then, on December 7, 1941, the radio announcement of the bombing of Pearl Harbor hit the country like a sledgehammer. New Concord and Muskingum College were no exception. All the proclivity towards pacifism evaporated that Sunday afternoon.

John Glenn Jr. was driving up College Drive towards Brown Chapel in his red '29 Chevy to hear Annie Castor's senior organ recital, when he heard the war bulletin on his car radio. After the concert John and Annie discussed the situation. He knew he had to postpone his college career and enlist. He joined the U.S. Naval Air Wing and in time reported to the training center at Corpus Christi, Texas.

John and Annie married on April 6, 1943, in College Drive United Presbyterian Church, New Concord, Ohio. In his new uniform, John Glenn posed with his bride Annie Castor and his parents, Clara Sproat Glenn and John Herschel Glenn Sr. As the United States frantically built up its forces and strained to supply, feed, and train hundreds of thousands—soon to be 15 million service people—village and college life continued. Then week by week young men disappeared from classrooms and village streets; they were off to serve the country.

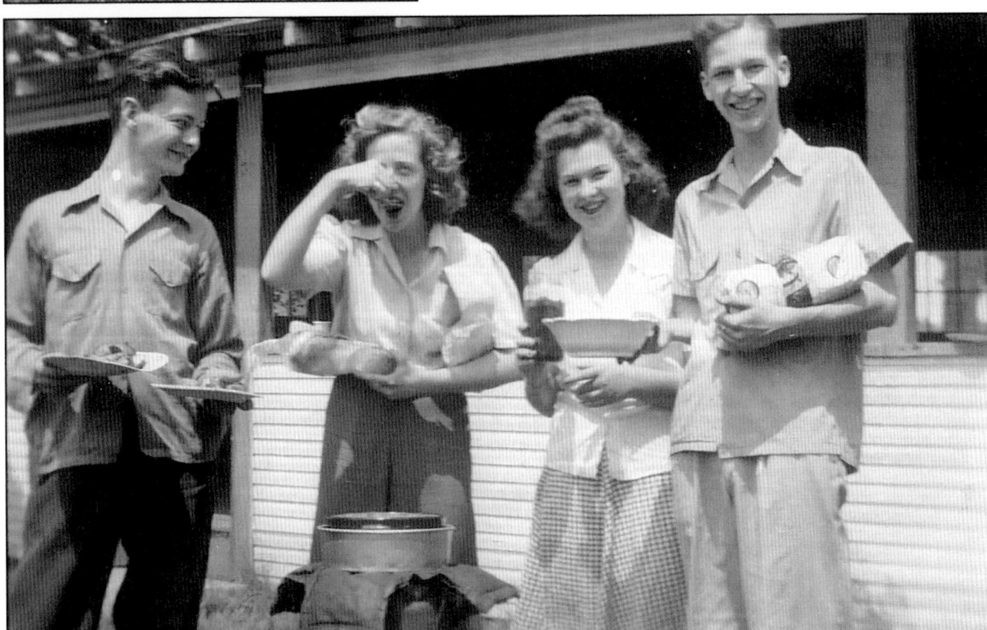

During New Concord High School's "Senior Walkout" in May 1942, Malcolm Law, Mary Bailey, Dorothy Brown, and Bob Morehead play at Maple Grove west of town. Soon the boys would be in uniform.

Merle Rife Jr., son of Muskingum College's Classics professor, had starred in the high school play in 1941; in 1942, he was wearing navy blue.

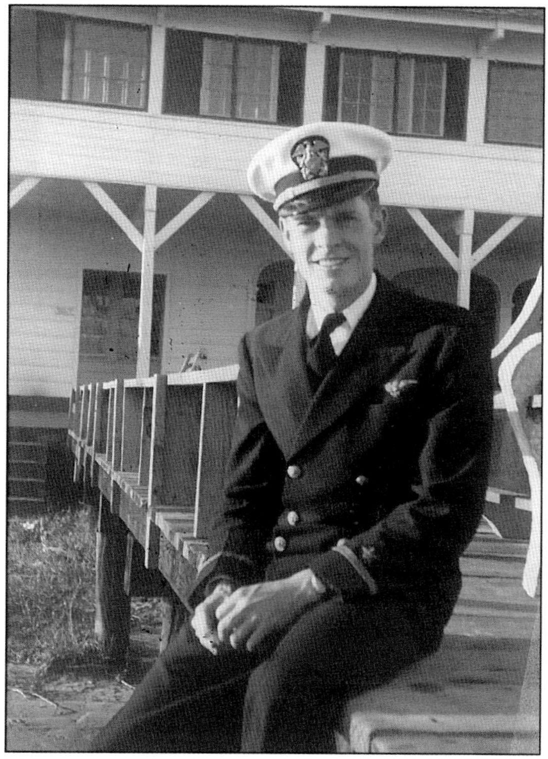

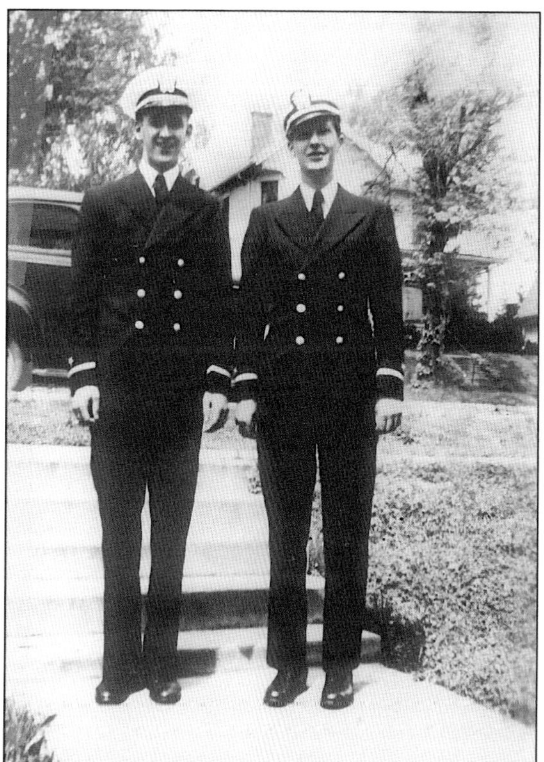

Francis Carpenter and Bob Morehead soon joined him.

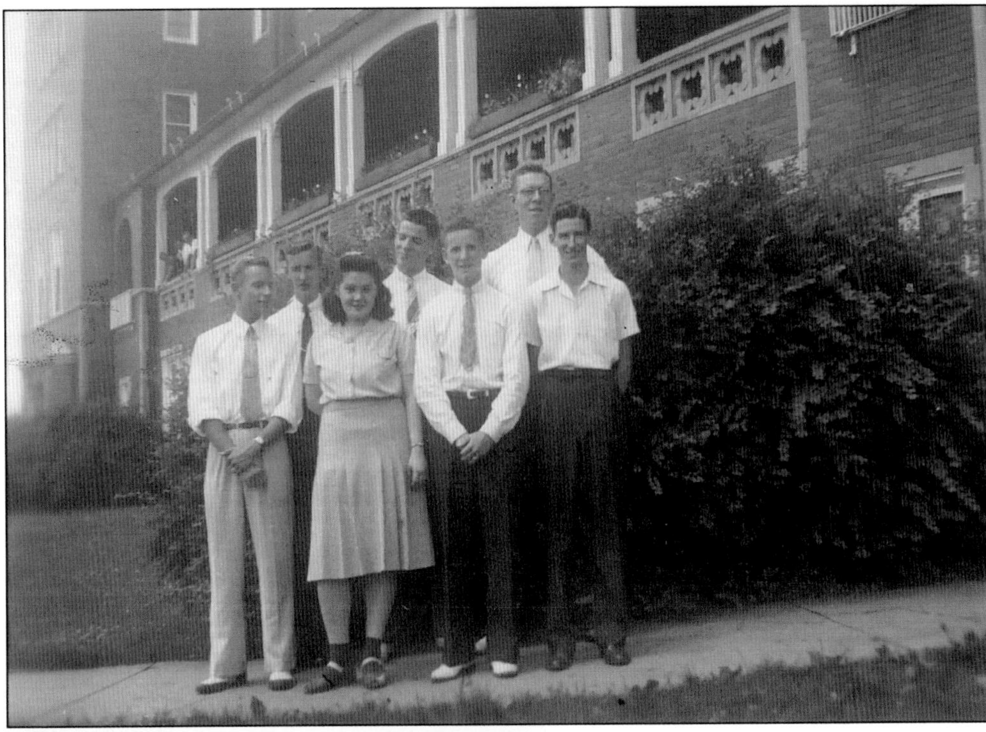

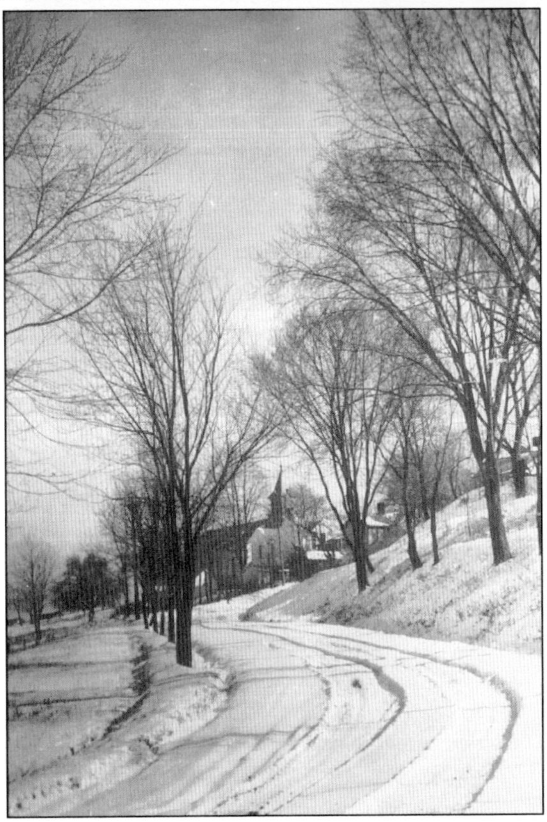

Bill Ballantine (front, left) and six other "Muskies" worked as waiters at Muskingum College's Patton Hall for a Christian Church summer conference in July 1942. By January 13, 1945, he was dead, killed in action in Belgium.

Waiting to be called up, John Glenn Jr. plowed fields for labor-starved farmers and pondered the future:

From the seat of the tractor I took in the Ohio countryside in which I'd grown up and which had shaped me. The land, the contours ordered by the plow, separated by tree lines and fences, rich and bountiful, was unimaginable in the hands of some invading force bent on destroying America.

—John H. Glenn Jr. A *Memoir*

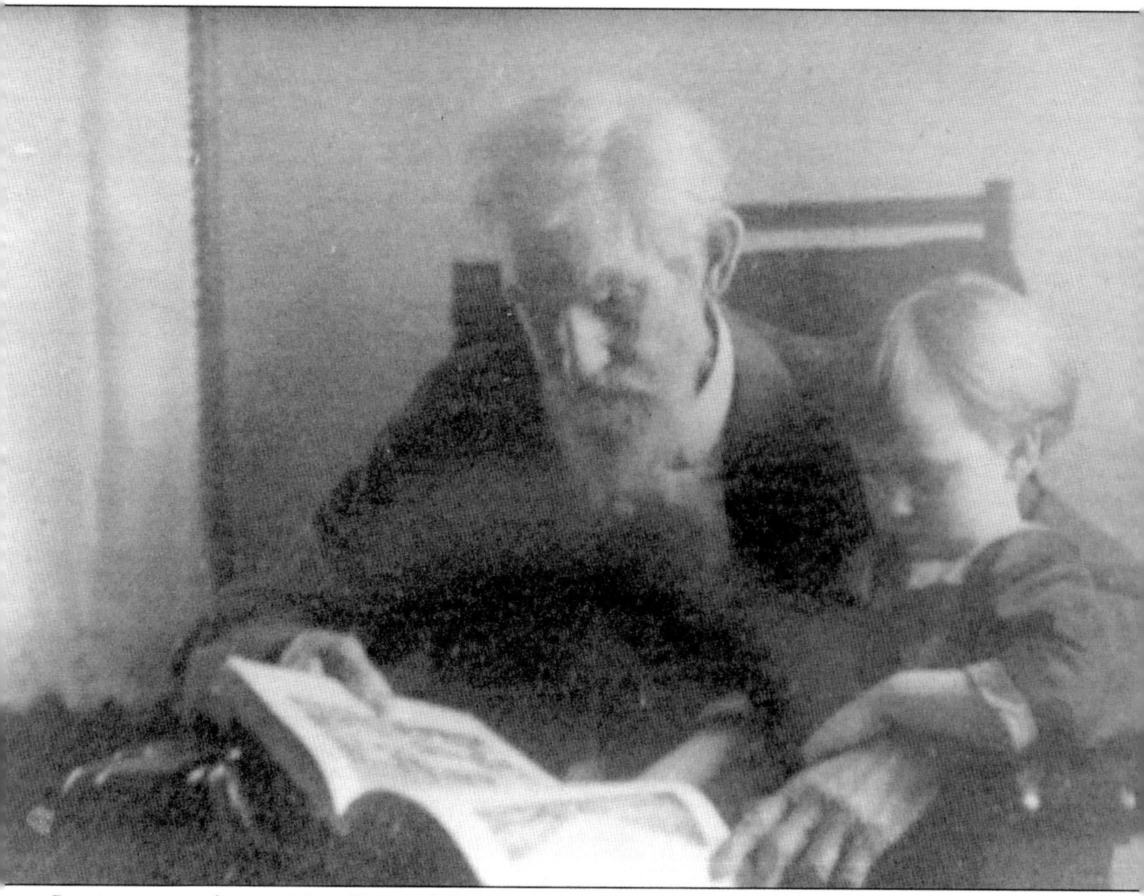

Patriotism ran deep in New Concord. When the World War II men and women were children, Civil War veterans still walked the streets of the village, sat in the park, and reminisced. Dr. Henry McCreary had been a hospital steward in the 78th Ohio Volunteer Infantry. Following service at Shiloh and Vicksburg, he studied medicine. He shared war memories with as much as 70 percent of Union Township's male population. Dr. McCreary is shown with his granddaughter, Betty Grace Garrison Cupoli, a childhood friend of the Glenns.

Memorial Day, Armistice Day, and July 4th were major village holidays. Herschel Glenn, wearing his WW I uniform and a red crepe paper poppie, stood in the Covenanter Cemetery (Friendship Drive) and played taps. John Glenn Jr. stood over the hillside and played an echoing taps on each of those sacred days.

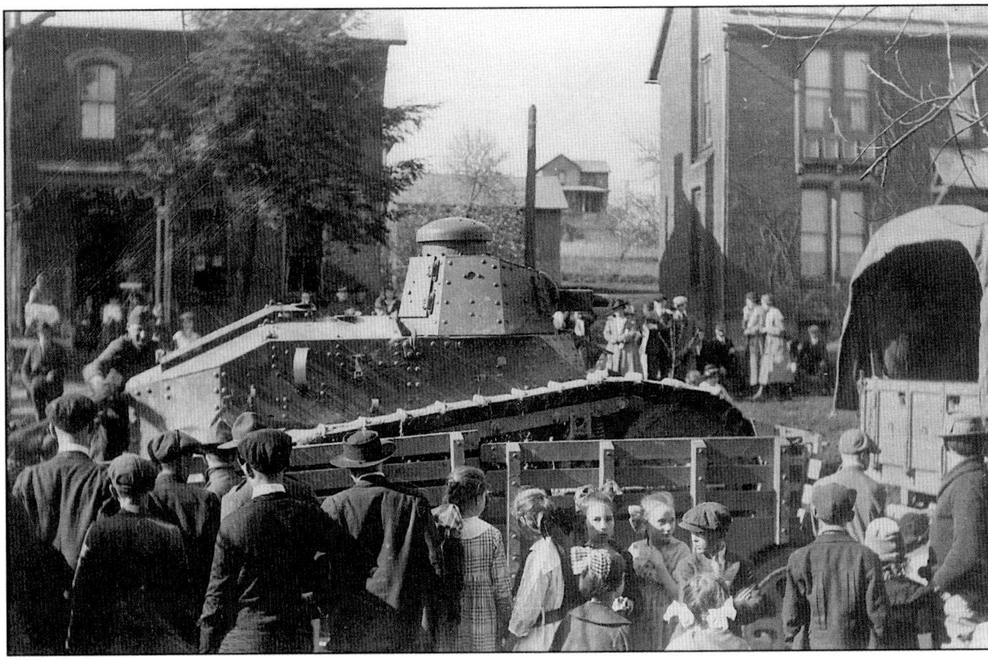

Many local men, including John Herschel Glenn, had seen service during World War I. After that war, the veterans secured an army cannon as a memorial. These scenes depict the military parade which brought the cannon to town. It was moved into place on the Muskingum College campus (site of the College Library) by a tank. During a World War II scrap drive, the World War I cannon was sacrificed to the new war effort.

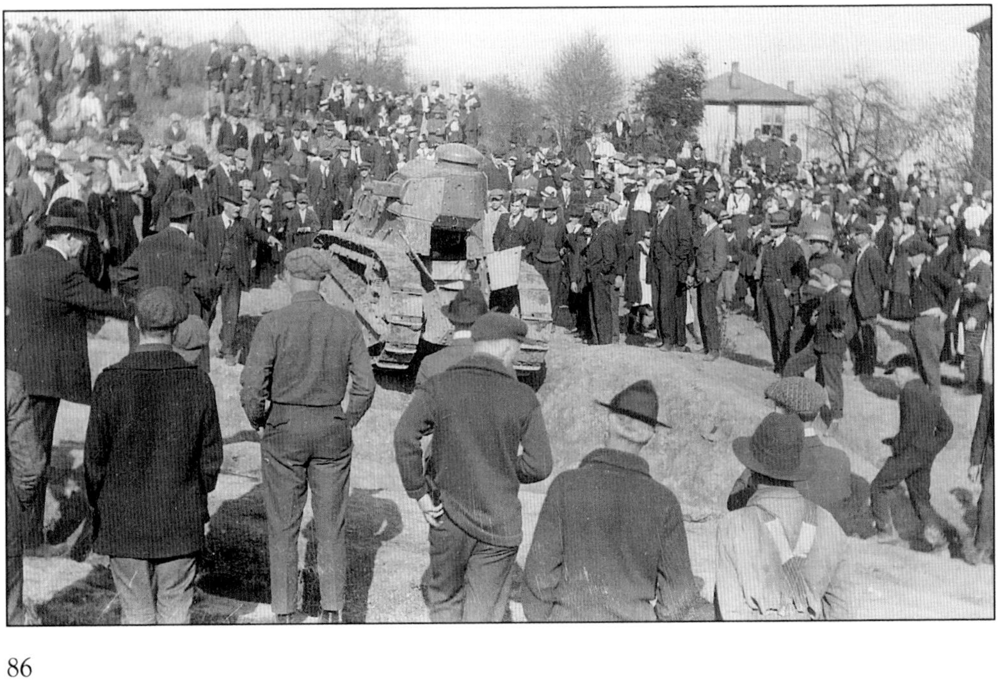

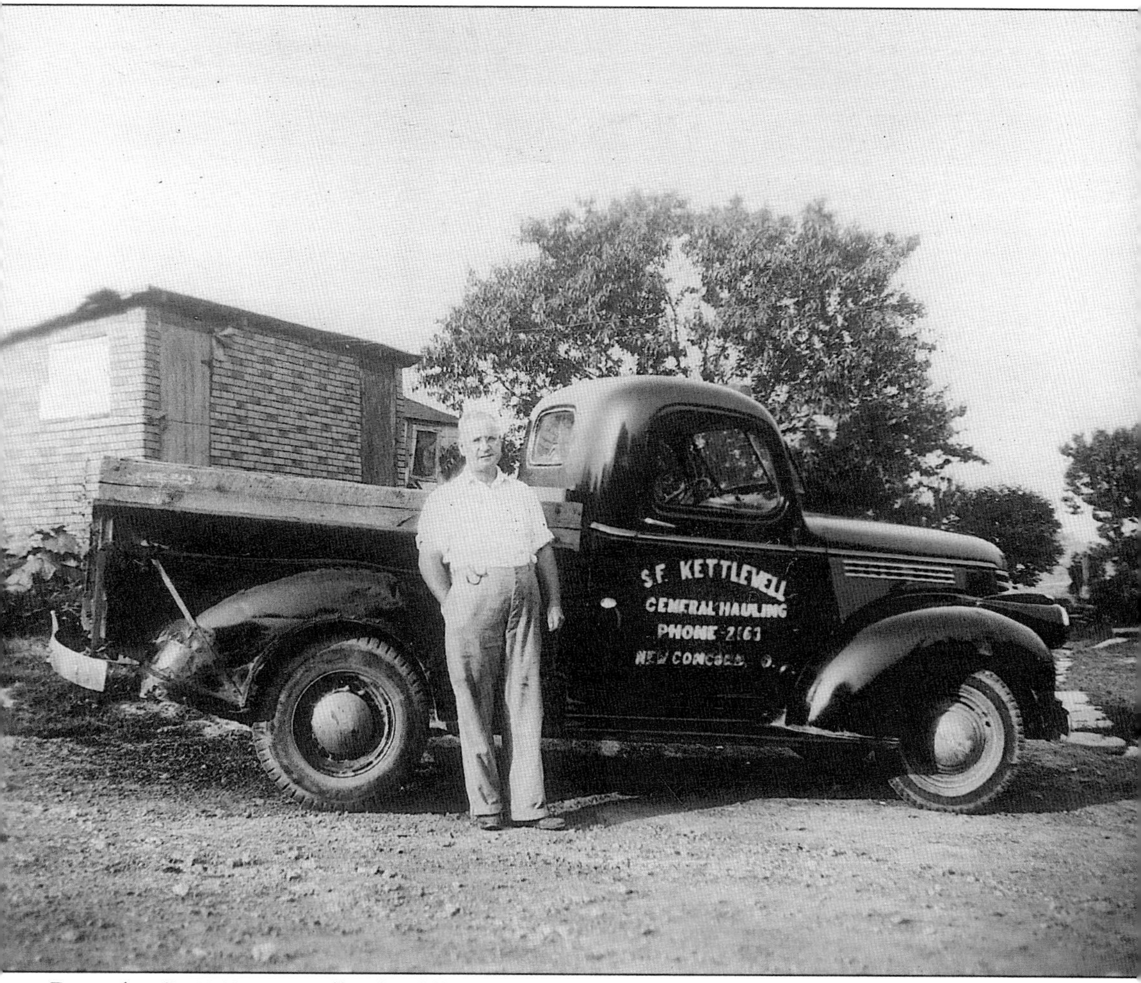

December 7, 1942, ironically also fell on a Sunday, as had the fateful day a year before. John Glenn Jr., a Marine/Naval Air Cadet, sat in his barracks in Corpus Christi and, thinking of two buddies already dead in training accidents, wrote a grateful letter to his pastor, Rev. C.E. Houk, thanking him for his inspiration.

Glenn's experience in the Marine Corps meshed with "all the components of the Community that was New Concord, Ohio," in honing a code of conduct. He never forgot his good fortune or love for his hometown and the Marine Corps. Glenn flew 59 missions in the Pacific during the war. His plane was hit five times.

The war effort consumed the country. In New Concord, there were fund drives for Finnish and Ethiopian relief. War-bond drives went "over the top," with the Muskingum College President, "Doc Bob" Montgomery, literally selling the shirt off his back as a premium. Ellis Duitch, John Glenn's science teacher, headed up village defense, and organized scrap drives and lard drives. A Red Cross sewing station operated in the Village Hall, and all men and women aged 21–35 were registered; volunteerism was extremely high.

S.F. Kettlewell continued his rounds as a "honey dipper" (cleaner of privys). He and other village men participated in home guard defense and assisted the children in unending scrap drives.

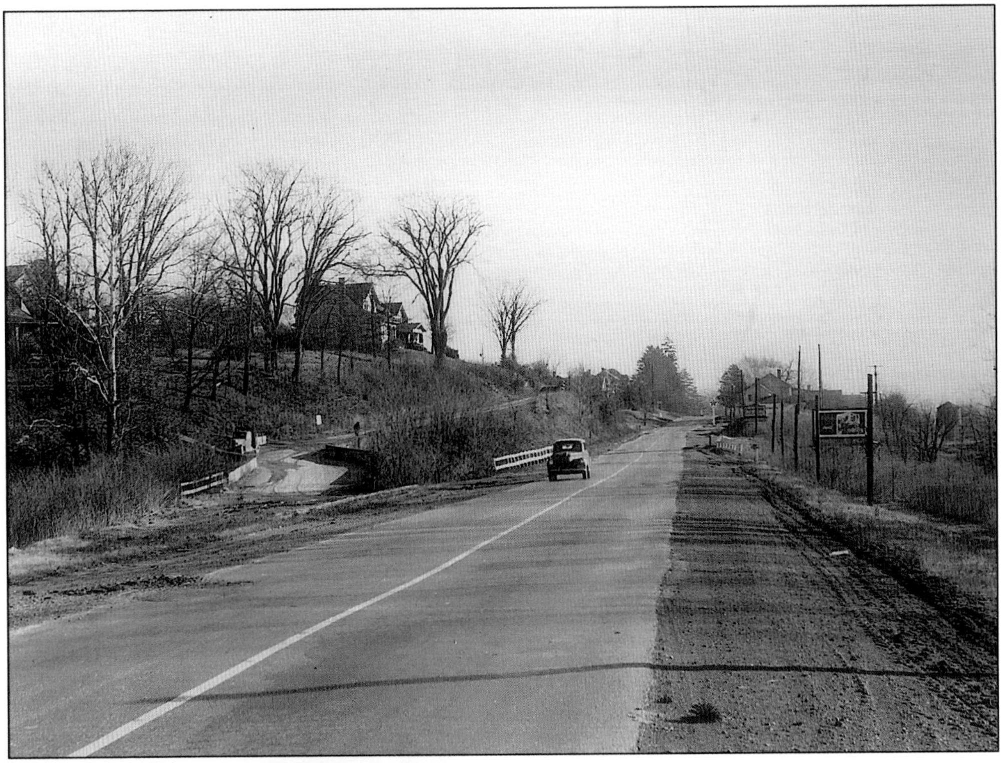

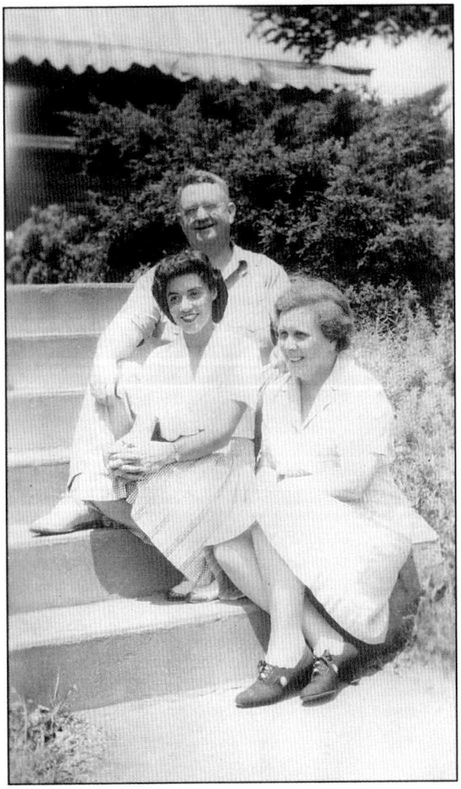

Fighting World War II was America's most challenging frontier. Widening U.S. 40 was a part of the gigantic effort. There was a crying shortage of labor; convicts and soldiers were detailed to the high priority job. The Glenn home would be destabilized by the huge cut at the "S" Bridge and would eventually be moved across a corn field to a site on "Friendship Drive" (known then as State Route 75). In this photo McCloud and Glenn homes perch on Shadyside Terrace. (Courtesy of Ohio Historical Society, Norris Schneider Collection.)

Annie Castor Glenn, Herschel, and Clara Glenn sit on the steps of the Glenn home for a picture Annie sent to John in the Pacific.

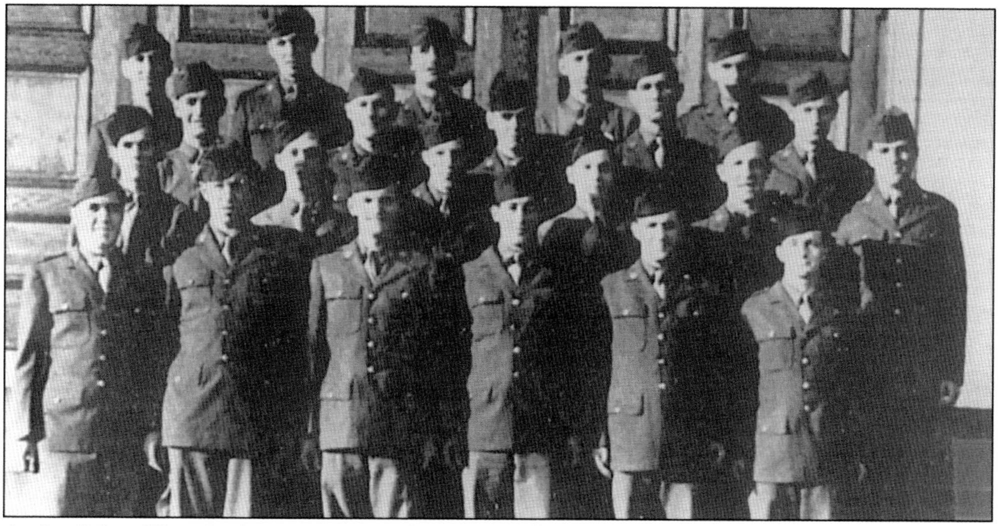

At Lt. John Glenn's alma mater, Muskingum College, potential army officers trained in the ASTP (Army Specialized Training Program).

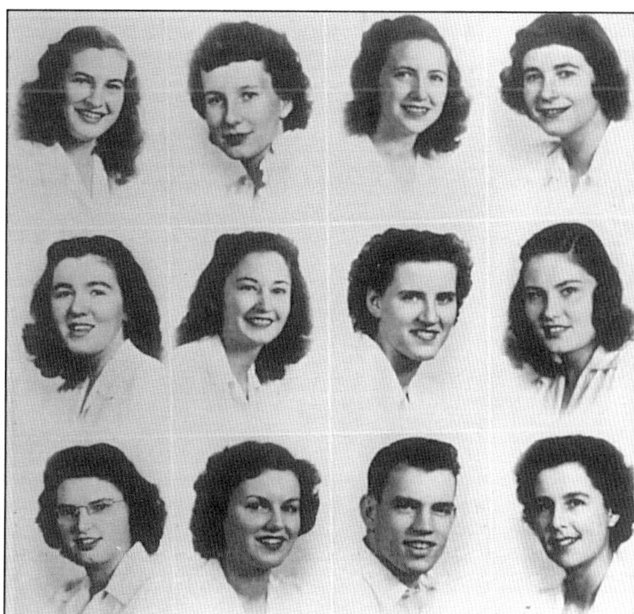

By 1944, these men and a few medical and ministerial students were the only males on campus.

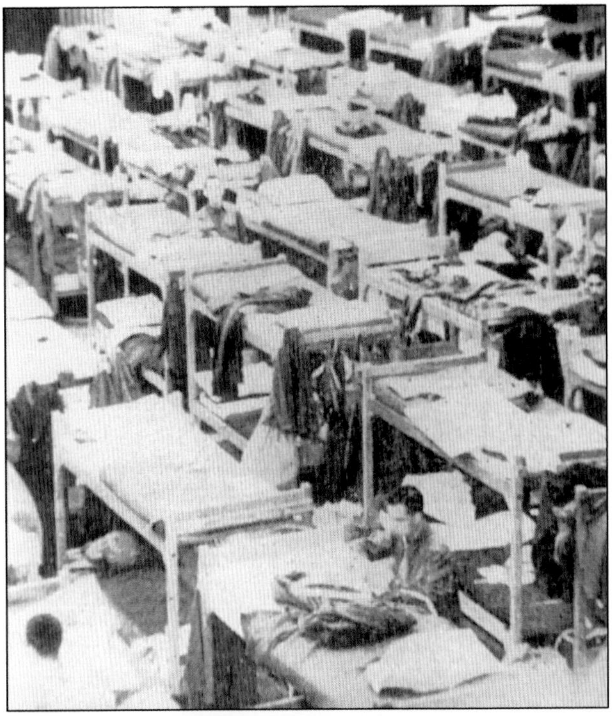

America's slumbering economic wealth was roused by the need to fight World War II. America literally fed, clothed, and armed the Allies. With unprecedented energy, factories reopened to meet the need. Unemployment vanished.

The American military went from less than 500,000 to more than 15,000,000 men and women. With a mighty effort of organization, discipline, dedication, and self-sacrifice, America marched off to war. The war cost 15 times what World War I had cost. Americans spent $330 billion in the effort. At peak performance, in production and military action, the effort cost $250 *million* a day.

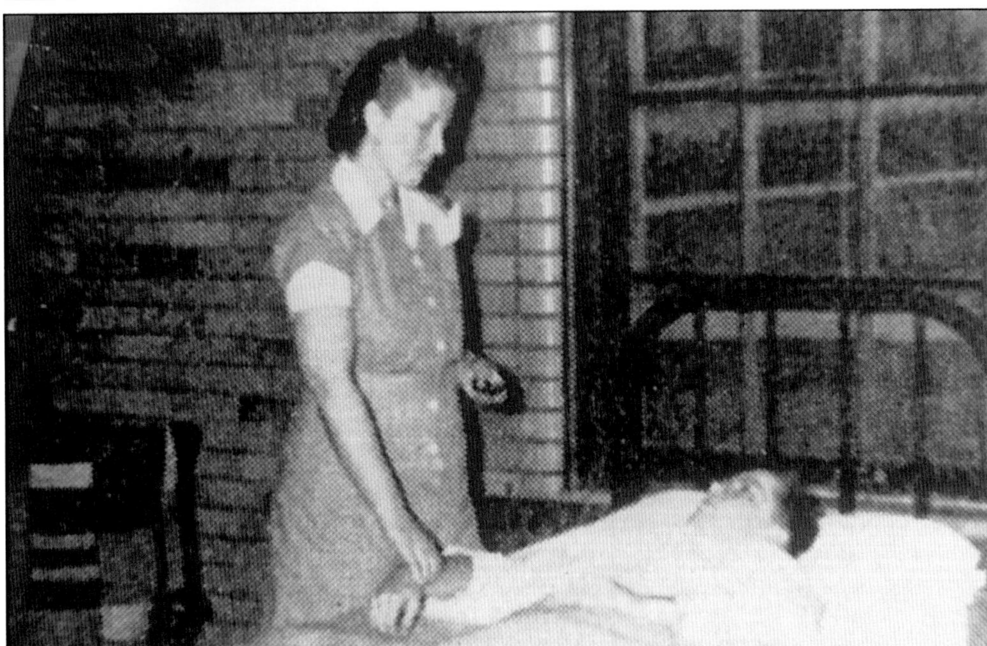

The war effort was both national and grass-root. Tiny New Concord, Ohio, was typical of grass-root efforts. The crying need for officers required colleges across the country to become training facilities. Muskingum College's gymnasium (now the John Glenn Gym) became a military barracks. Local New Concord women, including "Mrs. Doc Bob," (Ruth Montgomery, wife of Muskingum College President Robert Montgomery), volunteered as nurses in the barrack's "sick bay."

Following Pearl Harbor, the fear of Japanese invasion of the Pacific states was very real. This led to the relocation of Japanese-Americans from California, Washington, and Oregon to interior states. The same action took place in Canada, Mexico, and Peru.

Appalled Japanese-Americans protested their patriotism and would win acclaim for their people by heroic service in the 442th Infantry Battalion's Italian campaign. This battalion became the most decorated unit in American military history. A small but steady criticism of this violation of civil liberties endured throughout the war. The American Friends (Quakers) acted by placing Nisei (Japanese-Americans born in this country) in American colleges. Five Nisei came to Muskingum College. They were popular and energetic students.

Mary Yamashita Doi
McGhee, Arkansas
English
Wawyin; Sigma Tau Delta; Pi Gamma Mu; Home-Ec Club; Editor of "Bubble Work."

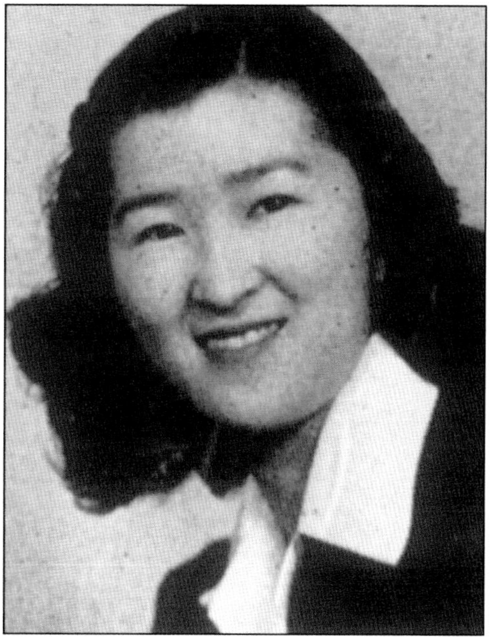

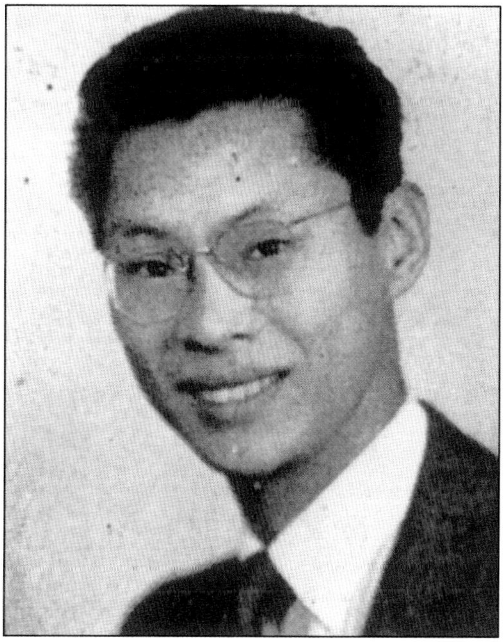

Harold S. Shirakawa
Boulder, Colorado
Biology
Alban, Pres.; Sr. Class Pres.; O.O.O.O.; Who's Who; Student Council; YMCA Cabinet; Homecoming Committee; Co-chairman Sejuna; Co-chairman Winter Carnival; Interclub council; Social Chairman, Co-chairman of Homecoming Variety Show; Cheer Leader.
Ph.D. Mycology, University of Notre Dame.

Cadet Nurses

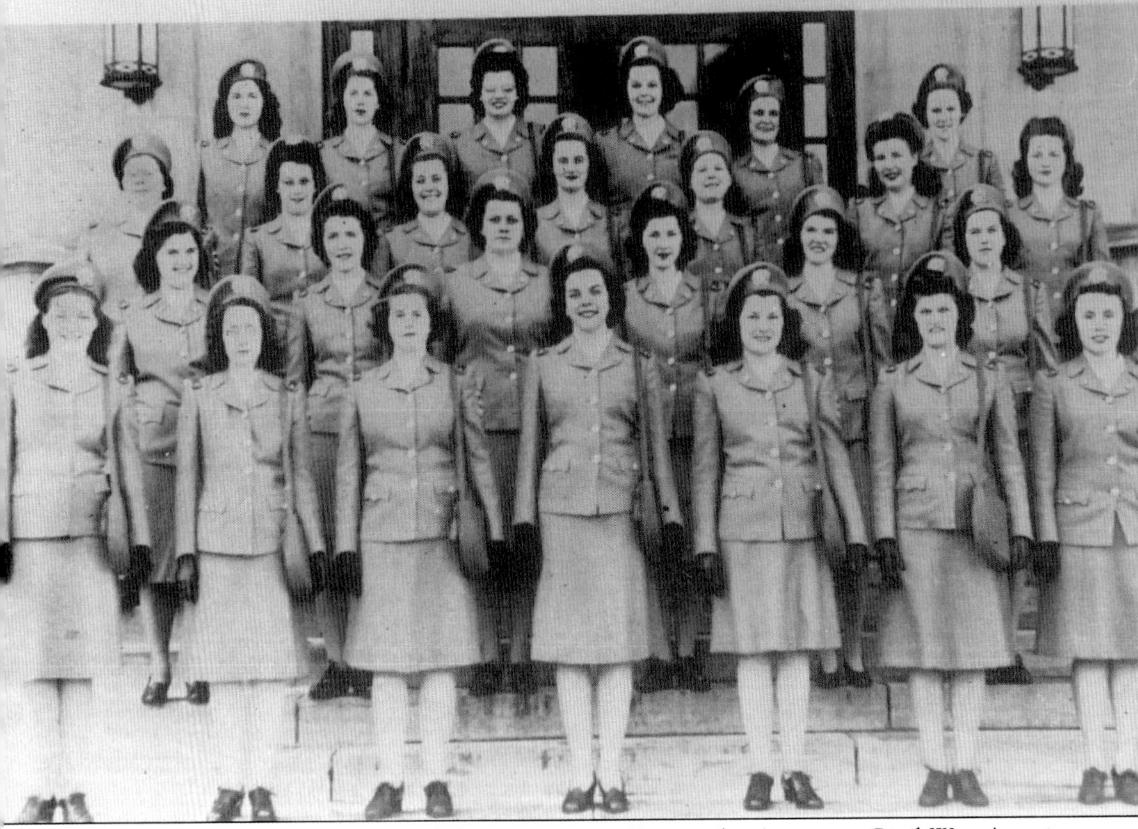

Social changes are rapidly-paced during war time. During the American Civil War, American women became heads of households at an alarming rate. They also became shopkeepers and seamstresses. During World War I, they "manned" production lines, and a few of them joined the military. During World War II, American women became epitomized by "Rosie the Riveter." The war effort would not have been successful without women in the work force. Another 200,000 women served in the military, as did many military nurses.

Student nurses from Bethesda Hospital in Zanesville were among women across the country who received academic and military training at colleges. This group trained at Muskingum College.

The first year of war (1941), 50 Muskies joined the military; the second year, 184. In 1943, there were 415 students in the college—only 80 of these were men. In total, 882 Muskingum men wore uniform in war time. Many Muskies served in the102nd Infantry during the Battle of the Bulge. Forty Muskingum men, 8 New Concord High School graduates, and 22 ASTP men were killed in action during the war. "Memorial Hall" and the Hollow and its pioneer cabin at Muskingum College were dedicated to their memory.

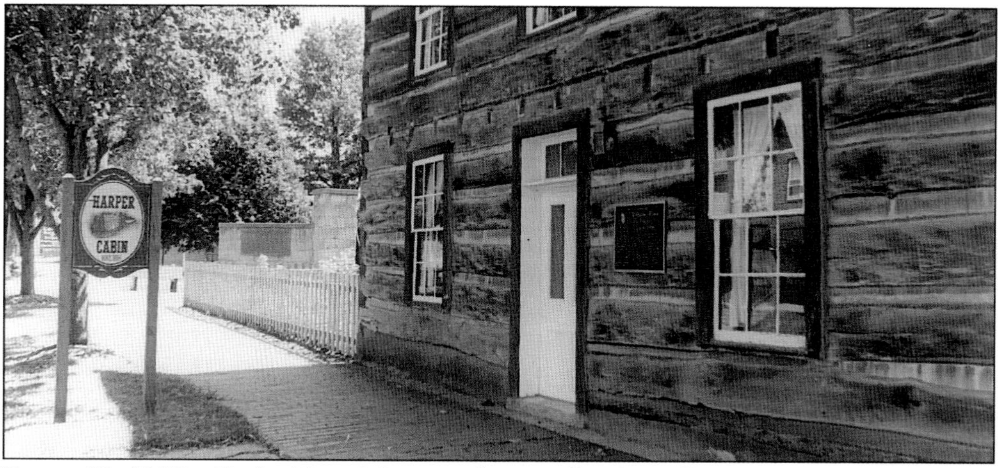

During World War II, the United States military suffered a million casualties—one third of these were deaths. The nation recognized that sacrifice with gold stars. Gold stars hung in several New Concord homes. The Village of New Concord war memorial at Harper Cabin Park records the sacrifice of many young men and their families. The men with stars before their names died in service. Muskingum College students' homes also sadly flew the Gold Star Flag.

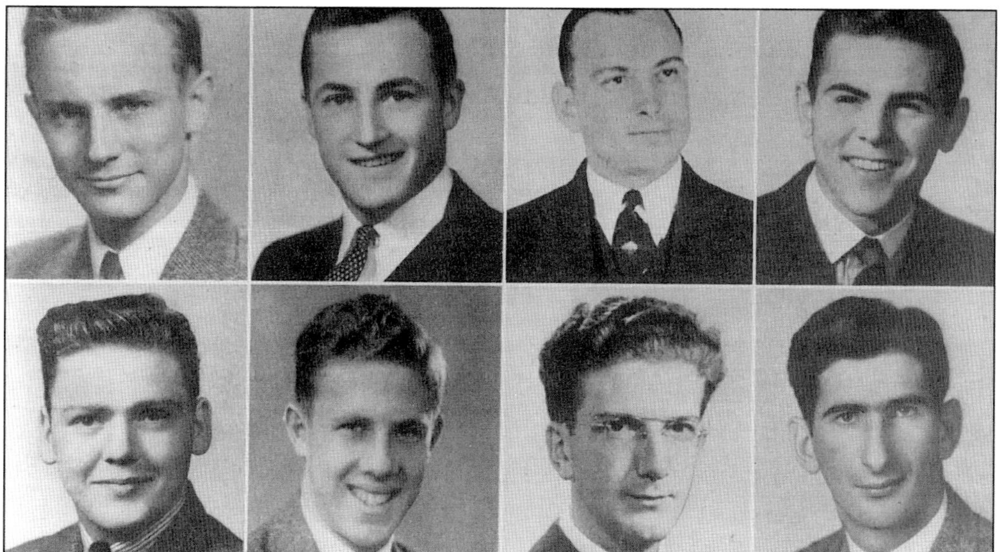

PVT. WILLIAM J.D. BALENTINE, x '45
New Concord, OH.
Army, Belgium, Jan. 13, 1945

LT. (J.G.) JACK BECHDEL, '42
McDonald, PA.
Navy, Philippines, Nov. 1944

SGT. JOHN FLOYD CONRAD, x '41
Freeport, OH.
Army, Germany, May 14, 1945

PVT. TED L. COOK, '39
Bellevue, PA.
Army Air Corps, U.S. Nov. 3, 1944

LT. (j.g.) CLARENCE R. COPELAND, x '43
Pittsburgh, PA.
Naval Air Corps, South Pacific
Feb 5, 1945

1st LT. RONDEL L. COX, x'38
Cuyahoga Falls, OH.
Army Air Corps, U.S., July 14,1942

PFC. WILLIAM DEAN, x '45
Cleveland, OH.
Army, Germany, March 1945

LT. JOSEPH DUBINSKY, '42
Washington, PA.
Army Air Corps, Japan,
July 27, 1945

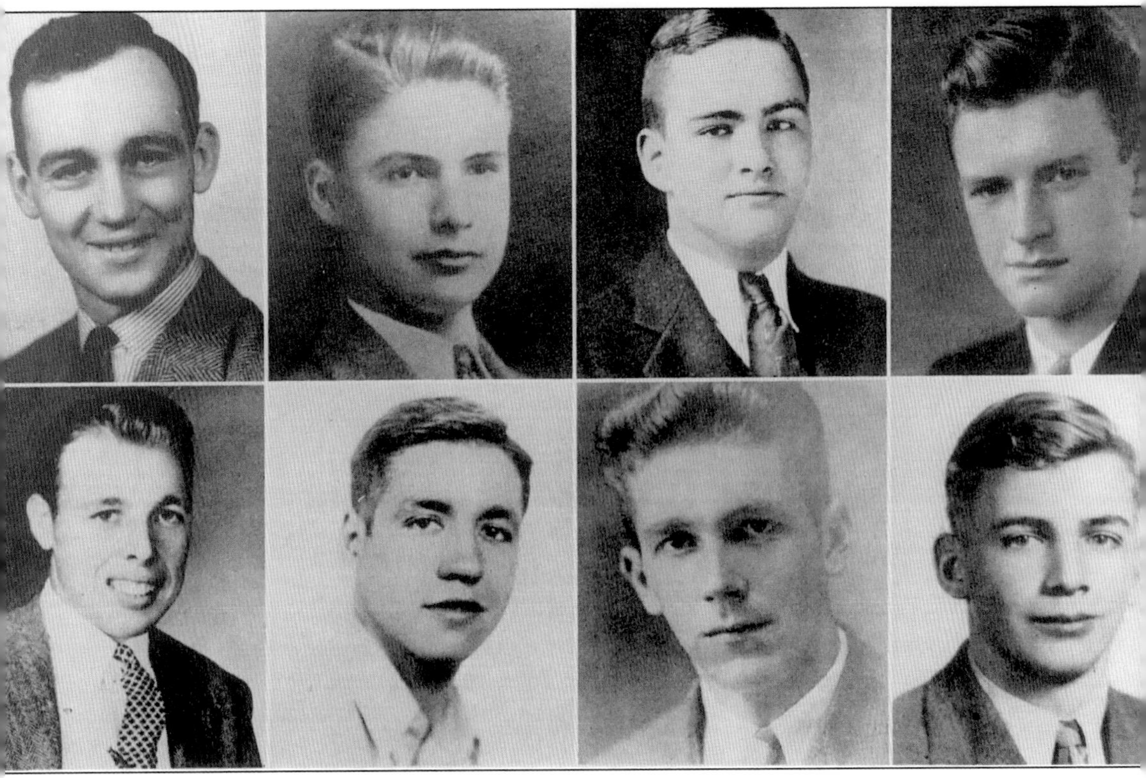

Some Muskingum College Dead:

LT. (j.g.) DAVID EVANS,
Hudson, OH.
Naval Air Corps, Pacific
April 19, 1945

S/SGT. HOWARD FERGUSON, x '32
Burgettstown, PA.
Army Air Corps, United States,
Feb. 1945

LT. CLARENCE GRAHAM, JR., x '40
Columbus, OH.
Army, Germany
Jan., 1945

CAPT. JOHN C. GREGG, x '37
Washington D.C.
Army, France
Jan. 18, 1945

LT. THOMAS HARDESTY, x '42
Ravenna, OH.
Army Air Corps, North Africa
Jan., 30, 1945

LT. RICHARD HUGHES, x '41
Steubenville, OH.
Army, Germany
April 22, 1945

ROBERT HUGHES, FC 3/c, x '27
Gibsonia, PA.
Navy, Pacific
July 30, 1945

DAVID JACKSON,
Fire Controllman, 3/c, x '42
Holloway, OH.
Navy, Mediterranean
April 20, 1944

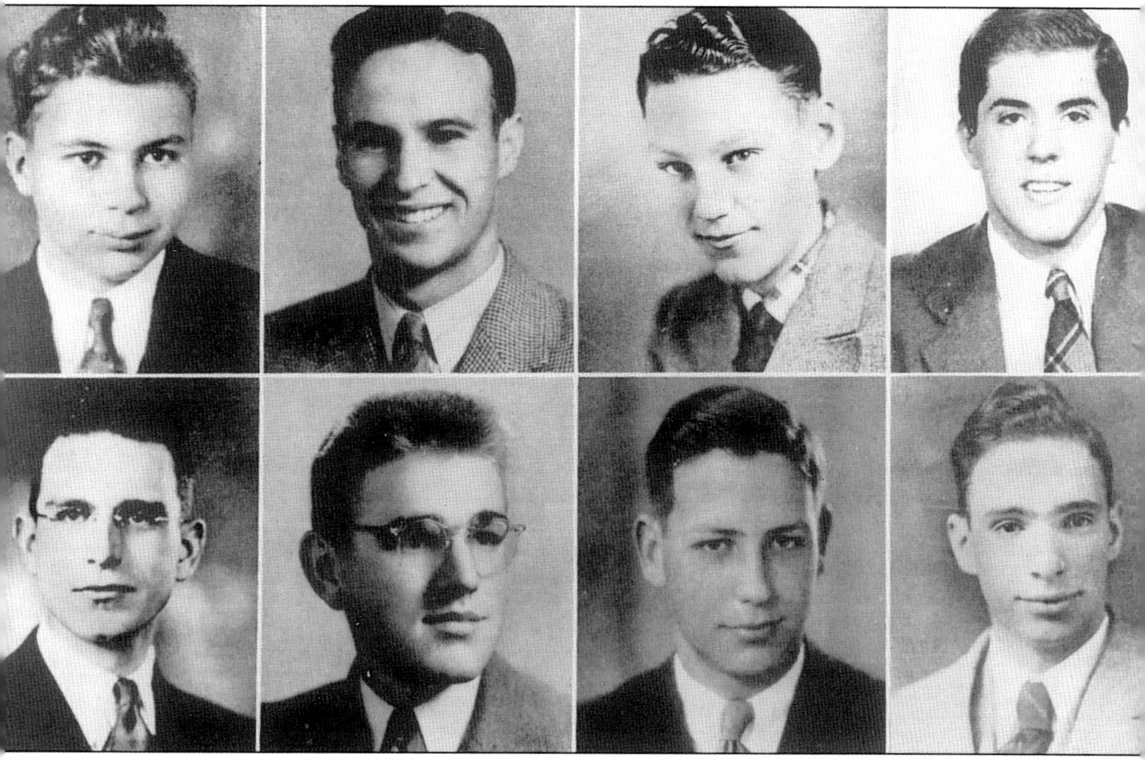

CAPT. GEORGE KAPPES '39
Zanesville, OH.
Army, South China Sea,
Oct. 24, 1944

ENS. DORN L. KILE, x '39
West Jefferson, OH.
Naval Air Corps, United States
May 23, 1945

ENS. JOHN LONGBRAKE x '41
Belle Center, OH.
Naval Air Corps, United States
Sept. 15, 1942

ENS. DARRELL MAXWELL, x '44
Sharon, PA.
Navy, Pacific
Jan. 3, 1945

PFC. WALTER W. MCCORKLE, '31
Elmira, NY
Army, France
Sept. 3, 1944

PFC. JOHN PAUL MCCREARY, x '45
College Corner, OH.
Army, France
Dec., 1944

LT. JOHN M. MCILVAINE, x '38
Houston, PA.
Army Air Corps, France
Aug. 9, 1943

PFC. REED McROBERTS, '28
Murraysville, PA.
Army, Philippines
Dec. 12, 1941

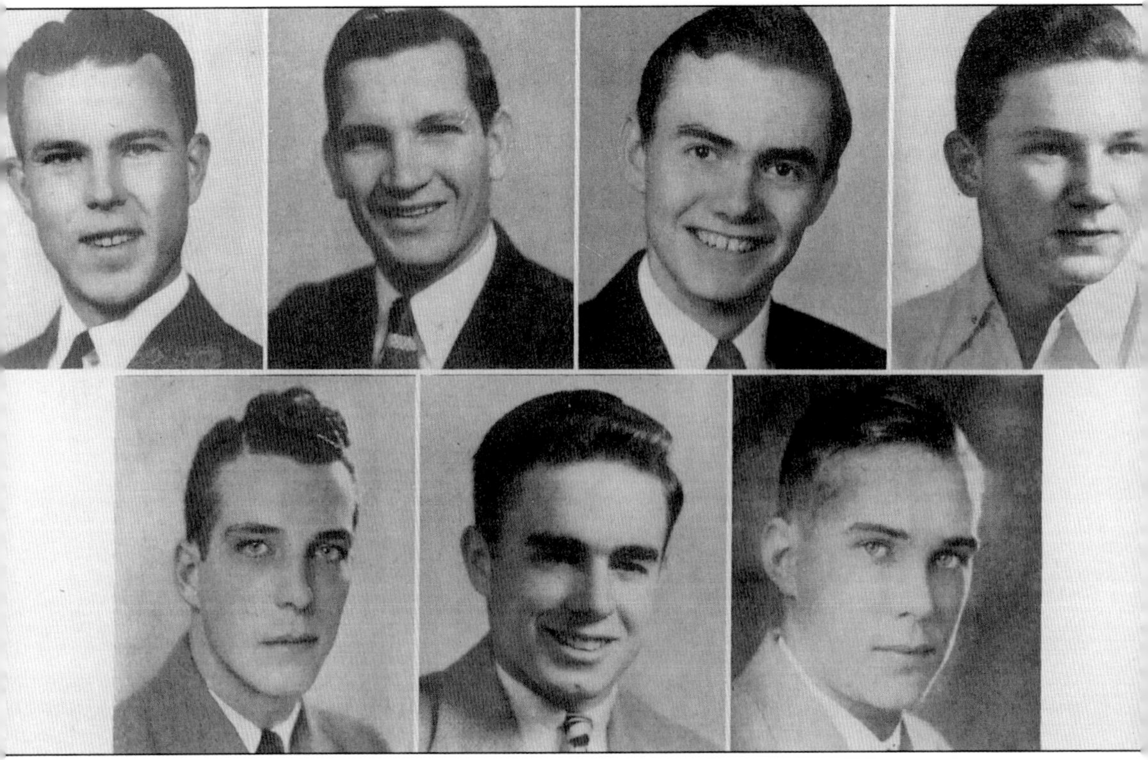

LT. RICHARD NOBLE, '40
New Concord, OH.
Army Air Corps, Germany
May 12, 1944

AC WILLIAM L. PRIAULX, x '43
Cambridge, OH.
Army Air Corps, United States
April 23, 1944

LT. ROBERT SCHIERTZ, x '43
Bellevue, PA.
Army Air Corps. Italy
Aug. 14, 1944

LT. PAUL J. SCHULTZ, x '44
Stratton, OH.
Army, France
July 18, 1944

Bottom Row

CAPT. GEORGE F. SLATER, x '37
New Concord, OH.
(Chaplain) France
Dec. 14, 1944

S/SGT. NOBLE WOOD, x '46
Allison Park, PA.
Army Air Corps, Austria
Dec. 1944

LST. LT. DAVID W. YECKEL '36
Lawrence, PA.
Army, India
Aug. 1945

Six

The Cold War and Beyond

In 1946, New Concord and Muskingum remained microcosms of the national scene. Service men returned and picked up the threads of their lives. Like Herschel Glenn and other "Great War" veterans, the world view of these young/old men had been broadened, and they set out to remake their world on a broadly democratic pattern.

After the war, the G.I. Bill (arguably the most successful American government program on record) brought back married veterans and new students to the Muskingum College campus. "Trail Wood Heights" was the "Married Muskie" compound north of Patton Hall on Lakeside Drive.

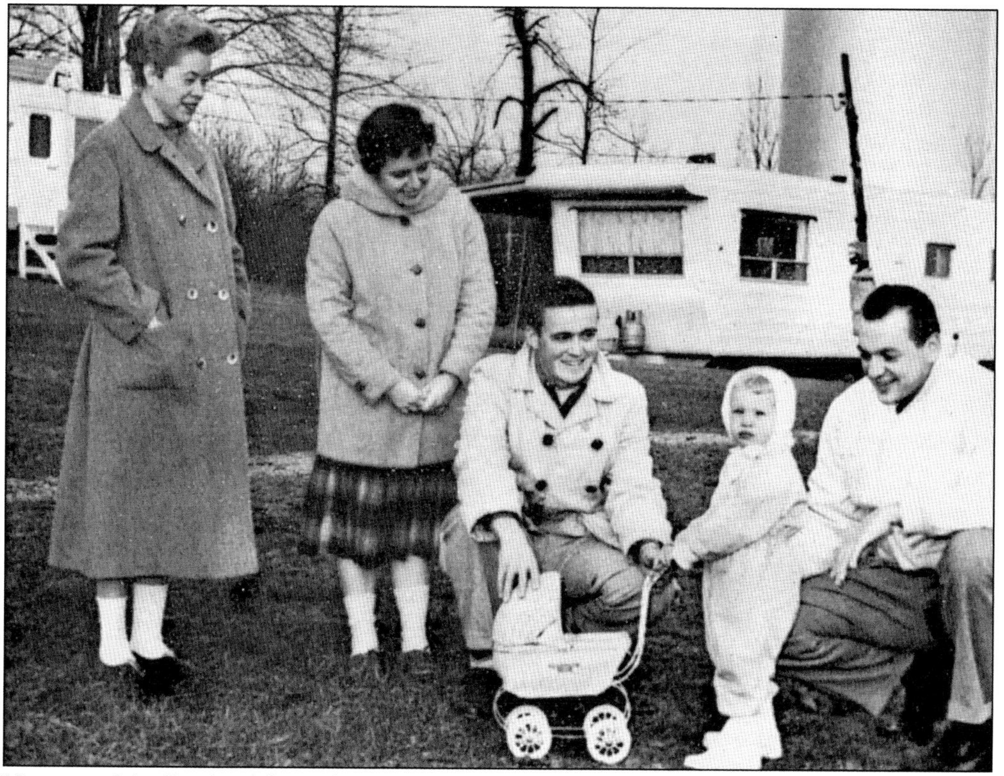

Veterans of the Battle of the Bulge, Saipan, Normandy, Iwo Jima, and all points east and west in this Greatest War abandoned rifles, tanks, flame throwers, and planes to concentrate on English Literature, Philosophy, and Biology. Mostly, the married Muskies concentrated on their children.

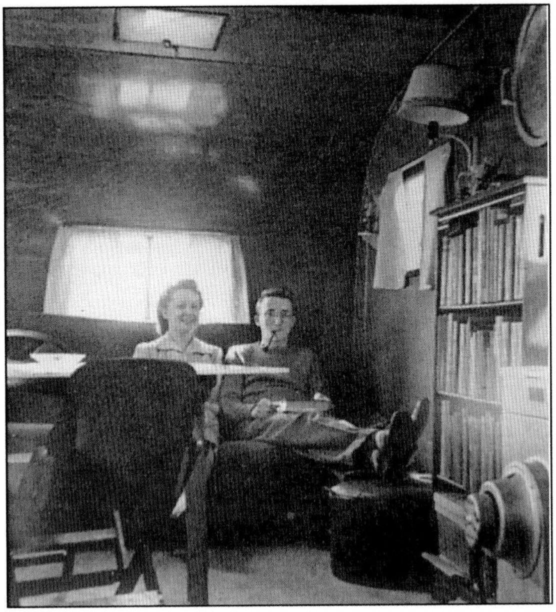

Muskingum College's student body slowly changed as the G.I. Bill encouraged huge numbers of men and women—who normally would never have attended college—to enter that world. Muskingum College and the village of New Concord were the better for the veterans' presence. George and Beryl Besore settled into their new "quarters," one of the government-issue trailers on Lakeside Drive. Beryl was one of several "war brides" on campus. She met George in the south of England at the end of the war. Beryl came to the United States on November 23, 1946. She and George were married three days later and immediately boarded a train for New Concord, Ohio.

Beryl Besore remembers:

Our trailer park we called 'Trailwood Heights.' These trailers did not contain bathrooms, so the college erected two bathrooms, one for the men and one for the women. We cooked on a Coleman gasoline stove and heated our unit with a kerosene stove. The iceman brought us ice twice a week. The Ohio winters were cold. I got a job at the Mosaic Tile Company in Zanesville and rode the Greyhound bus to work. George worked part-time at an auto body shop in New Concord.

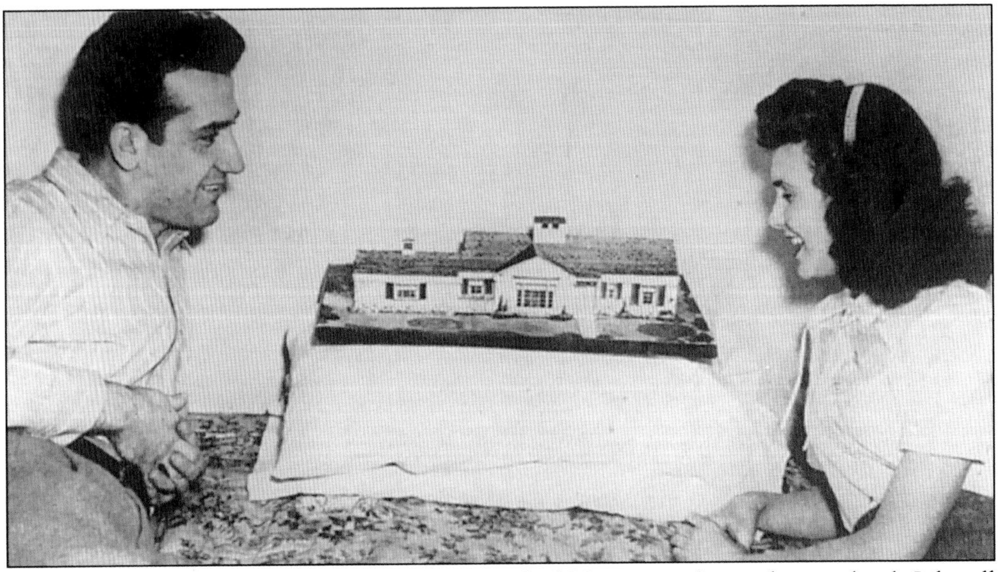

George graduated in 1948 and enrolled at Stanford University for graduate school. Like all the Married Muskies—veterans across the land—the Besores dreamed of their own home. The building boom triggered by the pent-up demand of war-time revolutionized American society. "Suburbs" were invented. The whole dynamic of American life sailed into uncharted seas in the 1950s.

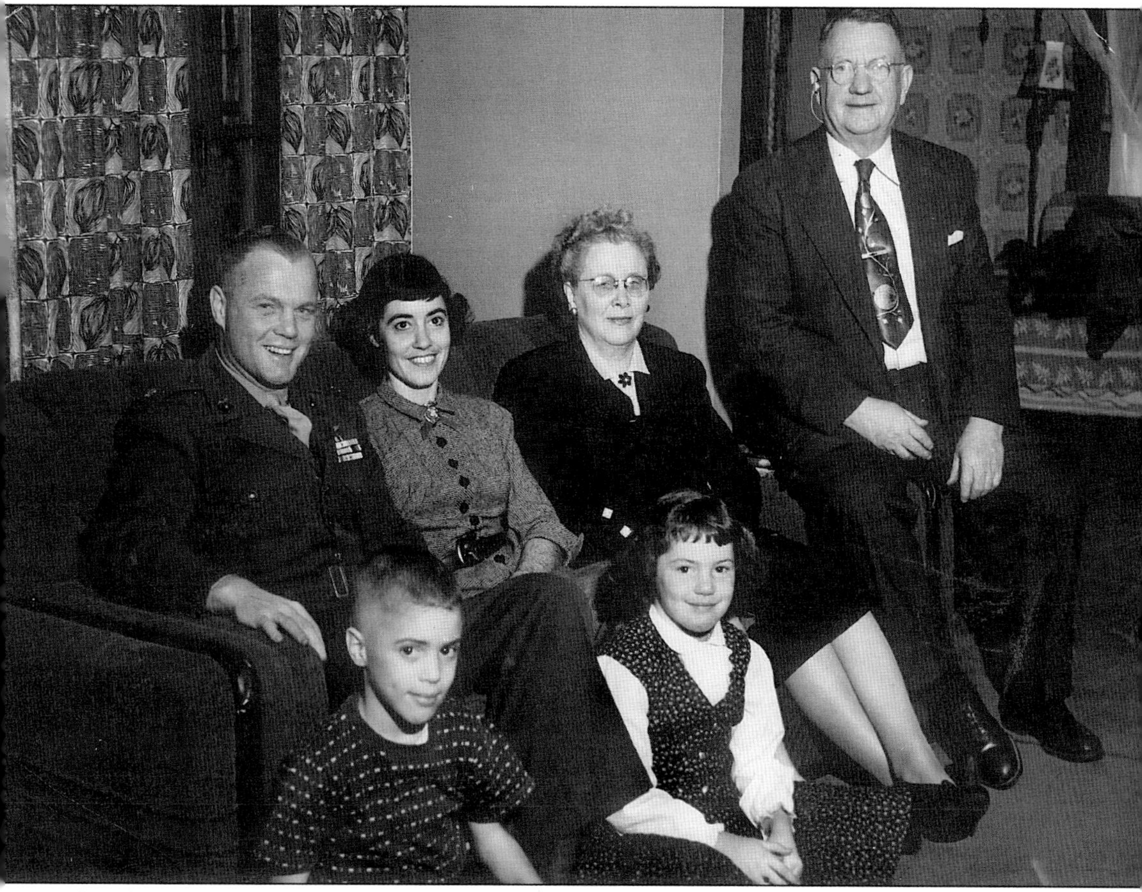

After the war, the American economy exploded. There was giddiness that the country had successfully endured and conquered both Depression and war. But the looming military power of the Soviet Union cast a pall on the cheerful mood. In 1950, the Korean War broke out, and once again American men were in combat half a world away. John Glenn Jr. distinguished himself in the Korean Action as "The Mig Mad Marine," flying F-5 Panther jets with baseball legend Ted Williams as his wing man. Glenn earned five distinguished flying crosses and the Air Medal with eight clusters. The Korean War halted in Armistice in 1953, but John Glenn Jr. had proved his worth to the Marine Corps and to the country.

Annie continued what was to be a career as a Marine Corps wife, eventually moving her family more than two dozen times. Each move was a torture because of her speech impediment, but Annie Glenn demonstrated tremendous courage in tackling necessary jobs, and she was successful. John and Annie Glenn introduced their children David and Lyn to the "old hometown" with a visit to Clara and Herschel Glenn in New Concord, in spring 1954.

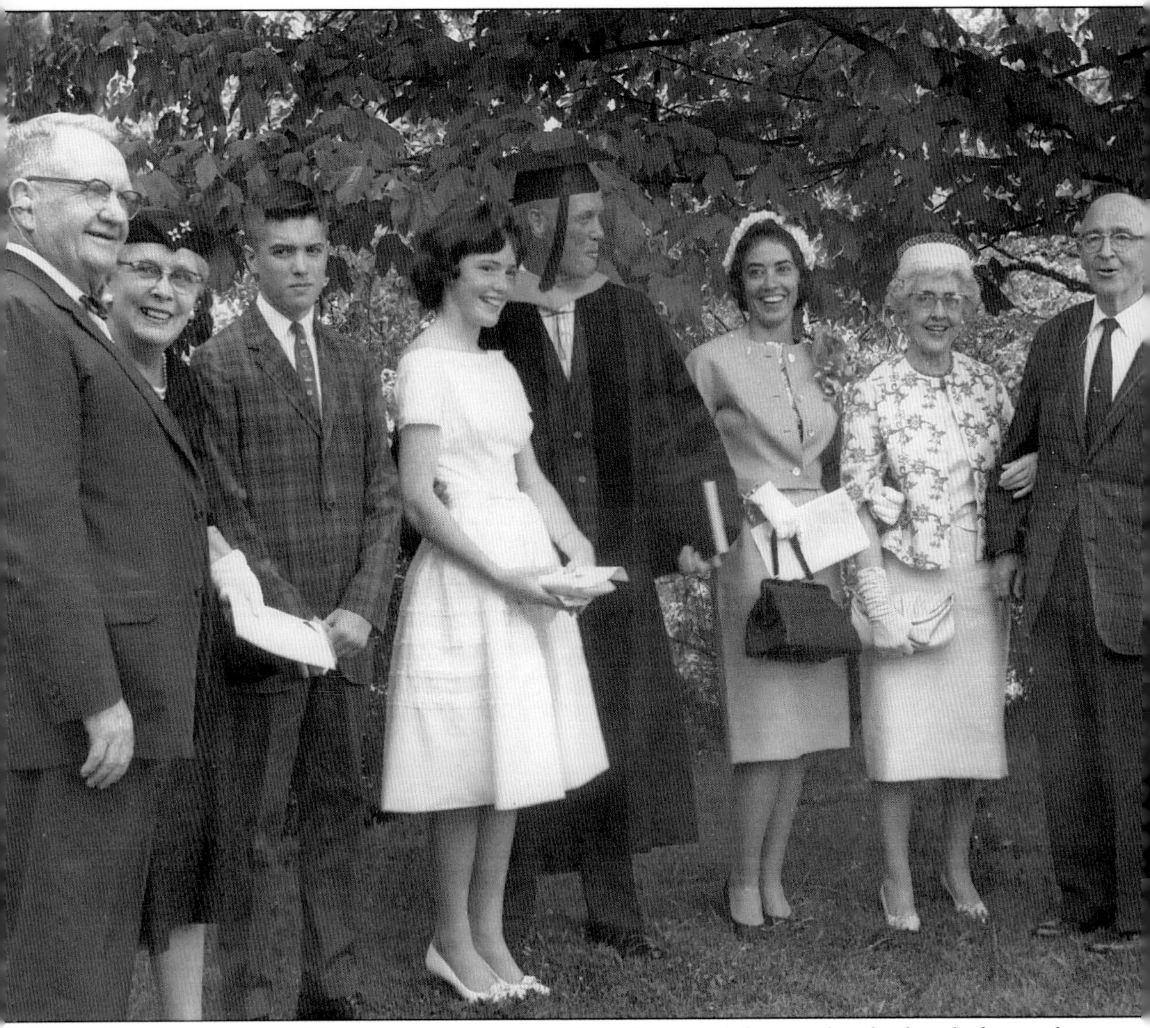

Remaining in the U.S. Marine Corps, John Glenn Jr. joined the tiny brotherhood of test pilots at the U.S. Naval Test Pilot School in Maryland. All his childhood fascination with speed and flight drove him to plan and execute "Project Bullet"—an attempt to beat the speed of sound in a plane. On July 16, 1957, the boy who had "souped up" his father's tractor and climbed the tallest sycamore tree in town to conquer fear, took off and set a cross-country supersonic record of three hours and 23 minutes with an average speed of 726 miles. A "howdy" sonic boom resonated over New Concord as he barreled by. Glenn received his second Distinguished Flying Cross for this mission.

In 1959, his alma mater, Muskingum College, presented him with a special award. Pictured, from left to right, are those sharing the day: John Herschel Glenn Sr., Clara Sproat Glenn, David Glenn, Lyn Glenn, the Marine hero, Annie Castor Glenn, Margaret Alley Castor, and Dr. Homer Castor.

Slowly, a more normal life returned to the village and the college. Dr. Robert Montgomery and four-time Academy Award nominee and Emmy winner, Agnes Moorehead, then Muskingum College's most famous alumna, are pictured in 1947. Miss Moorehead grew up on a farm near Rix Mills. She was a member of Orson Welles "Mercury Theatre," and made her debut on film in *Citizen Kane* (1941). Her flare for waspish and neurotic roles earned her theatrical and film acclaim.

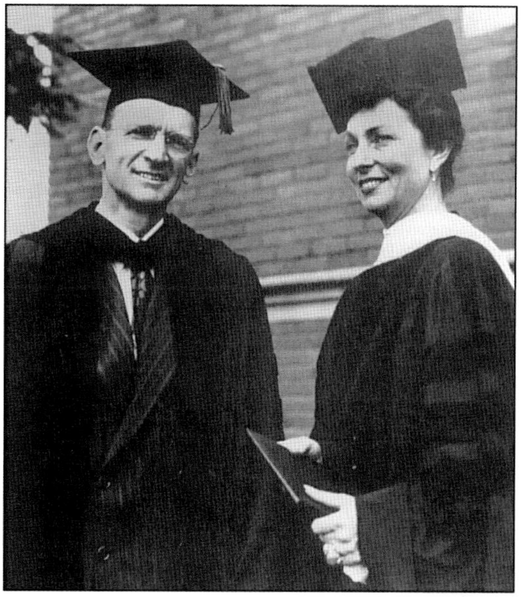

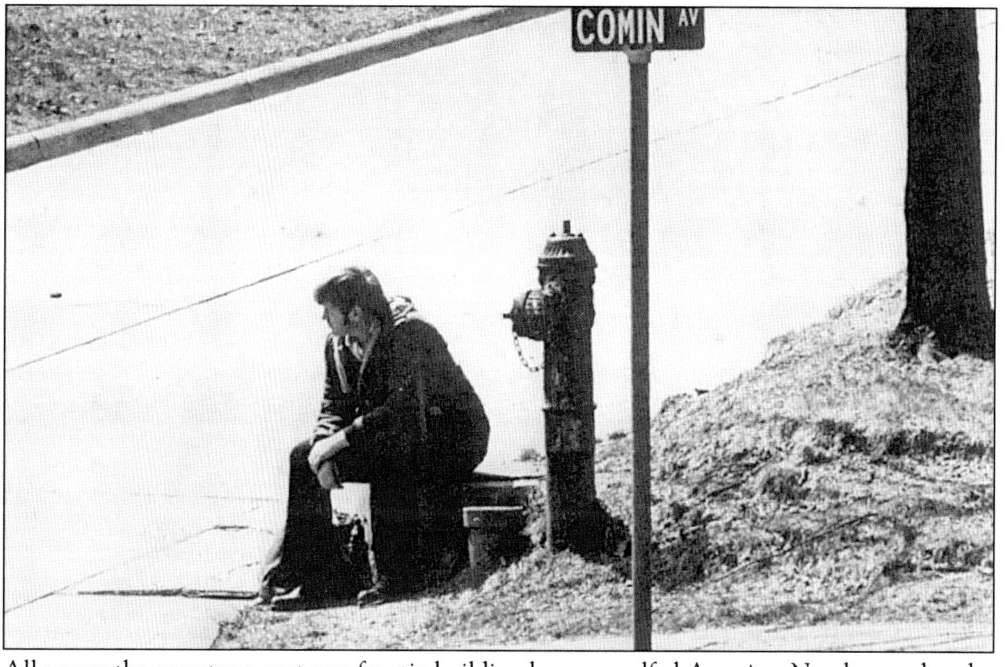

All across the country a post-war frantic building boon engulfed America. Nearly two decades of privation and sacrifice fed a huge national appetite for housing, for cars, and for progress. Part of that expansion was the Interstate Highway System. President Dwight D. Eisenhower was acutely aware of the difficulty of moving troops and supplies in war time. His desire for rapid coast-to-coast transportation changed America . . . and New Concord. Years earlier the National Road had bypassed the pike town of Norwich, stunting its growth. Now I-70 bypassed New Concord, with similar results. Businesses dried up as access to major towns became easy. Increasingly New Concord became a service center. Within the town, the importance of Muskingum College as the largest employer was magnified. New Concord's and Muskingum College's fates have always been intertwined.

As the new Interstate opened in the early 1960s, the economic life of the village of New Concord changed. All four car dealerships closed. Increasingly, rapid transportation fed shoppers to larger towns and to the newly developed "malls." New Concord settled into its role as a "bedroom" community college town. "Suburbs" began to sprout: Wedgewood Acres, Colonial Heights, Sunrise Acres, Morgan Manor, and Meadowwood. The East Muskingum School District (comprising all eight townships originally settled by Scotch-Irish) served as a magnet for new families. In the 1960s, the Scotch-Irish enclave began to break down and a new community, still embracing the traditional values of John Glenn's youth, began to develop. A need to "keep up" and perhaps compete with Cambridge and Zanesville led to the destruction of much that was old in the village. The Village Hall was demolished in 1959. The train depot —no longer servicing passenger trains—came down a decade later. The First National Bank building (and the Muskingum House) fell in 1968.

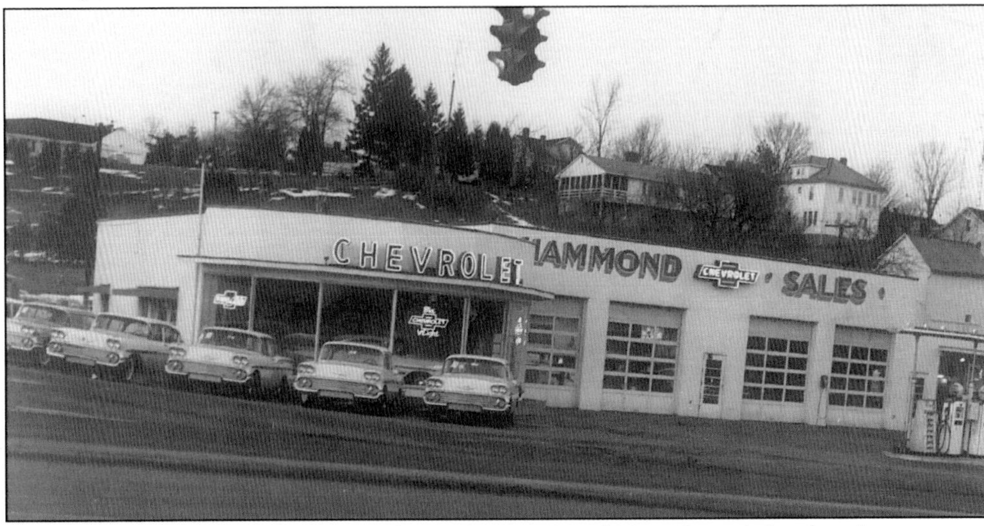

Hammond Chevrolet Sales (corner of State Route 83 and Main Street) developed into various gas stations and restaurants.

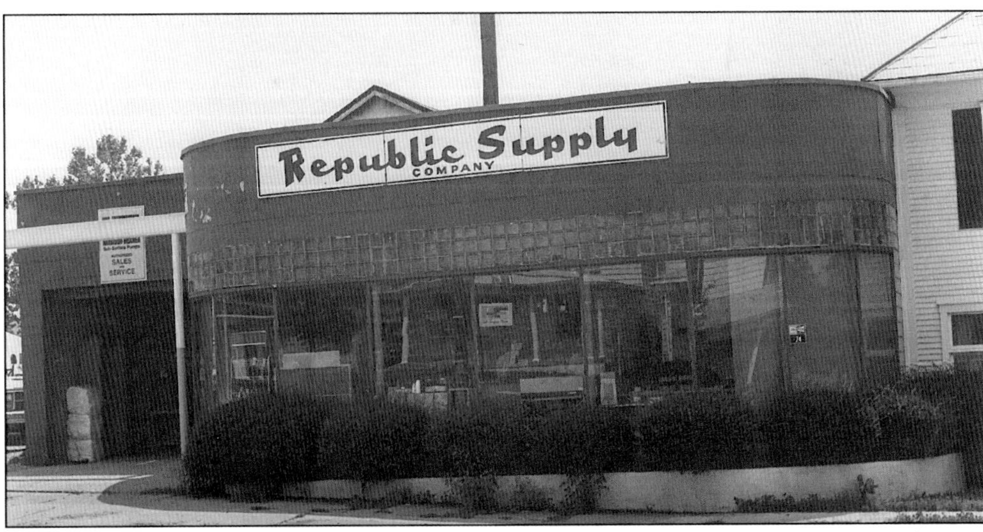

The Ford Dealership (Park Garage) on Main Street became an oil field supply office during a local oil/gas boom in the 1970s. This is the site of the Glenn Homestead/Museum.

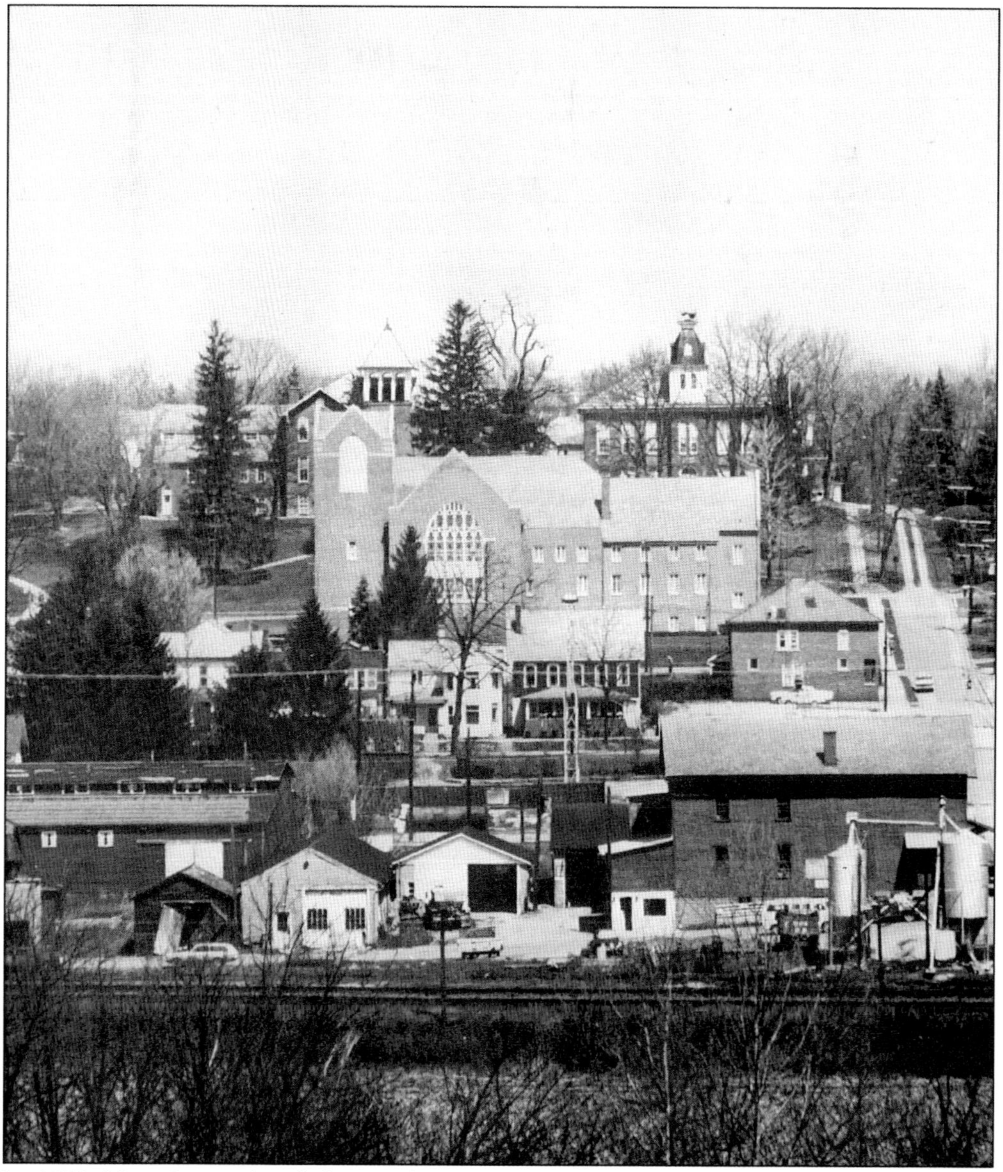

In 1957, New Concord and the people in the larger East Muskingum School District were bound together by the ideals of religion, education, and service. John Glenn reflected that culture. World War II service set him on a life that he has lived "with supersonic speed and the constant possibility of sudden death." (*Time*) A career Marine flyer, he served commendably in the Korean Action and then blazed a brilliant career as a test pilot—during which he and fellow flyers "went to more funerals than we'd like to."

Glenn, and a handful of other men, would need their courage when on October 4, 1957, the balance of world power shifted out of America's favor. The Soviet Union successfully sent an artificial earth satellite, *Sputnik*, into orbit around the earth. The Soviet leader's threat that "Americans will sleep under a Soviet moon," seemed all too possible. The United States put its infant space program (NASA) into high gear. John Glenn with his love of speed and of flying, yearned to be part of this mission. He was, however, 37 years old; his candidacy would be a longshot.

The race to the moon was, I think, the quintessential story of the American Century.

Walter Cronkite, American Television Journalist

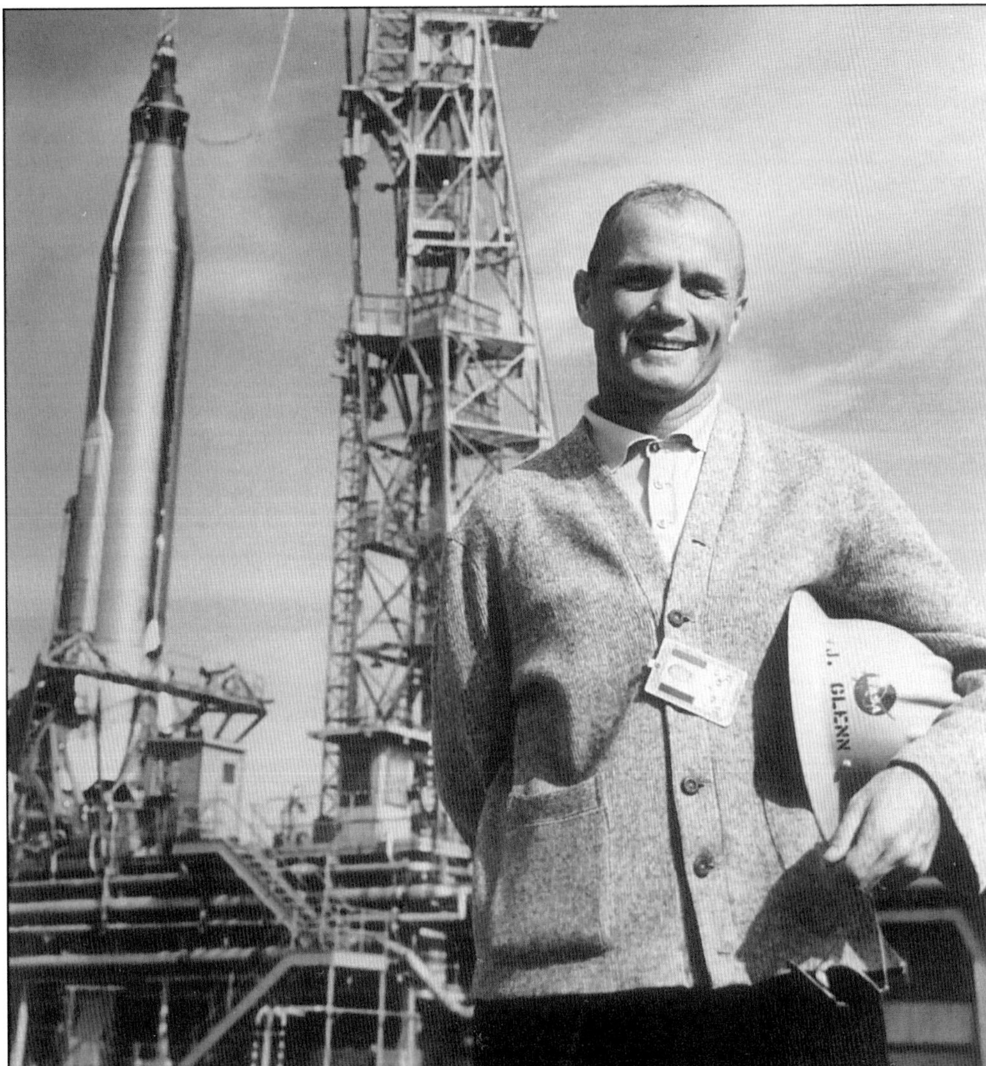

John Glenn was one of more than 500 candidates for the *Mercury* Program—America's manned flight experiment. He was ecstatic when he was accepted into the program. In press conferences, Colonel Glenn remembers, "vintage New Concord, Ohio, came pouring out," meaning that his hometown sense of patriotism and service was articulated in his answers. The astronauts had no idea what lay ahead of them; the Soviet experiments had been in secret. The open American efforts suffered many failures. When in April 1961, Yuri Gagarin, a Soviet cosmonaut, became the first human to orbit the earth, America fell into panic. Bomb shelters were built in back yards, and air raid rehearsals were mandatory in schools and workplaces.

The American experiment was imperative. Both Alan Shephard and Gus Grissom blasted off on preliminary suborbital missions. On December 5, 1961, Lt. Colonel John H. Glenn Jr. was chosen for the full orbital mission. Americans held their breath. No one knew if he could achieve orbit, or if upon return, the craft would skip off the earth's surface and fly out into space, never to return. John Glenn's cheery smile masked the anxiety that NASA, his colleagues, and his family felt.

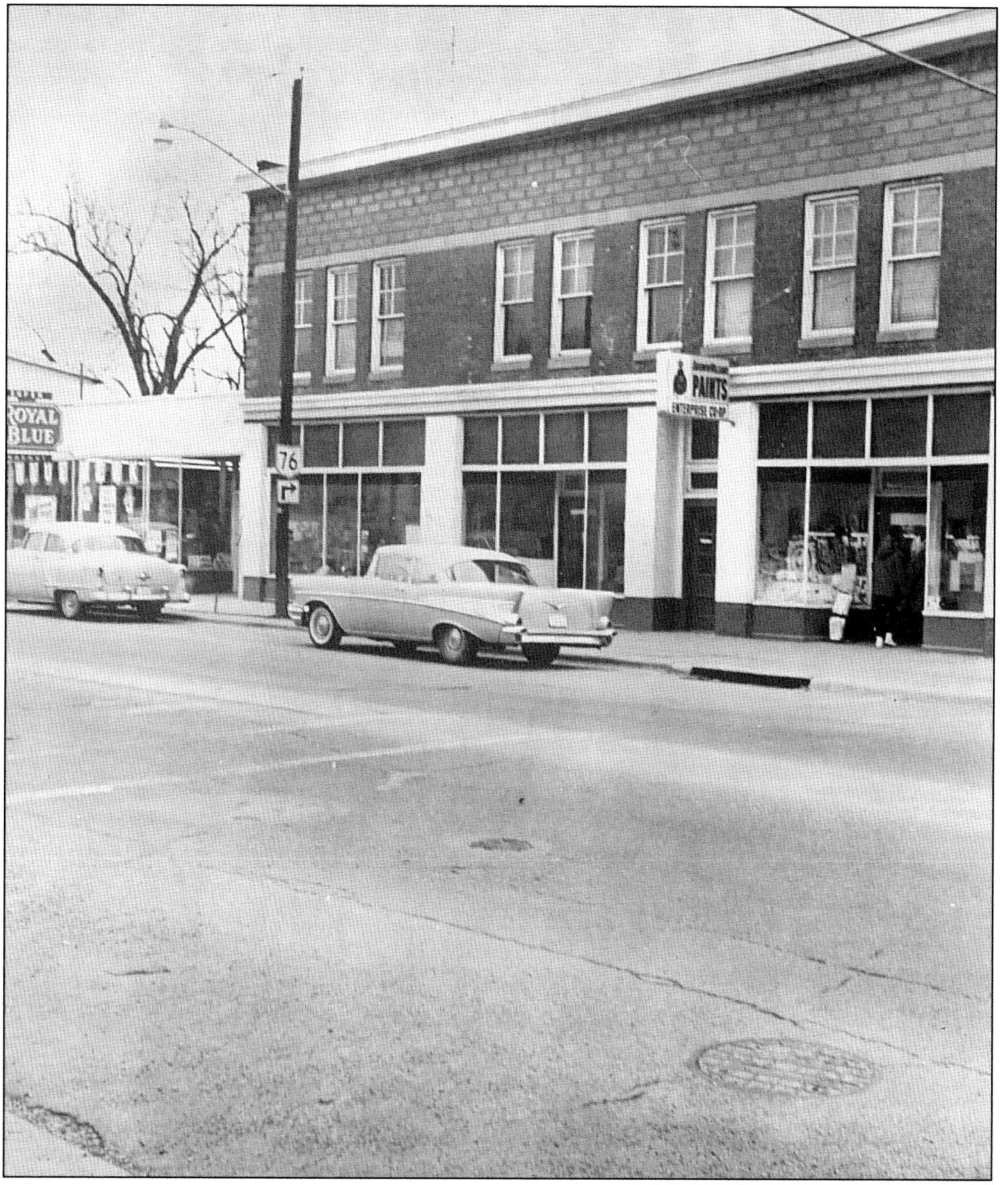

Hordes of press crowded into tiny New Concord in anticipation of the orbit attempt which was scheduled for January 27, 1962. Delay after delay followed, ten in all, and the village's streets became a staple on U.S. television. Muskingum College students, and every man, woman, child, cat, and dog in the village were interviewed. Everyone waited . . .

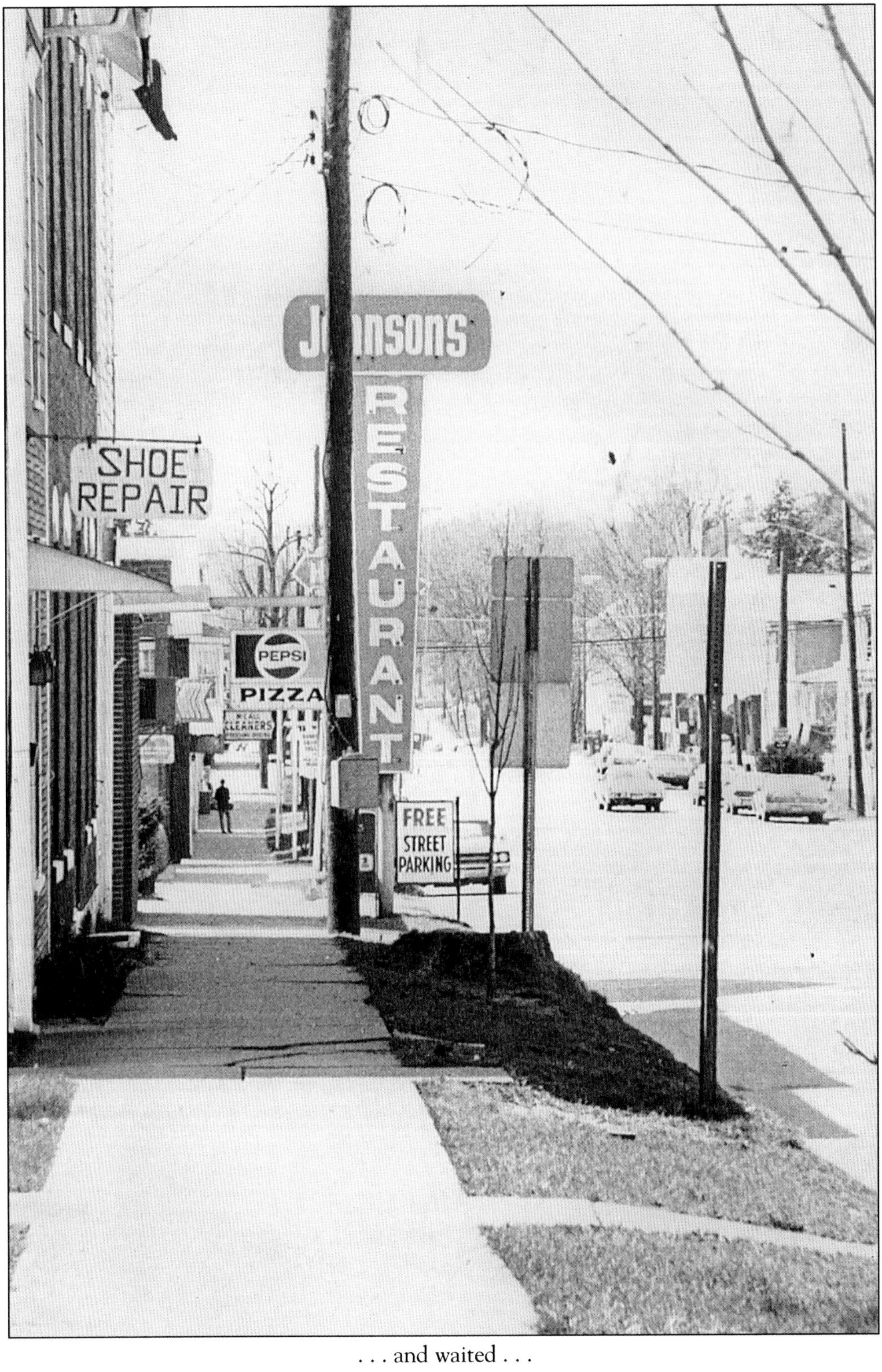
SHOE
REPAIR
RESTAURANT
PEPSI
PIZZA
CLEANERS
FREE
STREET
PARKING

. . . and waited . . .

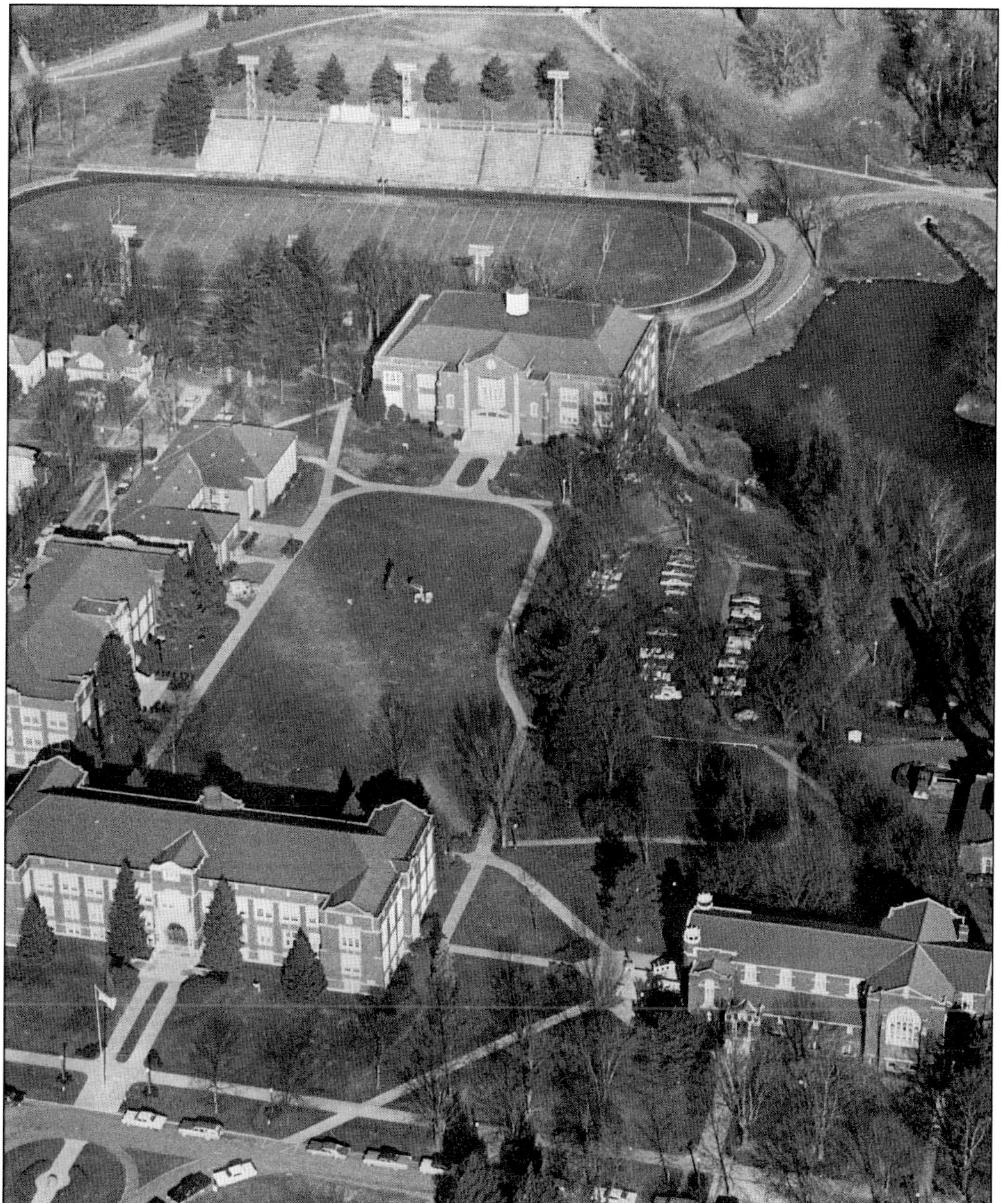

. . . and waited . . .

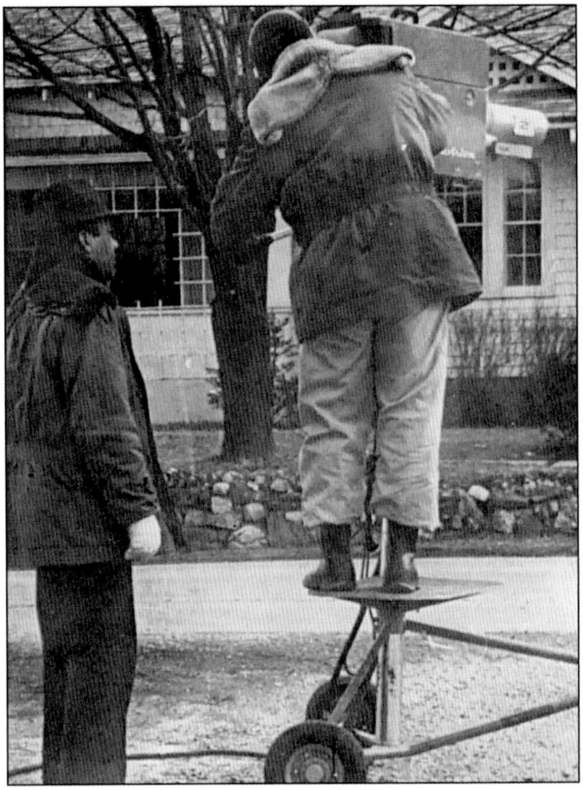

. . . and waited.

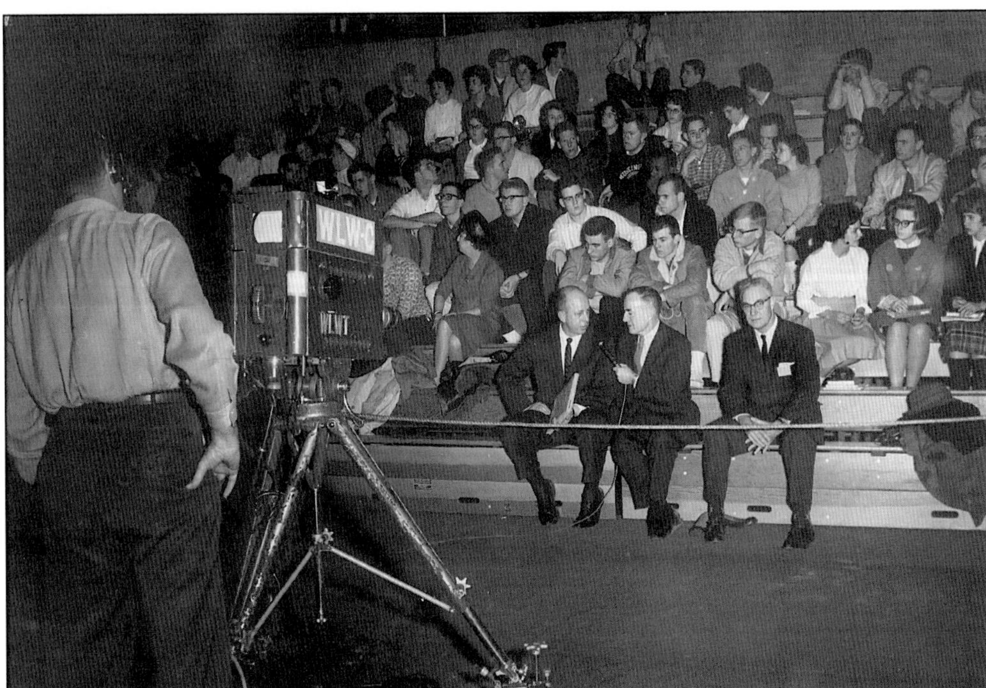

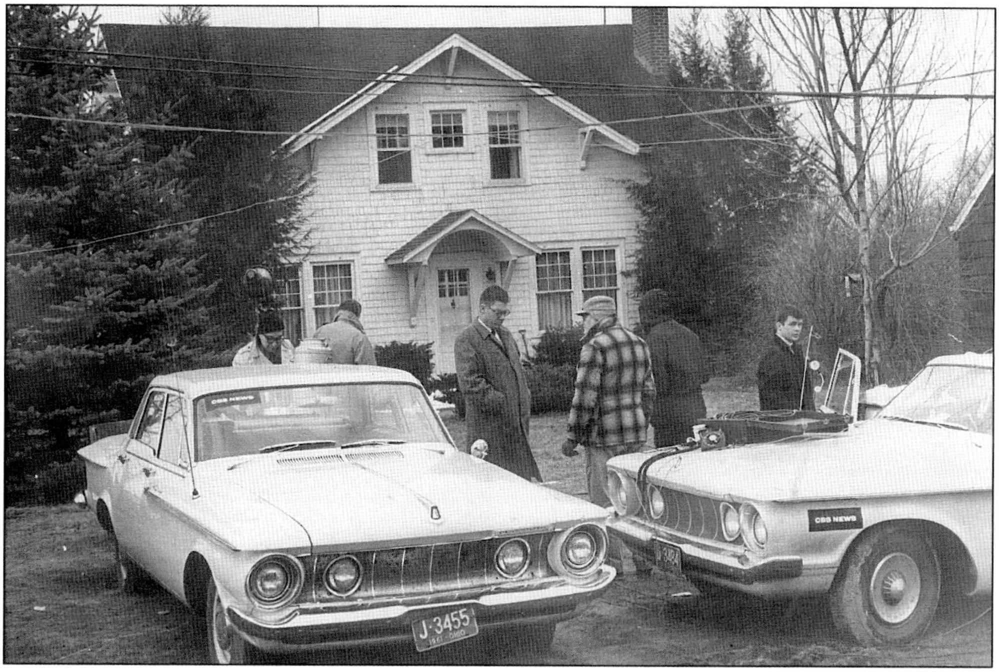

The brisk February weather did not deter the national media from "camping out" on the lawn of Herschel and Clara Glenn's home in New Concord. Colonel Glenn's parents were unfailingly gracious to the media throughout the long delays.

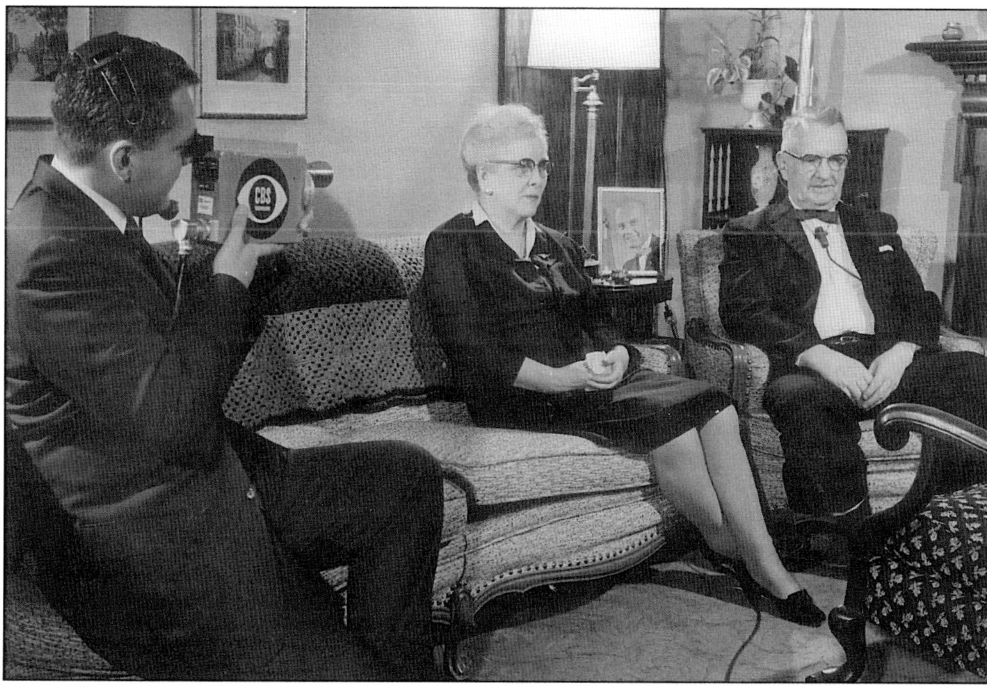

Mrs. Glenn even invited a representative of the Muskingum College newspaper staff in for milk, warm gingerbread, and a memorable interview. Here the Glenns are captured waiting for their son to rocket into space.

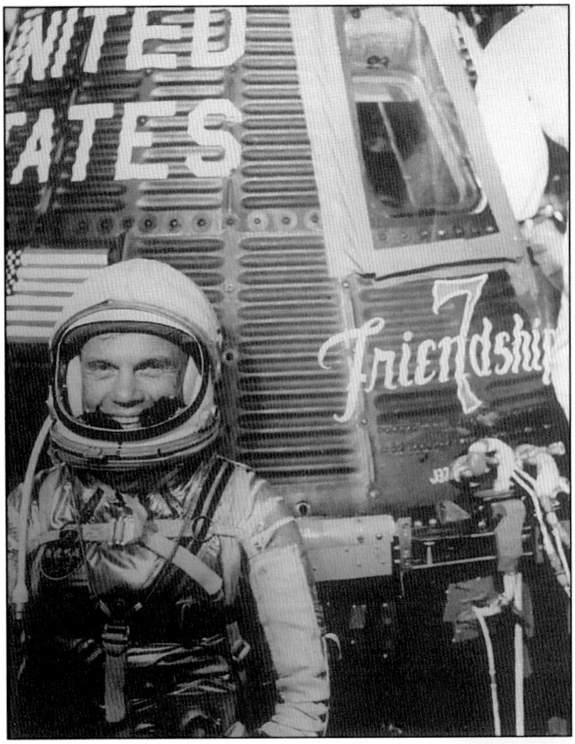

On February 20, 1962, John Glenn returned for the 11th time to the tiny space capsule and settled in. A technician closed the hatch.

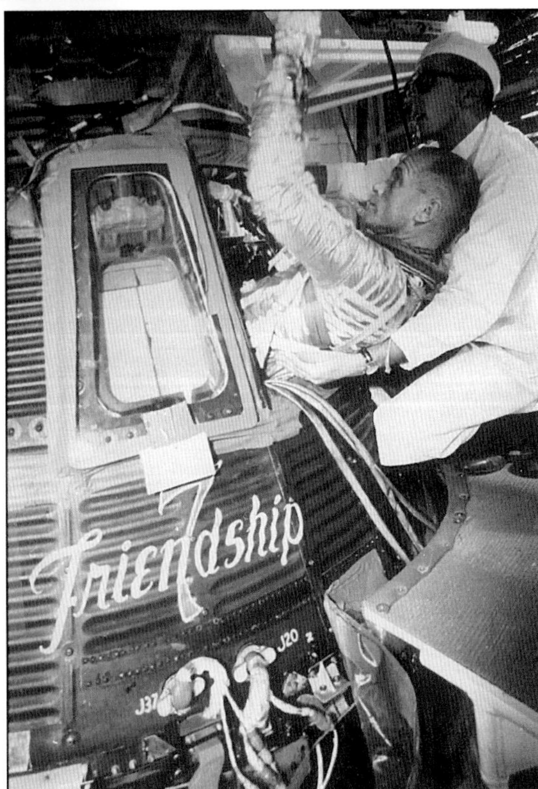

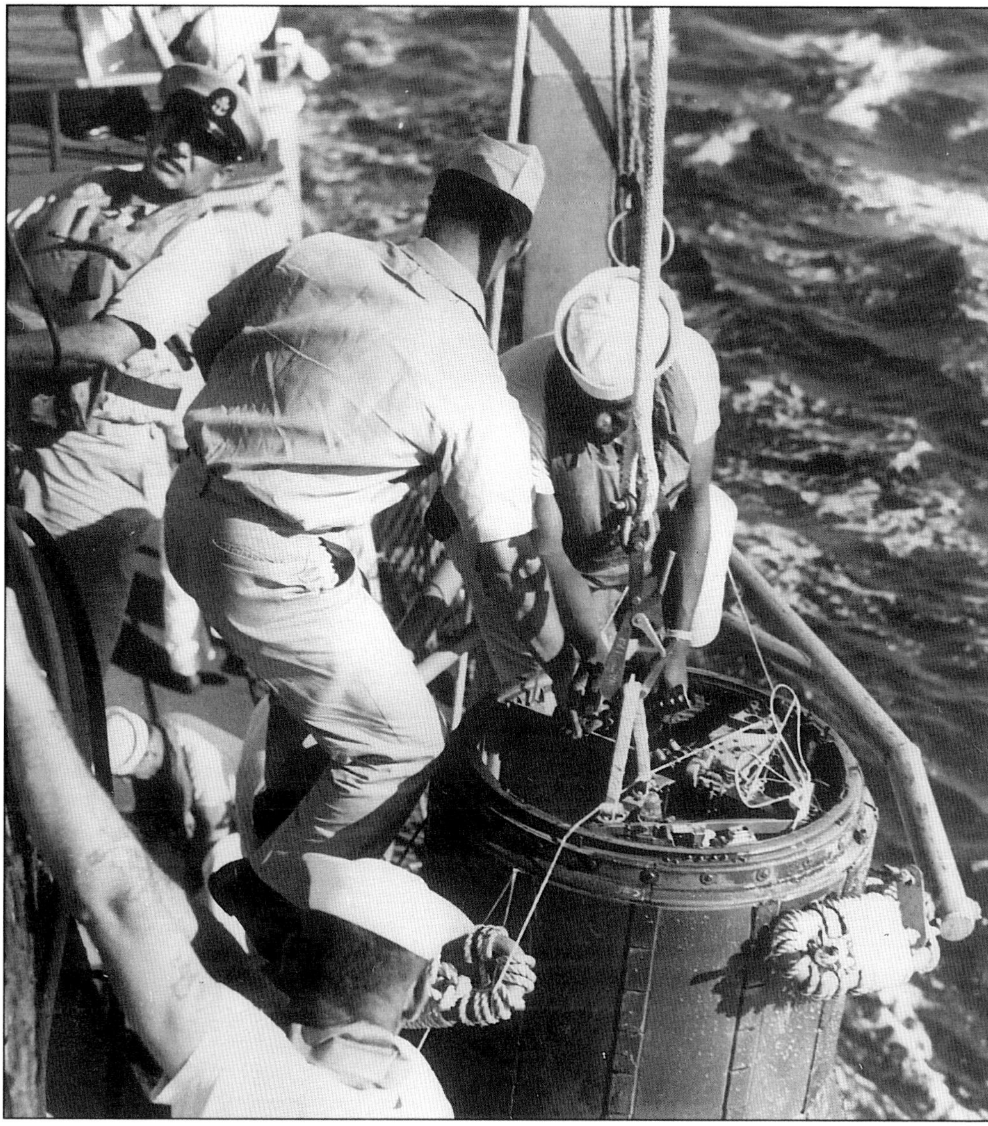

At 9:47 a.m., on February 21, 1962, lift-off was achieved. The NASA Flight Director, Cris Kraft, intoned "God Speed, John Glenn," a phase that became part of American history.

Suddenly, the launch was on, and John Glenn became "a latter day Apollo, flashing through the unknown." (*Time*): the most famous American hero since Lindberg.

After three orbits of the earth and a frightening few moments of reentry, *Friendship 7* splashed down in the ocean. To rousing cheers, sailors of the *USS NOA* retrieved Colonel Glenn's space capsule. Throughout America, and especially in the family homes in New Concord and Arlington, Virginia, the Glenn/Castor family breathed easier and thanked God for His aid.

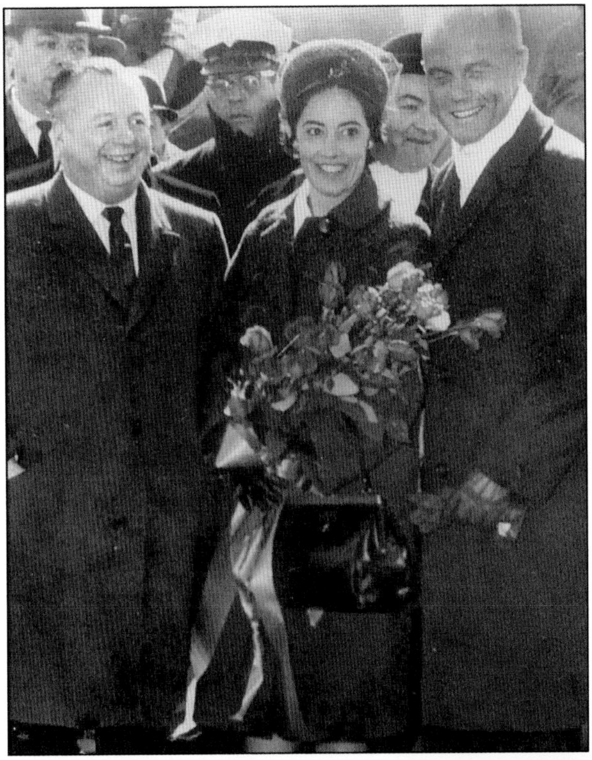

The euphoria following Glenn's return was the greatest since VJ-Day. Massive crowds greeted the astronaut and President John F. Kennedy in Washington and New York. His hometown secured the third parade for March 3, 1962.

Seventy thousand people poured into New Concord (the Interstate was under construction). The old National Road/U.S. 40 had never seen such a throng. The Depression-era gym was renamed John Glenn Gym. The new district high school on State Route 83 (renamed Friendship Drive), became John Glenn High School.

Ohio Governor Mike DiSalle greeted John and Annie Glenn at the Zanesville airport and, traveling back country roads, brought them into New Concord on Lower Bloomfield Road.

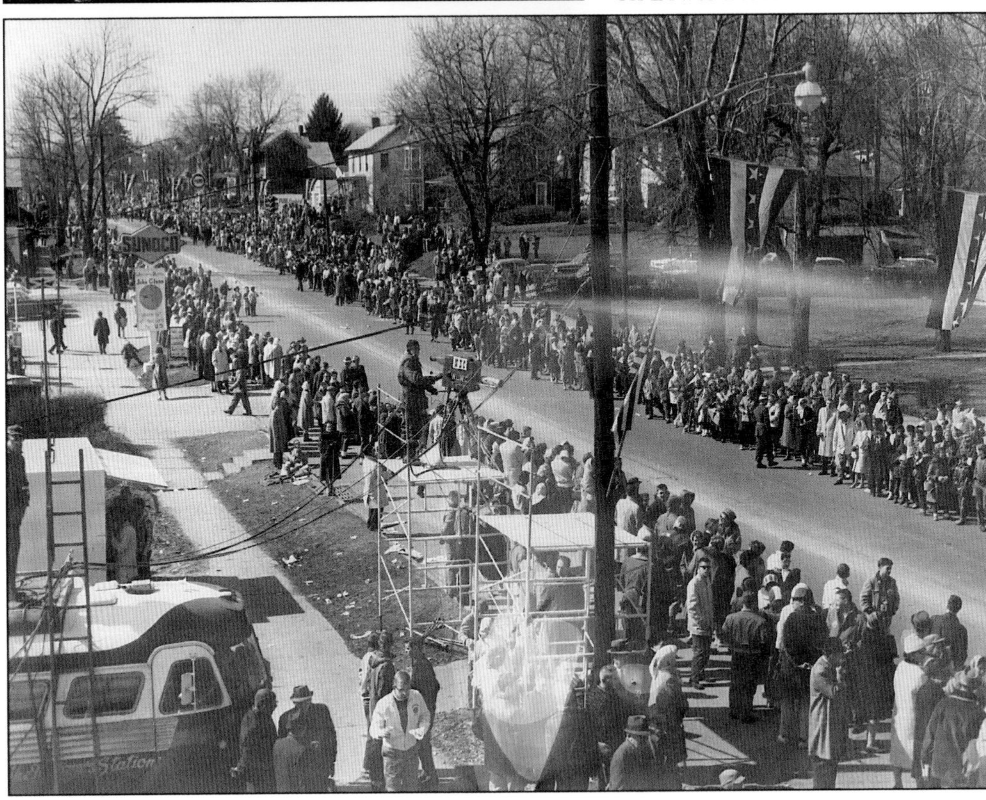

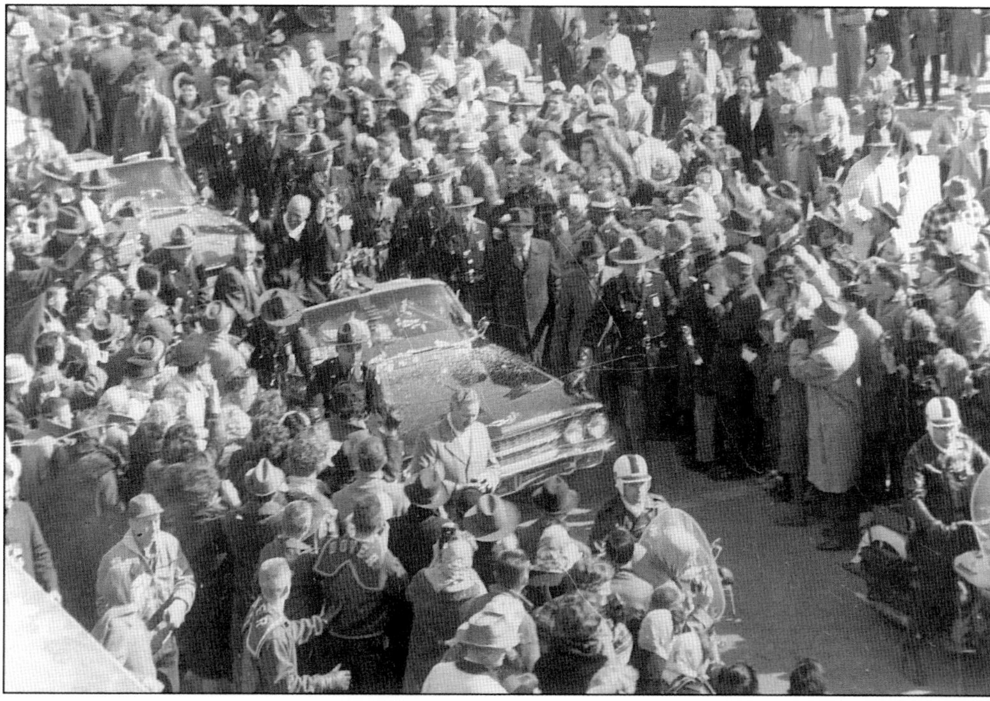

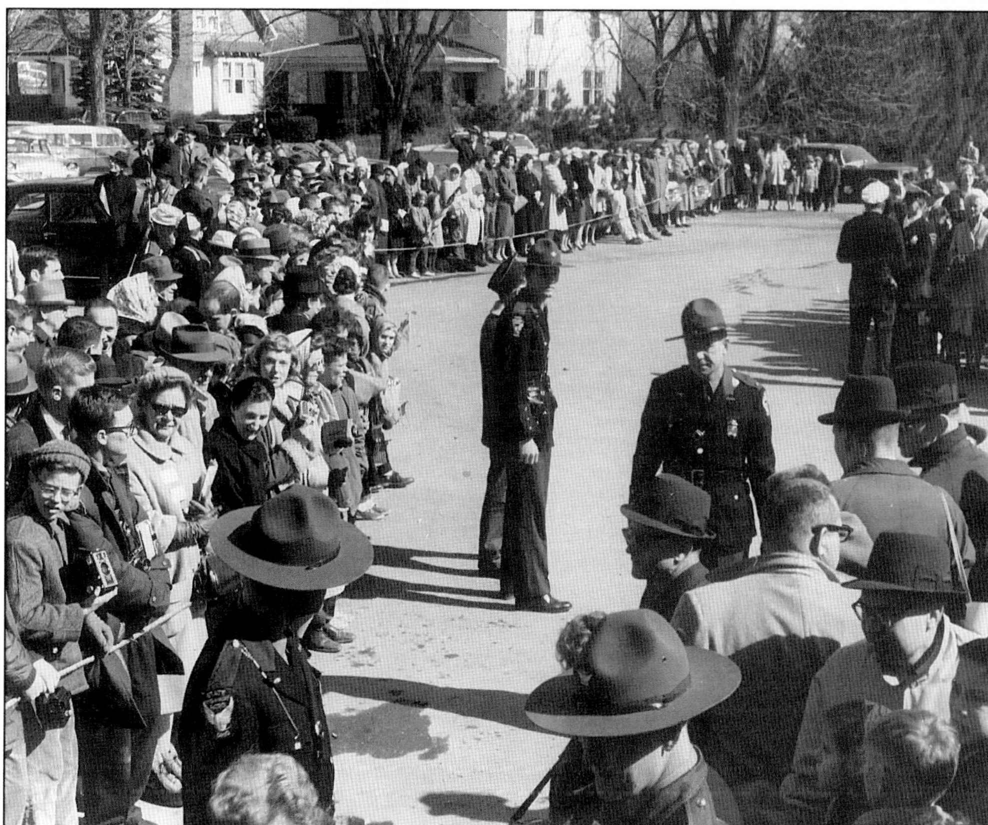

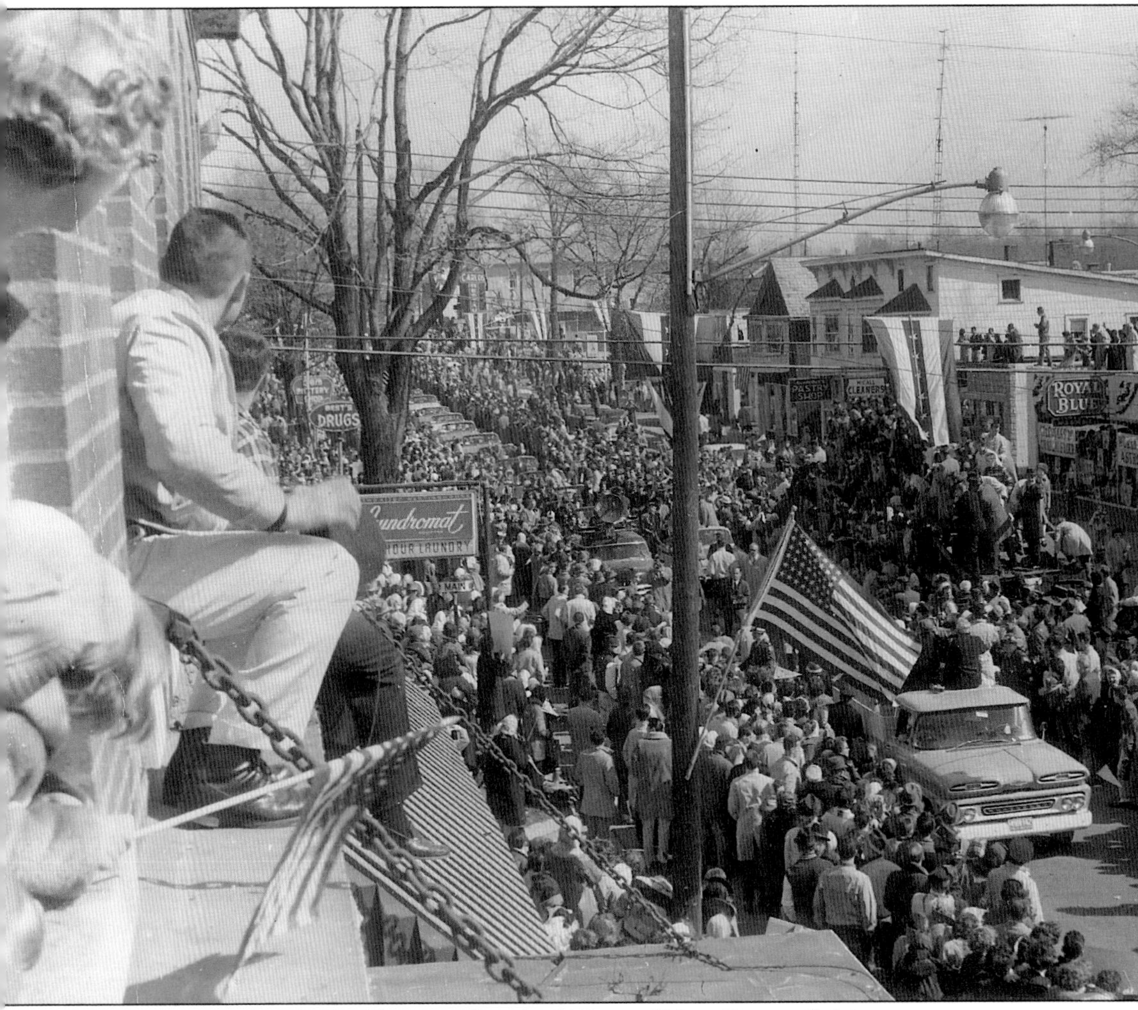

Nothing like this day had happened in the Village of New Concord's history.

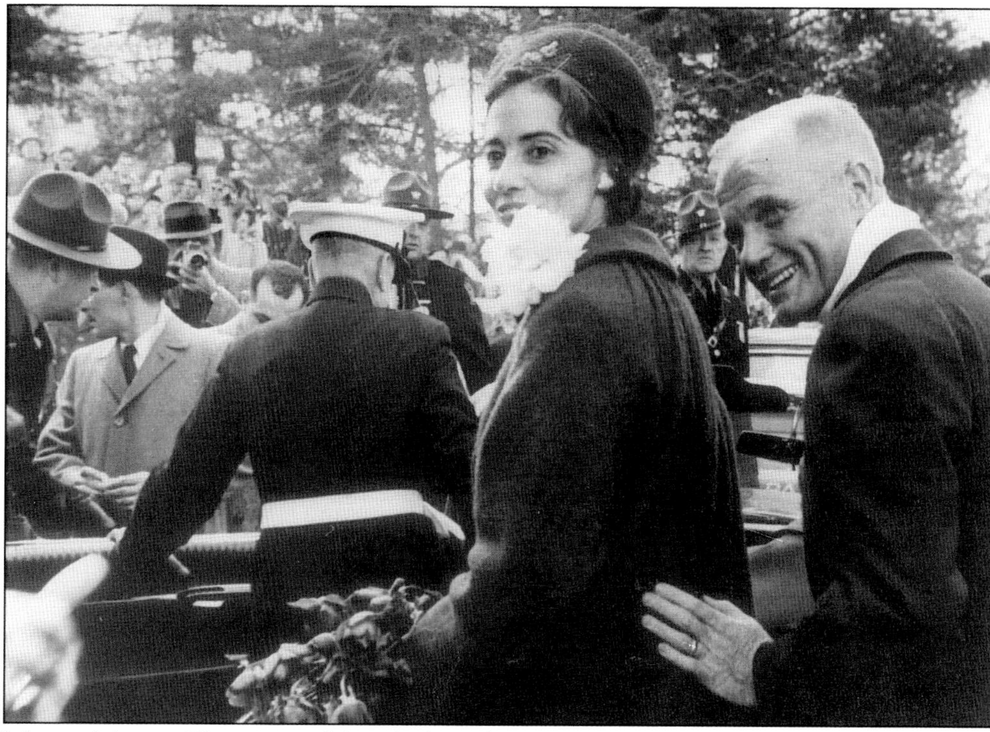
John and Annie Glenn greeted friends throughout the parade.

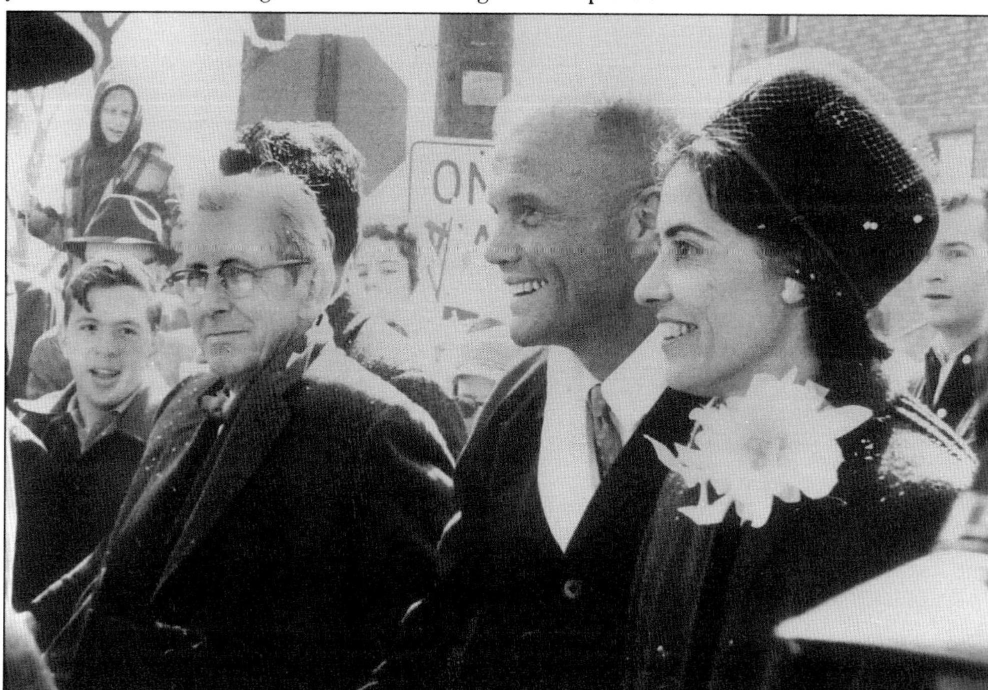
Village Mayor James K. Taylor, who had orchestrated the indoor ceremony at the end of the parade by issuing two tickets to every holder of a village water meter, enjoyed the parade with the Glenns.

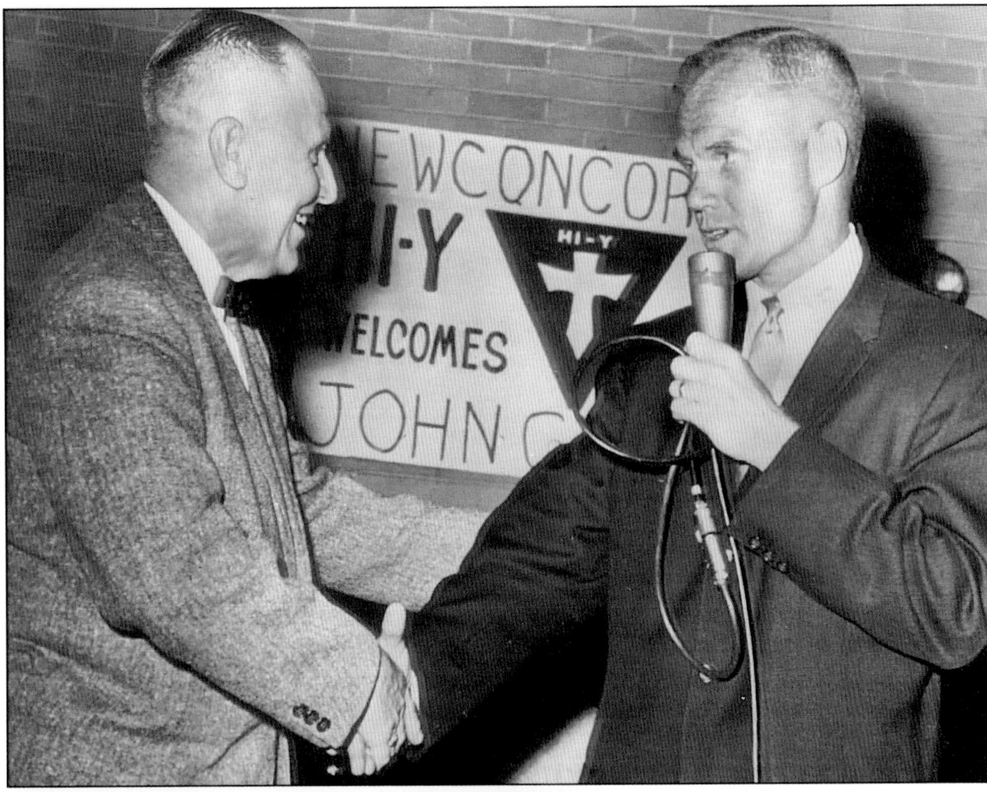

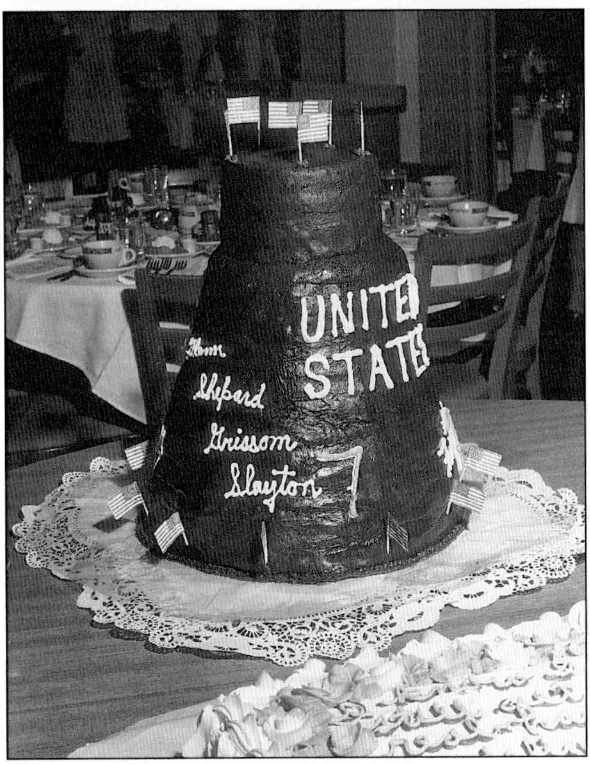

During his news conference, Astronaut John Glenn paid tribute to "the finest teacher I ever had"—his government teacher, H.A. Steele, principal of the New Concord High School.

A creative baker celebrated the success of *Friendship 7's* ,mission for the banquet in the newly renamed John Glenn Gymnasium, Muskingum College, New Concord, Ohio. Colonel Glenn jokingly admonished a table full of former teachers that they should "clean up my gym" after the meal.

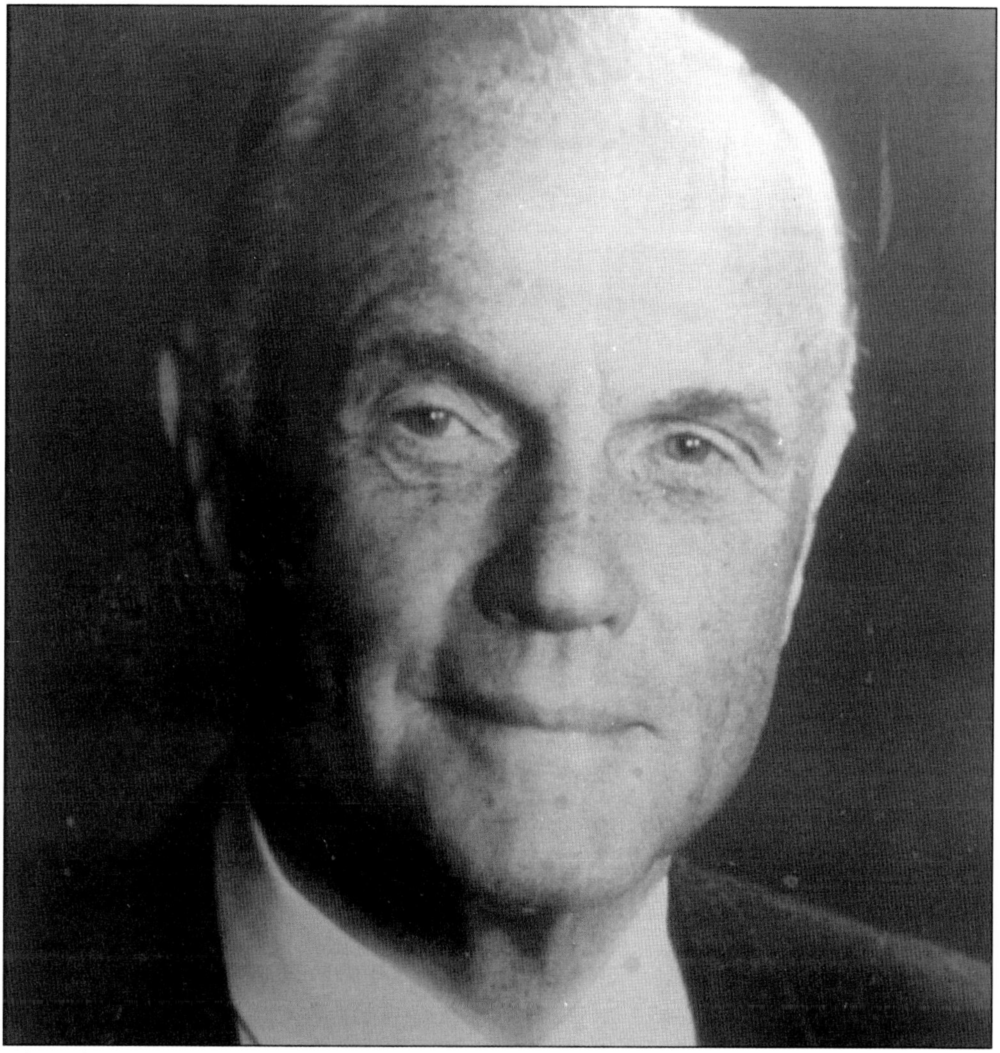

John Glenn's career as a spokesman for NASA flourished, but, secretly, fearing a demoralizing accident, President John F. Kennedy refused to let the astronaut fly again. Yearning to fly, but unable to get such an assignment, reluctantly, John Herschel Glenn Jr. resigned from his beloved Marine Corps.

After a successful period of business, Glenn, whose political sense had been energized by his friendship with John and Robert Kennedy, ran for national office. He was elected to the U.S. Senate from Ohio in 1975, eventually becoming the longest serving Senator from Ohio in history. Respecting his hometown roots, Senator Glenn launched his presidential attempt of 1984 at the high school named for him and at the end of his Senatorial career in 1997, he returned with Annie to Brown Chapel on Muskingum College, to announce his retirement from the U.S. Senate.

I've been privileged to serve my country in war, peace, and in one of the most exciting frontiers in all of human history. But nothing I have ever done in my life has been more rewarding or made me any prouder than serving for the past 24 years in the United States Senate.

But Senator Glenn was distressed by low civic participation in government and by the distrust of government which dogged society. He was determined to devote his life to changing these things.

It is 1998, the millennium speeds towards us, and John Glenn flies out to meet it because there is a scandalous shortage of heroes (in our national life).

Steve Lopez, *Life*

After months of lobbying, to fulfill a personal dream, and to reanimate interest in NASA's programs, Senator John H. Glenn, passed rigorous physical exams to join the crew of the *Discovery* space flight in October 1998. He would become the oldest human to experience space flight and would subject himself to an enormous battery of geriatric tests while on the mission.

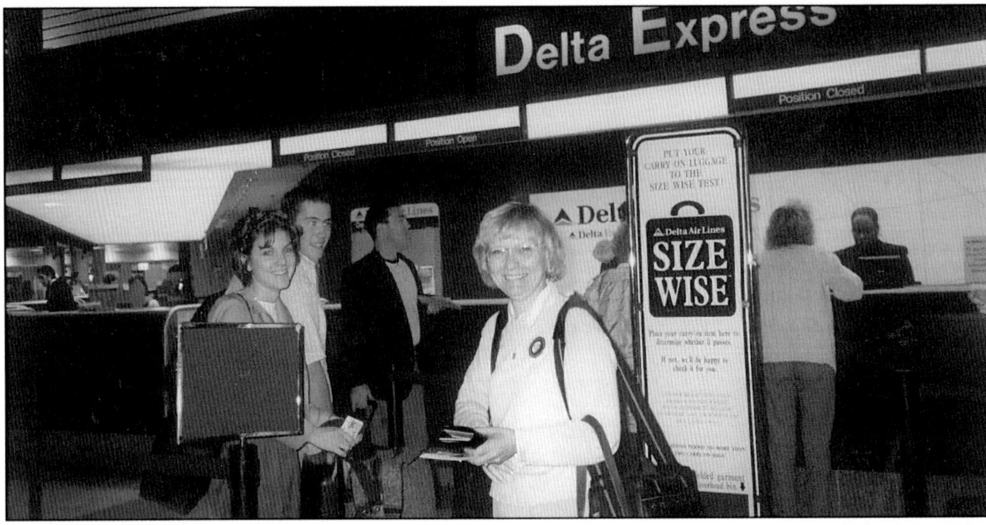

Students Renée Morrow and Levi Shegog and Faculty Advisor Mary Ann Devolld of the John Glenn High School newspaper (the *Jon Jee*) set out on the great adventure.

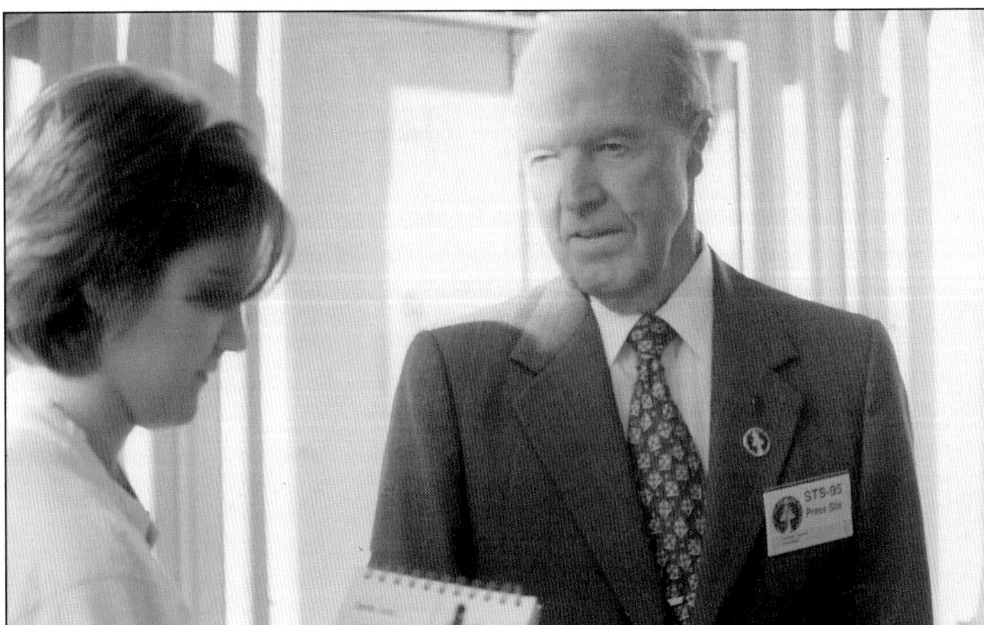

Renée Morrow interviewed Astronaut Gordon Cooper at Cape Kennedy. The staff, in turn, was interviewed by national media.

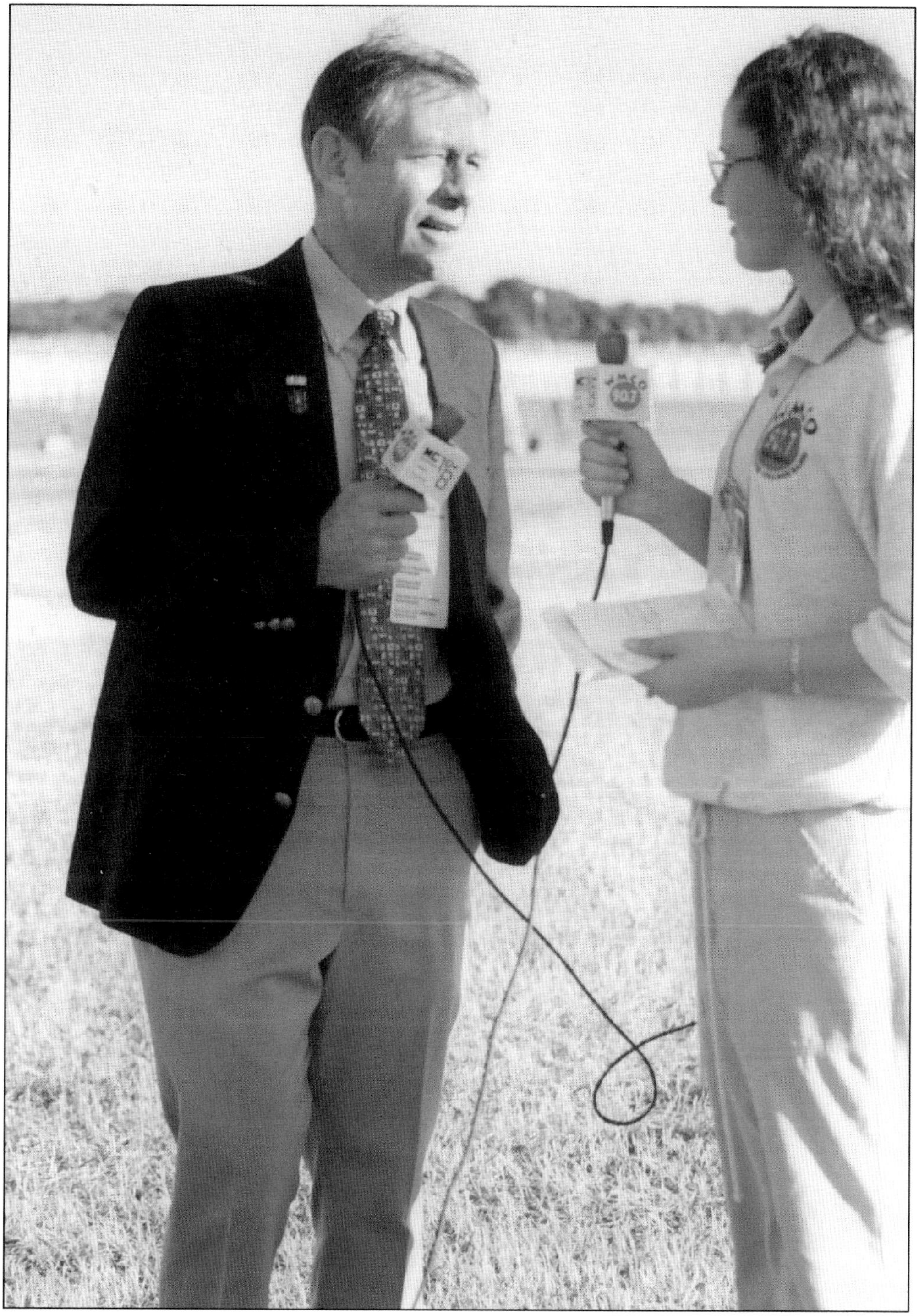

Muskingum College interviewer Maria Rittenhouse interviews Governor (later Senator) George Voinovich in Florida. Muskingum College radio station WMCO continued its month-long coverage with a lively account of the parade. WMCO won first place among all radio entrants in the country for its coverage of the *Discovery* launch.

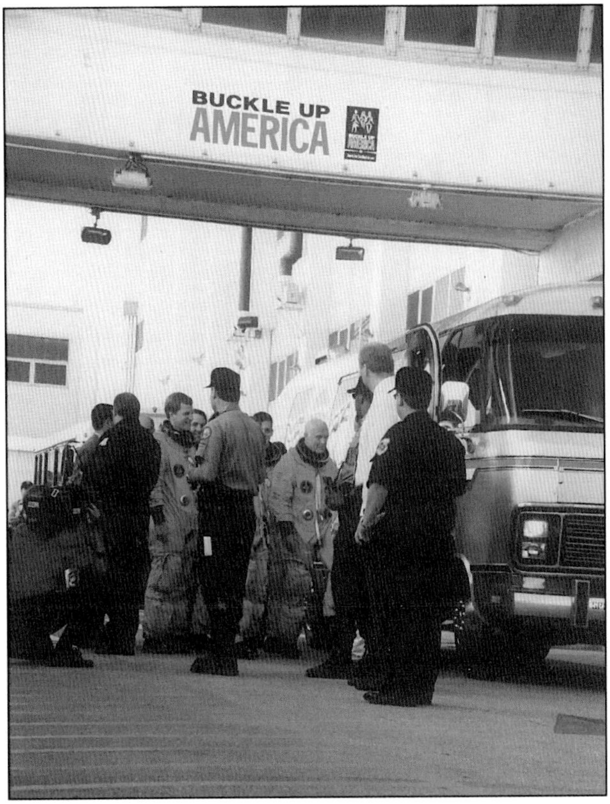

The *Jon Jee* staff was in the forefront to see Senator Glenn board the bus to the space shuttle.

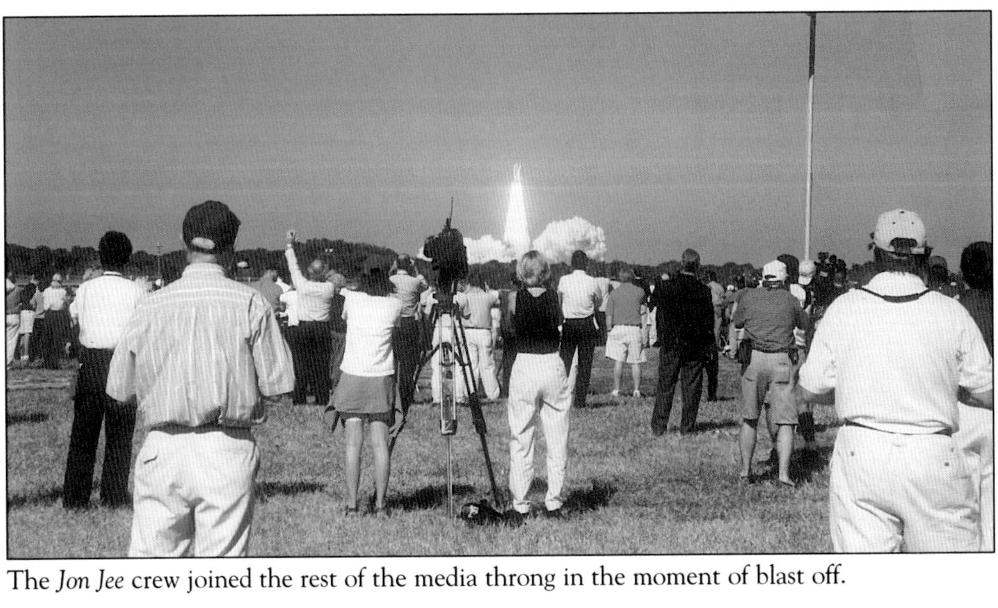

The *Jon Jee* crew joined the rest of the media throng in the moment of blast off.

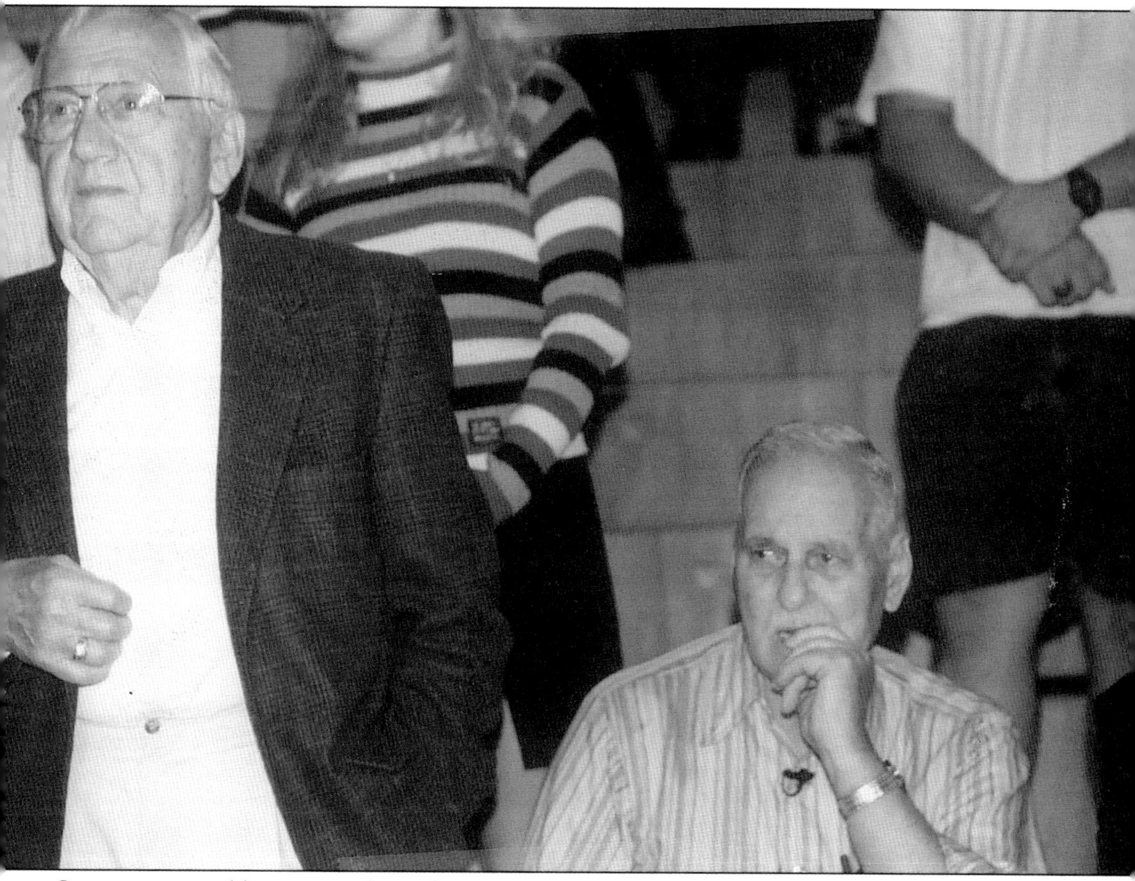

Once again, world attention focused on New Concord, Ohio, and Muskingum College. The Reverend Dr. Harold Kaser, Muskingum College Board of Trustees member and John Glenn's football teammate in 1939–40, and Rev. Lloyd White, Glenn's childhood chum and best man, are caught at the moment of launch, October 28, 1998.

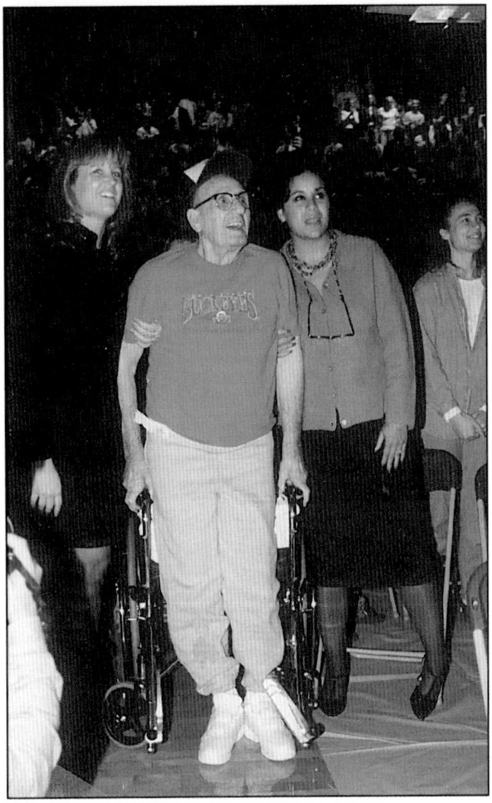

In the Muskingum College Recreation Center, a capacity crowd rose to its feet at the launch. This septuagenarian rose from his wheelchair in a moment of elation.

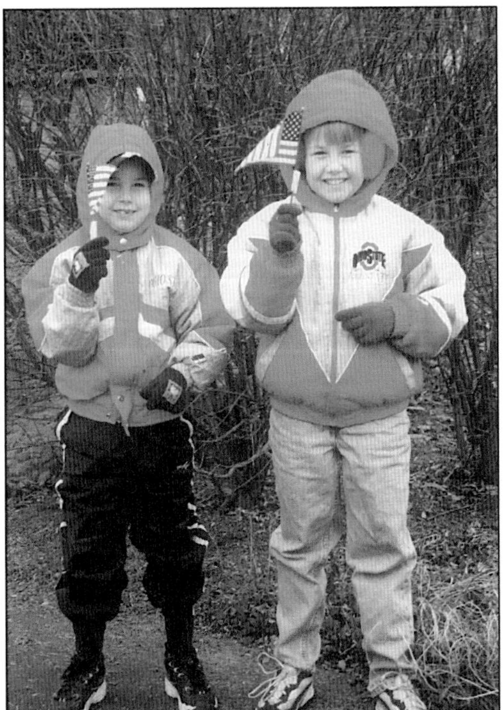

The enthusiasm touched all ages.

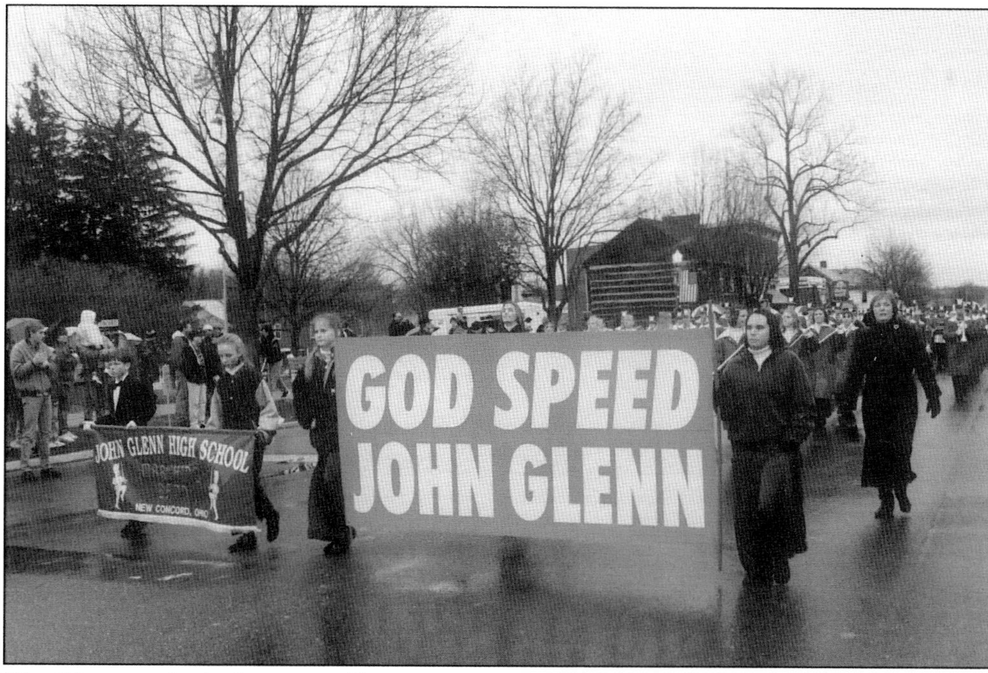

The Glenns embarked on a world tour to promote NASA's goals. But first they participated in parades in New York City, Columbus, Ohio, and their hometown, New Concord, Ohio. Echoing the famous 1962 blessing on blast off, the village of New Concord, the East Muskingum Schools, and Muskingum College welcomed John and Annie Glenn home.

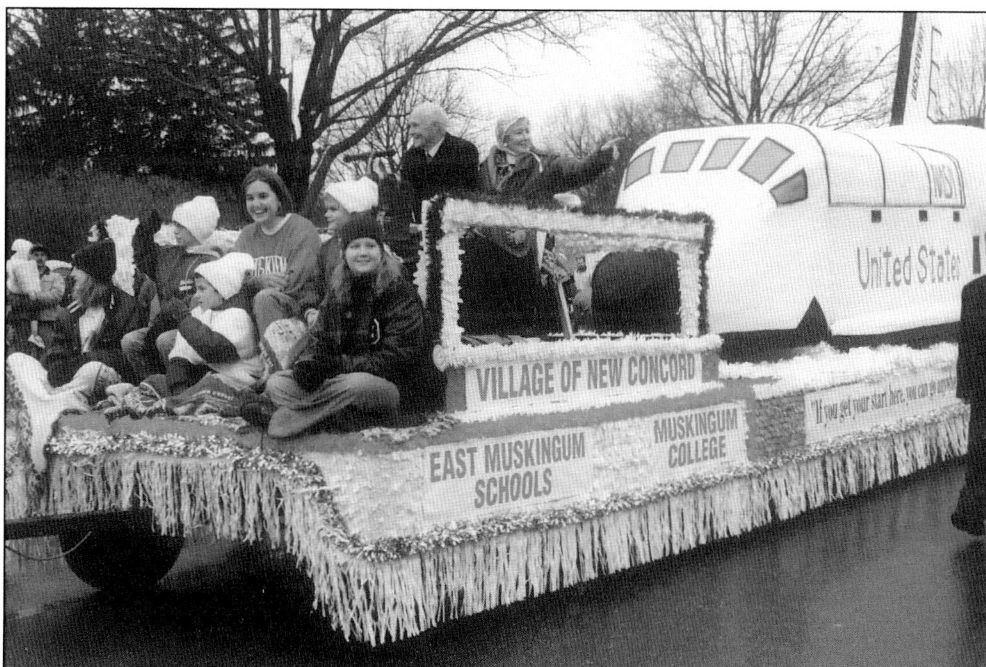

John and Annie Glenn greeted old friends along the parade route. Sharing the float with the Glenns were representatives of the local schools.

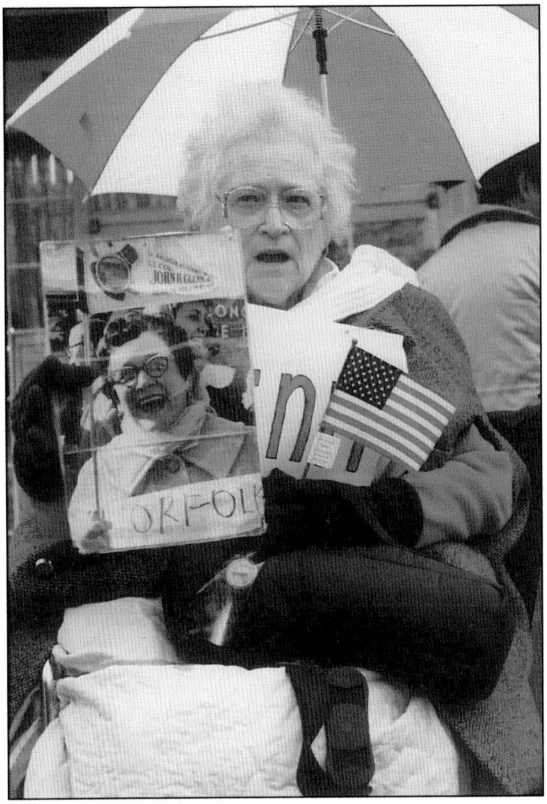

"Twice is better" shouted Evelyn Kettlewell Envoldson as she proudly displayed her photo taken during the original 1962 parade and published nation-wide.

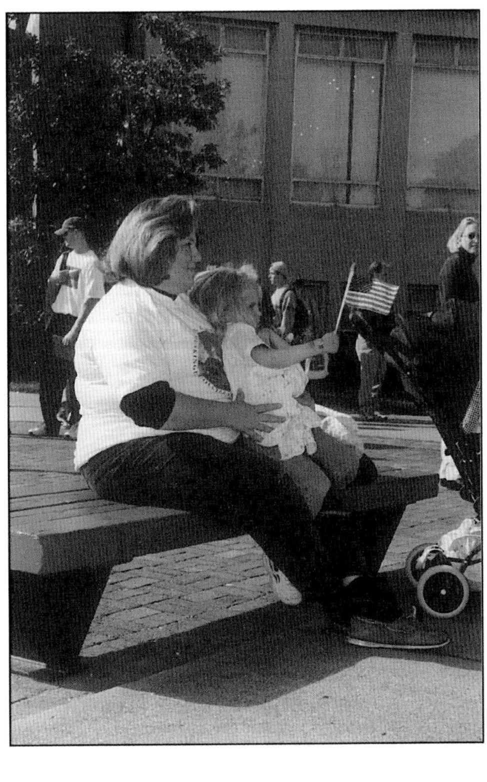

A sense of hometown companionship permeated New Concord.

The Muskingum College Band welcomed the Glenns home.

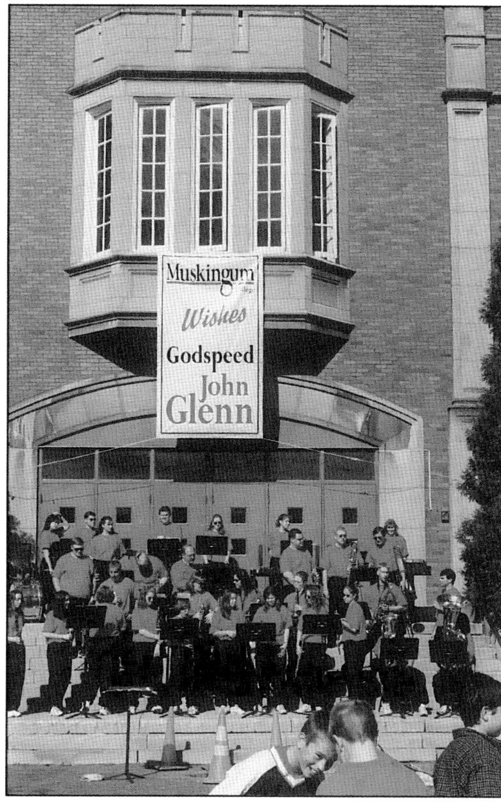

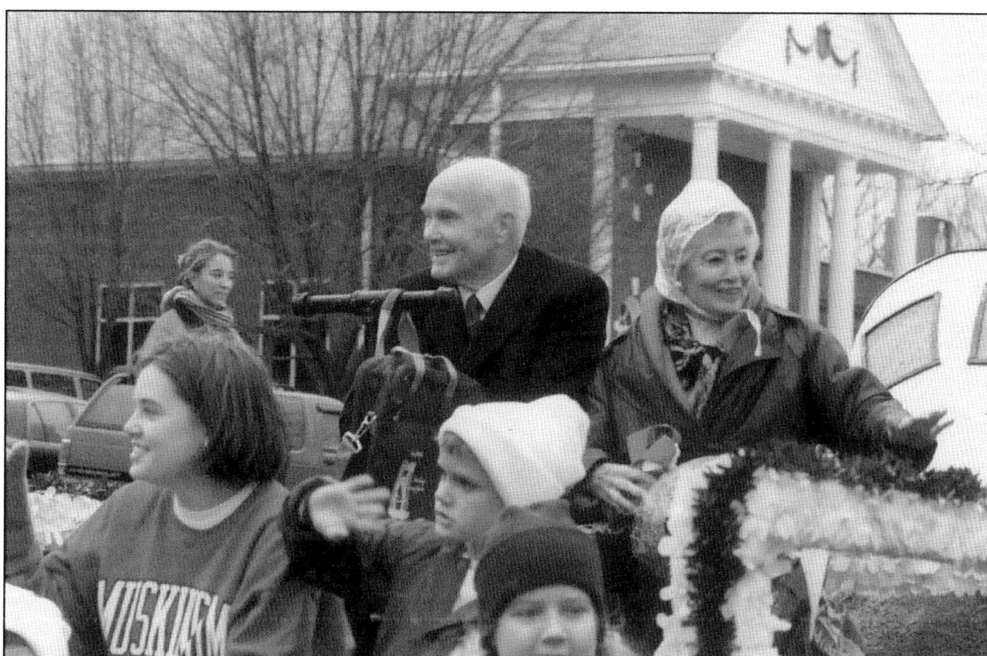

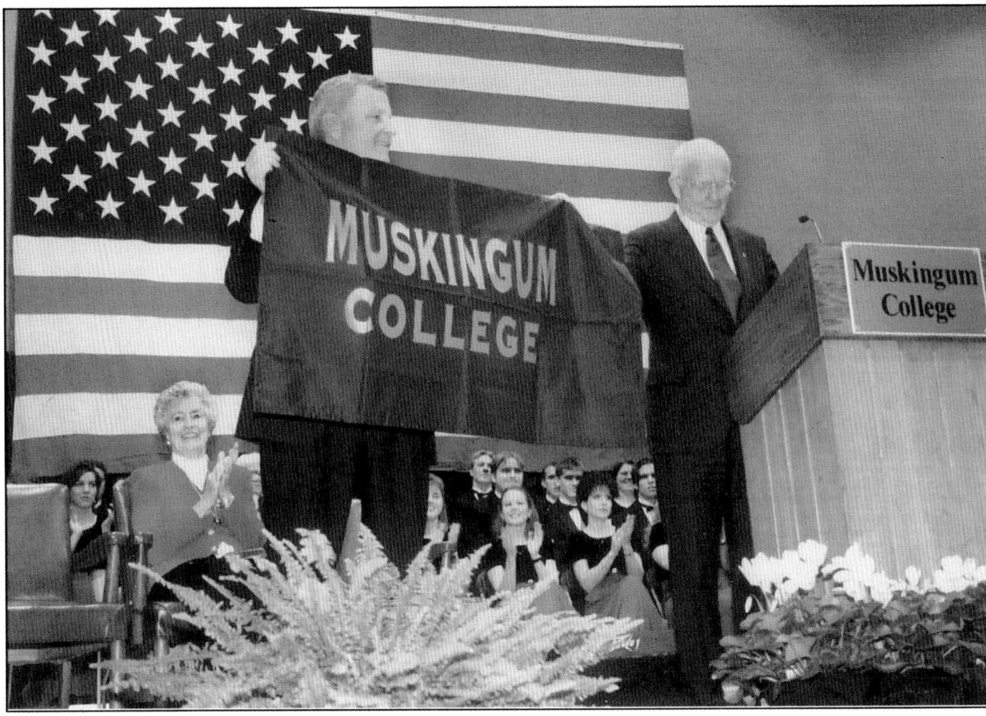

Muskingum College President Sam Speck proudly displays a Muskingum College flag, which Senator Glenn carried into space. John Glenn High School also received a unique souvenir—a student designed patch Senator Glenn carried with him in space.

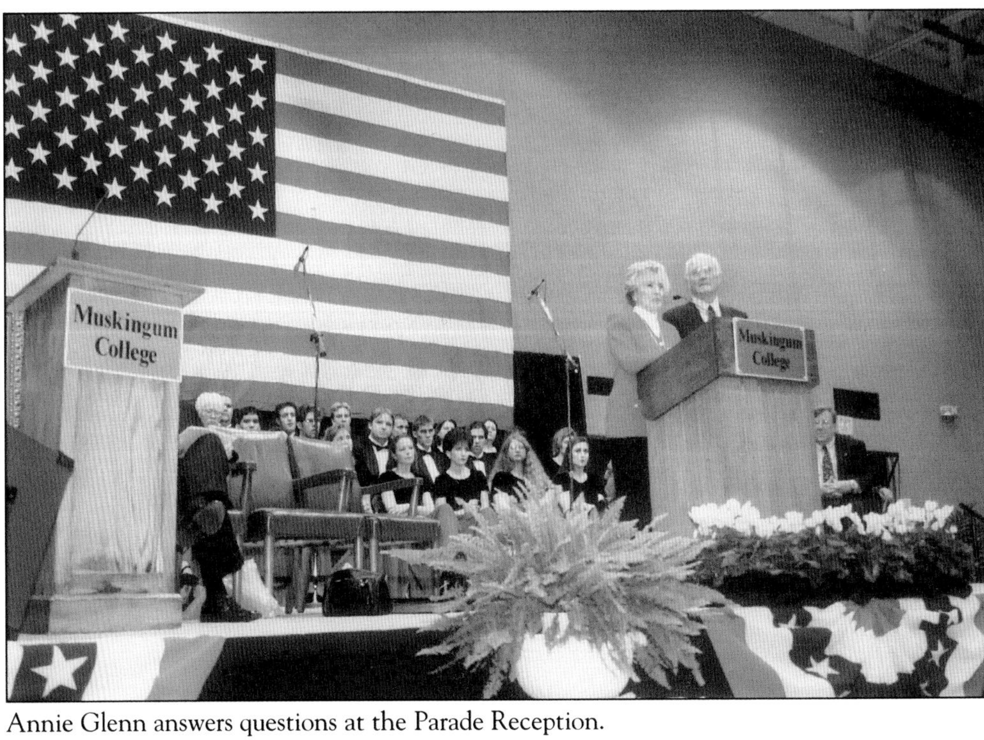

Annie Glenn answers questions at the Parade Reception.

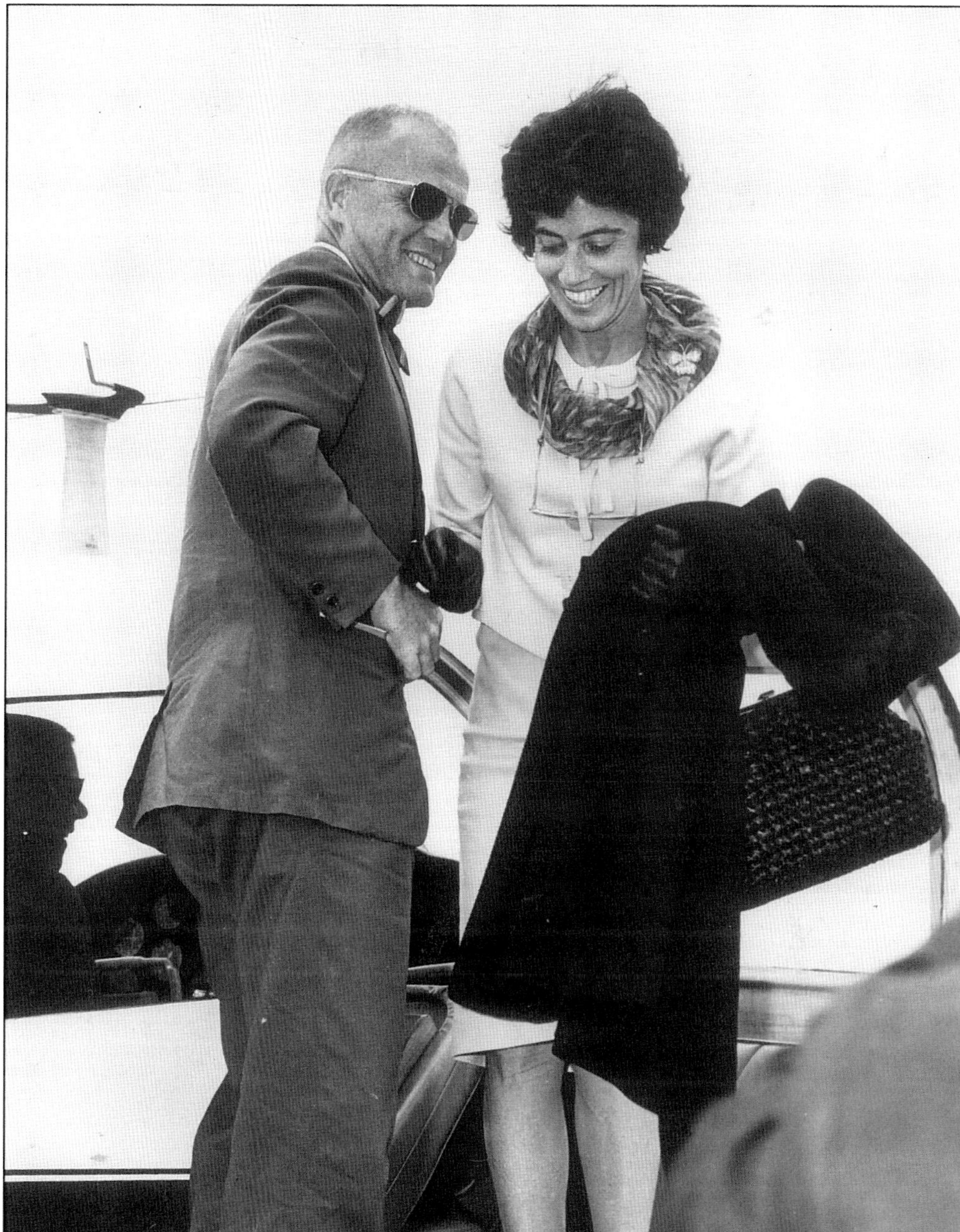

John Glenn is who he is because of his parents, his wife, his church, and his village. A *Life* editor wrote: "America gets two heroes for the price of one."

Annie Glenn moved her family 22 times during their military career. Each move was agony because of her speech impediment. The business of uprooting a family and simply getting there is difficult for anyone; how much more so if one cannot speak? Annie Glenn has been a rock during war and political onslaught. Then, in 1973, Annie's private miracle occurred—the Glenns saw a feature on *Today* about Hollins College stutter therapy. Heroic hard work by Annie gave her the gift of speech. As she says, "I couldn't read to my children, but now I can read to my grandchildren."

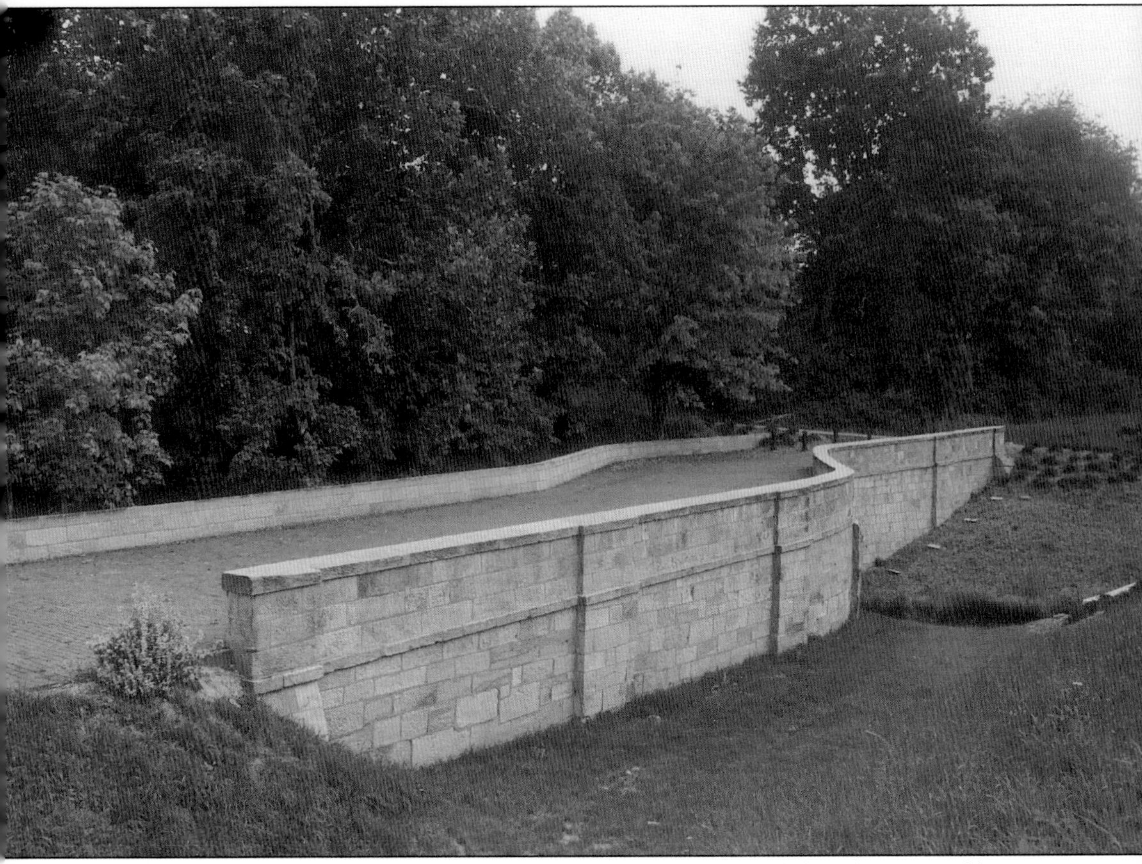

John H. Glenn and Anna Margaret Castor Glenn have devoted their lives to public service. However, their service is not yet over. They serve as Distinguished Alumni Professors at Muskingum College, have created the John Glenn Institute of Public Service and Public Policy at the Ohio State University, and are involved in the John and Annie Glenn Historic Site and Exploration Center in New Concord.

John Glenn says that he and Annie have lived through one-third of American history. He says he will devote the rest of his life to trying to reanimate in the American soul the American ideals which created him.

The purpose of the John and Annie Glenn Historic Site and Exploration Center is to bridge past, present, and future; to inform people of the past and prepare them for the future in the next frontier. Let us strive to fulfill that mission.